ISBN 978-1-333-65678-2
PIBN 10068448

1 MONTH OF
FREE
READING

at
www.ForgottenBooks.com

———◆———

By purchasing this book you are eligible for one month membership to ForgottenBooks.com, giving you unlimited access to our entire collection of over 1,000,000 titles via our web site and mobile apps.

To claim your free month visit:
www.forgottenbooks.com/free68448

English
Français
Deutsche
Italiano
Español
Português

www.forgottenbooks.com

Mythology Photography **Fiction**
Fishing Christianity **Art** Cooking
Essays Buddhism Freemasonry
Medicine **Biology** Music **Ancient
Egypt** Evolution Carpentry Physics
Dance Geology **Mathematics** Fitness
Shakespeare **Folklore** Yoga Marketing
Confidence Immortality Biographies
Poetry **Psychology** Witchcraft
Electronics Chemistry History **Law**
Accounting **Philosophy** Anthropology
Alchemy Drama Quantum Mechanics
Atheism Sexual Health **Ancient History**
Entrepreneurship Languages Sport
Paleontology Needlework Islam
Metaphysics Investment Archaeology
Parenting Statistics Criminology
Motivational

HUMOUR OF THE LAW

FORENSIC ANECDOTES

BY

JACOB LARWOOD

AUTHOR OF

"A HISTORY OF SIGNBOARDS," "ANECDOTES OF THE CLERGY," ETC.

A NEW EDITION

LONDON

CHATTO & WINDUS

1903

PREFACE.

A VERY wise man has said, "There is nothing new under the sun," and this seems fatally true in the matter of collections of anecdotes. All the good sayings given in this volume have appeared in print before; all the curiosities are gathered from printed sources. Like the dapper little gentleman in Washington Irving's *Art of Bookmaking*, I have dipped into a variety of books; fluttered over endless pages; taken a morsel out of one, a morsel out of another, line upon line—here a little, there a little. In fact, the contents of this little volume are as motley and heterogeneous as the witches' caldron in *Macbeth*—here a finger and there a thumb, toe of frog and blind-worm's sting, with my own gossip poured in as "baboon's blood," to make the medley "slab and good."

Such must necessarily be the case with compilations. Productions of that kind are merely to be considered as attempts, more or less successful, to hand over to the present fast-reading generation the good things locked up in volumes no longer within everybody's reach. Says old Dan Chaucer :—

> " For out of the olde fieldes, as men saithe,
>   Cometh all this new corne from yere to yere ;
> And out of olde bookes, in good faithe,
>   Cometh all this new science that men lere."

FORENSIC ANECDOTES.

A COSTLY COMMODITY.

JOHN HORNE TOOKE'S opinion on the subject of law was admirable. "Law," he said, "ought to be, not a luxury for the rich, but a remedy to be easily, cheaply, and speedily obtainable for the poor." Somebody observed to him how excellent are the English laws, because they are impartial and our courts are open to all persons without distinction. "And so," replied Horne Tooke, "is the London Tavern, to such as can afford to pay for their entertainment."

Never, however, was the formerly almost prohibitive cost of the law in divorce suits illustrated with more genuine wit, and in a more forcible manner, than by Sir William Maule. A poor man having been convicted before him of bigamy, the following conversation took place :—

Clerk of Assizes. What have you to say why judgment should not be passed upon you according to law ?

Prisoner. Well, my lord, my wife took up with a hawker, and run away five years ago, and I never seed her since ; and I married this other woman last winter.

Mr. Justice Maule. I will tell you what you ought to have done ; and if you say you did not know, I must tell you the law conclusively presumes that you *did*. You ought to have instructed your attorney to bring an action against the hawker for

B

criminal conversation with your wife. That would have cost you about £100. When you had recovered substantial damages against the hawker, you would have instructed your proctor to sue in the ecclesiastical courts for a divorce *a mensa atque thoro*. That would have cost you £200 or £300 more. When you had obtained a divorce *a mensa atque thoro*, you would have had to appear by counsel before the House of Lords for a divorce *a vinculo matrimonii*. The bill might have been opposed in all its stages in both Houses of Parliament, and altogether you would have had to spend about £1100 or £1200. You will probably tell me that you never had a thousand farthings of your own in the world ; but, prisoner, that makes no difference. Sitting here as a British judge, it is my duty to tell you that this is not a country in which there is one law for the rich and another for the poor."

This judicial sarcasm on the then existing state of the law was uttered only a few years prior to the creation of the court for the trial of matrimonial and divorce cases, and coming from such an experienced judge as Mr. Justice Maule, must have had its weight in the passing of the Act.

ONCE BIT, TWICE SHY.

ALDERMAN WATSON was in his youth a midshipman, and while bathing in the West Indies had the misfortune to lose his leg by the bite of a shark. Some years afterwards, when he and Wilkes were both in the House of Commons, and a tax upon attorneys was proposed, Alderman Watson spoke strongly in favour of the tax, and inveighed warmly against the attorneys in general. Somebody asked Wilkes what made his brother alderman so severe upon the attorneys ? " Why," said Wilkes, " my brother alderman was bit by a shark when he was young, and he has never forgiven it."

HAIR-TRIGGER JUSTICE.

WO or three generations back, the reputation of a duellist was by no means considered an impediment to promotion, even to the bench, in Ireland. It was a favourite boast of Chief Justice Toler (Lord Norbury) that he "began the world with £50 and a pair of hair-trigger pistols." They served his purpose well. A quarrel with Napper Tandy, one of those ephemeral demagogues in which Ireland is so prolific, was the immediate ladder by which he ascended the bench. To such compensation for such service Lord Clare, the then chancellor, was vehemently and naturally opposed. " Make *him* a chief justice ! " he exclaimed. " Oh no ; if he must mount the bench, make him a bishop, or an archbishop, or—anything but a chief justice ! " The luck, however, of the hair-triggers triumphed, and Toler not only became a chief justice, but the founder of two peerages, and the testator of an enormous fortune. After his promotion, the code of honour became, as it were, engrafted on that of the Common Pleas, the noble chief not unfrequently announcing that he considered himself a judge only while he wore his robes. A non-suit was never heard of in his time. Ill-natured people said it was to draw suitors to his court ; Toler's reason was, he was too *constitutional* to interfere with a jury ! Be this as it may, a non-suit was a nonentity. " I hope, my lord," said counsel in a case actually commanding one, " your lordship will for once have the courage to non-suit." In a moment the hair-triggers were uppermost. " Courage ! I tell you what, Mr. Wallace, there are two kinds of courage—courage to shoot, and courage to non-shoot, and I hope I have both ; but non-shoot now I certainly will not ; " and the argument was only a waste of time.

QUADRUPEDAL GRACE.

SERJEANT WHITAKER was one of the most eminent lawyers of his day, though the few memorials which have been preserved of him exhibit him more in the character of a wit than of a learned man, which he, however, undoubtedly was. One day, two ladies of rank and fashion were praising Mr. Serjeant Walker's dancing. Whitaker, who knew that his brother-*in-law* was remarkable for anything except grace, insisted that the ladies were mistaken as to the individual. When they declared that they were not, he begged leave to put one question to them : " Pray, ladies, was it upon his hind legs or his fore legs that Serjeant Walker moved so gracefully ? "

LEGAL OPINION.

WHEN Sir John Hayward, LL.D., in 1590, published his *First Part of the Life and Reign of King Henry IV.*, Queen Elizabeth considered this work so full of treason, that she sent its learned author to the Tower. Bacon having been consulted by her on the question, answered, "An please your highness, for treason I cannot deliver opinion that there is any ; but very much felony." The queen rejoiced at hearing this. "How, and wherein?" she exclaimed eagerly. "Because," he answered, "many of the sentiments and conceits are stolen out of Cornelius Tacitus."

"A BILL WITHOUT A NAME."

LORD BROUGHAM, in the House of Lords, said he remembered a case wherein Lord Eldon referred it, in succession, to three chief courts below to decide what a particular document was. The Court of King's Bench decided it was a lease in fee ; the Common Pleas, that it was a lease in tail; the Exchequer, that it was a lease for years. Whereupon Lord Eldon, when it came back to him, decided for himself that it was no lease at all.

NOT BEEF-WITTED.

JUSTICE FLETCHER, of the Common Pleas, about five o'clock every day became so ravenously hungry that the country people agreed he had a wolf in his stomach. On one occasion, just on the advent of the ominous hour, a circuit counsel of the name of French commenced a pompous cross-examination. Sundry and wryful were the contortions of Fletcher, and dogged in proportion became the pertinacity of French. At last the hour of six sounded. Flesh and blood—at all events flesh and blood like Fletcher's—could stand it no longer, and the outburst came, "Lord of heaven! Mr. French, do you mean to keep me here all night, like a bear tied to a stake?" "Oh no, my lord," answered French, bowing reverentially, "not tied to a *steak*."

"THE LAW AND THE LADY."

SIR FRANCIS BULLER was equally celebrated among both females and males, but not with equal admiration. While he is considered by the latter as one of the most learned of lawyers, he is stigmatized by the former as one of the most cruel of judges, since to him is generally attributed the obnoxious and ungentlemanly dictum, that a husband may beat his wife, so that the stick with which he administers the castigation be not thicker than his thumb. It may perhaps restore his memory to the ladies' good graces to be told that, though the story was generally believed and even made the subject of caricature, yet, after searching investigation by the most able critics and antiquarians, no substantial evidence has been found that he ever expressed so ungallant an opinion.

A PRIMITIVE MODE OF SEISIN.

SAINT COLUMBA wished to take heritable state and seisin of his little island of Hy, and resolved it would be best done by the interment there of one of his followers; but the question was, who should die and be buried for this end. Then Oran arose quickly, and spoke : " If you accept me, I am ready for that." " Oh, Oran," said Columkille, " you shall receive the reward of this." Oran then died, and was buried, and Columba founded the Church of Hy close to the grave of Oran. The cemetery of Iona at the present day is still known by the name of Relig-Oran. "This," says Mr. Cosmo Innes, the learned Scotch legal antiquary, " I have always thought to be the very first instance of symbolical seisin."

"FOR LACK OF A NAIL."

BARON WILLES, Chief Justice of the Common Pleas, to illustrate the absurdity into which judges would inevitably fall, unless they applied the rule of common sense to restrict the extent of liability for the breach of a con- tract of the class then under consideration, observed : " Cases of this kind have always been found to be very difficult to deal with, beginning with a case said to have been decided about two centuries and a half ago, where a man going to be married to an heiress, his horse having cast a shoe on the journey, employed a blacksmith to replace it, who did the work so un- skilfully that the horse was lamed, and the rider, not arriving in time, the lady married another, and the blacksmith was held liable for the loss of the marriage."

LEARNED SMOKE.

CERTAIN counsel, Mr. Marryatt, declared that he never opened any book, after he left school, but a law-book. But Mr. Marryatt was certainly no instance in favour of such a practice. Once, when addressing a jury, he was speaking of a chimney on fire, and exclaimed, " Gentlemen, the chimney took fire ; it poured forth volumes of smoke,— volumes, did I say ?—whole encyclopædias !"

A RAZOR CASE.

AN appeal came to the Sudder Court in 1854, in which thirteen parties as plaintiffs sued twenty-six barbers, to compel them to shave them. It appears that a succession of barbers, of a particular caste, had lathered and shaved the ancestors of the plaintiffs from time immemorial. From father to son the same razor had come down as an heirloom, destined to scrape the skins of certain families, their heirs and successors for ever. At last, however, prompted by some evil genius, the barbers absconded, and, as a result, the beards of the plaintiffs appeared ; this being repugnant to the spirit of the *shastras* (Hindu scriptures), the judge was asked to have the plaintiffs duly shaved, which he declined to do. In another case certain parties sued certain individual barbers, praying that the latter might be compelled to pare the nails of the former. The first court found that it had been the custom of the defendants to perform this service for the plaintiffs, and passed a decree compelling the defendants to perform it. The barbers, being indignant, appealed. The Lower Appellate Court held that such a suit will not lie, and, as is the custom of litigants in India, an appeal was immediately made to a higher tribunal. It was gravely urged in special appeal to the High Court that a suit will lie for the enforcement of an established usage having the force of law. The High Court, in its turn, solemnly say :

"We have carefully considered this argument, but, looking at the facts of the case, we think it should be governed by the decision of the late Sudder Court, 2nd November, 1854, p. 465, in which thirteen parties sued twenty-six barbers to compel them to shave them, and which appears to us to be on all fours with this. It is, indeed, urged in that case that any barber may have been resorted to, and here the individual defendants must perform the service, otherwise plaintiffs lose caste. But that was not the ground of that decision. It was that the claim was of doubtful principle, and not one of which the court could enforce execution." (*Weekly Reporter*, Vol. I.) The special appeal was accordingly dismissed.

Probably it was a fortunate circumstance that the court so decided, for if (in the shaving case at least) a decree for the plaintiffs had finally been made, both the judges and the plaintiffs would assuredly have found themselves under the tyranny of an exceedingly "doubtful principle." If the barbers had refused to carry out the decree, and had sullenly put away their razors, then, probably (as in the case where a defendant, being ordered, refuses to sign a document to the plaintiff, the judge may sign it in his stead), the honourable judges would have been compelled to consider the question, whether they should not shave the plaintiffs themselves. If, again, the defendants (barbers) had shown a cheerful disposition, and were prepared to shave the plaintiffs in terms of the decree, why, in that case, even, it is of exceedingly "doubtful principle," and a question the casuists have nowhere decided, whether it is just to a man's wife that he should intrust himself to the hands of a barber against whom he holds a decree carrying costs, which costs, at the time of shaving, happen to be still due and unpaid.

DIGEST OF THE LAW.

HE following is the way in which Lord Polkemmet described his own judicial preparation for the bench : " Ye see I first read a' the pleadings, and then, after letting them wamble in my wame wi' the toddy twa or three days, I gie my ain interlocutor."

"A LEARNED JUDGE."

OLERIDGE, in his *Table Talk*, mentions one of Lord Kenyon's illustrations borrowed from ancient history, which displays a felicitous ignorance that the whole race of Malaprops might have envied. "Above all, gentlemen, need I name to you the Emperor Julian, who was so celebrated for the practice of every Christian virtue, that he was called Julian the Apostle ! "

MURDER OF A HORSE.

R. HECTOR, in his *Selections from the Judicial Reports of Renfrewshire*, records one of the year 1721 for the *Murder* of a Horse. The major proposition for the indictment is as follows : " That where any person doth wilfully and of set purpose, stick, butt, or stabb ane other person's horse, without the owner's consent, with ane knife, sword, or other invasive weapon, especially where the wound given thereby proveth mortall, and the horse diyeth within a little time thereafter, the actor becometh guilty of the murder of the said horse, and is liable to condign punishment in his person and goods, being ane crime of ane high nature." The minor proposition in this logical document is worthy of its major, setting forth the particulars of the murder, even to the accused having been seen " *dighting the foresaid knife.*"

A CATCH LAW REPORT.

THE gravity of the poor-laws was enlivened, and the aridity of settlement cases agreeably refreshed, by a catch introduced by Sir James Burrow into the report of the King *v.* Norton. The reporter says : "I do not find the case of Shadwell and St. John's Wapping [which had been cited in the argument] in any printed book or manuscript. But I guess it to be the same case which I have heard reported in the form of a catch to the following effect, if my memory serves me right :—

> A woman having a settlement,
>   Married a man with none.
> The question was, he being dead,
>   If what she had was *gone.*

> Quoth Sir John Pratt : * Her settlement
>   *Suspended* did remain
> Living her husband ; but, him dead,
>   It doth *revive* again.

> *Chorus of Puisne Judges.*

> Living her husband ; but, him dead,
>   It doth revive again.

Chief Justice Pratt's decision having been reversed by Chief Justice Ryder, his successor, the report was amended in this fashion :—

> A woman having a settlement
>   Married a man with none ;
> He flies, and leaves her destitute ;
>   What then is to be done ?

> Quoth Ryder, the Chief Justice,
>   In spite of Sir John Pratt,
> You'll send her to the parish
>   In which she was a brat.

---

* Then Lord Chief Justice.

Suspension of a settlement
Is not to be maintained ;
That which she had by birth subsists
Until another's gained.

Chorus of Puisne Judges.
That which she had by birth subsists
Until another's gained."

LAUGHING ON CONTINGENCY.

CURRAN was just rising to cross-examine a witness, before a judge who would not comprehend any jest that was not written in "blackletter." Before he said a single word the witness, in his nervousness, began to laugh. "What are you laughing at, friend ?—what are you laughing at? Let me tell you that a laugh without a joke is like—is like——" "Like what, Mr. Curran?" inquired the judge, imagining he was at fault. "Just exactly, my lord, like a *contingent remainder* without any particular *estate* to support it." The joke was quite to his lordship's fancy, and rivalled with him all "the wit that Rabelais ever scattered," but, as I am afraid few but my legal readers will understand the admirable felicity of the similitude, I may add that a "contingent remainder" is, according to Blackstone, "an estate in remainder which is limited to take effect upon a dubious and uncertain event."

"ALL MY EYE !"

HARRY DEANE GRADY, an eminent Irish Nisi Prius lawyer of the earlier portion of this century, revelled in drollery. To a rich fund of genuine Irish fun and constitutional vivacity, he mischievously added on many occasions a vulgarity not his own. One of his most efficient weapons was his right eye, which he constantly used in winking at the jury when he wished them to note some particular answer from an adverse witness. By mere dint of winking it seemed smaller than the left one. Appearing in Court one morning in rather depressed spirits, which for one of his joyous temperament was very unusual, a sympathizing friend said, "What's up, Harry? You are not as lively as usual." "My dear fellow," was the answer, "I'm ruined outright; *my jury eye is out of order.*"

SUUM CUIQUE.

AN indictment for a libel was once tried before Justice Maule. The learned counsel for the defence said to the jury, "This, gentlemen, is a shameful, an infamous, I may say, a diabolical prosecution." When the time came for summing up, Maule said : "Gentlemen of the jury, you are told that this is a diabolical prosecution ; but, gentlemen, you must give the devil his due, and find the defendant guilty." This happened accordingly.

HOW TO DEAL WITH THE ATTORNEYS.

LADY CHATTERTON, in her *Rambles in the South of Ireland in the year* 1838, gives the following picture of the Arcadian manners of the people of Dingle, a small town in the south-west of Ireland. "Law, sir," repeated the man of Dingle, with a look of astonishment and affright ; "law, sir ! We never mind the law in our court. We judge by the honesty of the case that comes before us. And let me tell you, sir, that if every court were so conducted there would be but few attorneys, and the country would be quiet and happy." "But what would you do if any person brought an attorney these twenty-two long miles, and hilly roads, from Tralee, and introduced him into your courts ; and if he started some points of law, which required professional skill to reply to?" "I'll tell you what I did myself," was the reply to this apparently perplexing question. "When I was deputy-sovereign, two fools in this town employed each of them an attorney, whom they brought at a great expense from Tralee. When the attorneys went into court and settled themselves, with their bags and papers all done up with bits of red tape, and one of them was getting up to speak, 'Crier,' said I, 'command silence.' 'Silence in the court!' says he. So I stood up, and looking first at one attorney, and then at the other, I said with a solemn voice : 'I adjourn this court for a month.' 'God save the king!' said the crier ; and then I left them all. And I assure you," he added, "that from that day to this no attorney ever appeared in our court ; and, please God, we never will mind law in it, but go on judging by the honour and honesty of the cases that come before us."

A CHICKEN IN THE LAW-PROFESSION.

IT is a well-known fact that occasionally when a joke or a pun has been uttered in the not very lively precincts of St. Stephen's, honourable gentlemen fasten eagerly upon it, "keep the pot a-boiling," as street boys say, each tacking his little joke to the lucky or unlucky expression which has given cause to such a flow of wit. A remarkable instance of this bantering took place in a debate on the Westminster scrutiny in 1785, on which occasion Mr. Michael Angelo Taylor first acquired the name of "the chicken." Mr. Taylor, then a young beginner, observed, "That he always delivered his legal opinion in that house and elsewhere with great humility, because he was young, and might with propriety call himself a chicken in the profession of the law." Soon after this modest declaration, which excited a smile through the house, Mr. Bearcroft, who advocated the scrutiny against Mr. Fox, adverted to the expression used by Mr. Taylor, and said, "for his part, with regard to legal opinions, he should never be biased by them, whether they came from chickens or old cocks." This was enough for Sheridan, who immediately followed, and in a humorous desultory speech, which produced repeated peals of laughter, he took notice of the diffidence of Mr. Taylor as connected with another observation of the same gentleman, " that he should on that occasion vote with the opposition, because they were in the right ; but that in all probability he should never vote with them again," thus presaging that for the future they would be always in the wrong. " If such be his augury," said Sheridan, " I cannot help looking upon this chicken as a bird of ill omen, and wish that he had continued side by side by the full-grown cock [alluding to Mr. Bearcroft], who will, no doubt, long continue to feed about the gates of the Treasury, to pick up those crumbs which are there plentifully scattered about, to keep the chickens and full-grown fowls together."

A MANSLAUGHTERING SPEECH.

SIR THOMAS DAVENPORT, a man notorious for lengthy dull speeches, was retained on one occasion to argue an ejectment case on the Northern Circuit. The day was intensely hot, and, as the case excited great interest, the court was crammed full. Sir Thomas made a speech of three hours' duration, whose soporific influence, aided by the atmosphere of the court, was most irresistible. Before the proceedings commenced, a boy had managed to climb up to a window-sill at a considerable height from the floor, from which coign of vantage he watched for some time what was going on. At last the heat and the serjeant's dulness overcame him, and, nodding in his sleep, he lost his balance and tumbled down. He was reported, though untruly, to be dead. In consequence of this Mr. John Scott, at that time Attorney-General of the Northern Circuit—a jocular office on a court which generally held its sittings after mess,—indicted the serjeant at the Circuit Court at Appleby for " manslaughter, perpetrated by a long dull instrument, of no value, to wit a speech." He was convicted and severely fined in bottles of wine.

VALUE OF AN INDEX.

A SEARCHER after something or other, running his eye down the index of a law-book through letter B, arrived at the reference "Best—Mr. Justice,—his great mind." Desiring to be better acquainted with this assertion, he turned to the page referred to, and there found to his entire satisfaction : "Mr. Justice Best said he had a great mind to commit the witness for prevarication."

In the index of "Smith, Leading Cases," ed. 1867, we find this reference : "Eagle eyes—court will not always look with."

A PERFERVID WELSHMAN.

L ORD KENYON was born at Greddington, in Flintshire, and in his younger days had a touchy love for his native country, which his mercurial friend Dunning delighted to affront. One day, after Dunning had become M.P., Kenyon asked the new member to frank a letter to a relation in North Wales. Dunning signed his name, and wrote the address, adding after North Wales the words "near Chester." This addition so wounded the spirit of the ancient Briton that he threw down the letter, and exclaimed, "Take back your frank, Mr. Dunning ; I'll accept no more from you." Dunning interposed between him and the door, and soon pacified his choleric but useful friend.

LAWYERS OF THE OLDEN TIME.

O UR early lawyers were not remarkable for their eloquence. Roger Ascham (1570) speaks of some of them who "roared like a bull," and he adds, "They do best when they cry loudest." Sir Thomas Elyot, in his *Governor* (1531), observes in reference to the law, that, "inasmuch as the

tongue wherein it is spoken is barbarous, and the stirring of the
affections of the mind in this nature was never used, therefore
they lacked elocution and pronunciation, two of the principal
parts of rhetorick ; notwithstanding some lawyers, if *they be
well retained,* will, in a mean cause, pronounce right vehemently." Profound learning, it would appear, afforded in those
days the best title to success : and probably the most successful
advocate never aspired to do more than obtain the approbation
of the court and his brethren at the bar. There was not then
a public, watching with intense interest the proceedings of the
courts of law and justice, ready to reward with the meed of
praise the redresser of the wronged, or the protector of the
innocent. In examining the State Trials, which afford the best
records of forensic eloquence, it is amusing to trace in the tone
and the allusions of counsel, the taste, manners, and degree of
enlightenment of the times. From the earliest period of which
any account of these is preserved, until the time of the Revolution, we find the speeches of the advocates for the most part
marked with a spirit of bitterness and malice, repugnant to the
feelings of a more advanced stage of civilization, such as, un-
happily, may still be heard not unfrequently in French courts of
the present day. The speeches of our ancient lawyers abound
with false metaphors and quaint images ; they are interlarded
throughout with Latin and Scriptural quotations, and are full of
references to ancient history and mythology. This practice,
which arose with the revival of classic literature, at last came
to such a pitch, that Sir Thomas Brown observed that, "if ele-
gancie still proceedeth, and English pens maintain that stream
we have of late observed to flow from many, we shall, within
a few years, be fain to learn Latin to understand English."
Notwithstanding those vagaries, there is, however, in many of
the speeches of the ancient lawyers a force and spirit, often
denied to more correct and elegant productions.

ADVANTAGES OF EARLY TRAINING.

HE following dialogue is reported to have taken place some years ago at the Queen's County Assizes, in the cross-examination of a medical witness by a barrister :—

Mr. Hayes, the barrister. " If a person lying on wet straw, were deprived of all the comforts and necessaries of life, would it not hasten his death ?

Dr. Edge. That would greatly depend upon whether he had been accustomed to them.

Mr. Hayes. Do you mean to tell us, that if a person lived in a horsepond it would not be injurious to him?

Dr. Edge. I think not, if he had lived sixty or seventy years in it."

NOT ACCORDING TO DARWIN.

HERNE, the senior counsel employed by Archbishop Laud, though a poor reasoner, was very quick and witty. When Sergeant Wilde, who was one of the managers for 'the Commons, observed : " That though no *one* crime of Laud's amounted to high treason, yet *all* his misdemeanours taken together, by way of accumulation, made many grand treasons," Herne quickly replied : " I crave your pardon, Mr. Sergeant ; I never understood before that two hundred couple of black rabbits would make a black horse."

A LOST REPORT.

MEMORABLE repartee is recorded of Sergeant Wilkins on one of his circuits, not long after a destructive fire had destroyed a part of the Temple. Wilkins was defending a prisoner : " Drink," said he, " has upon some persons an elevating, upon others a depressing effect. Indeed there is a report, as we all know, that an eminent judge, when at the bar, was obliged to resort to 'heavy wet' in a morning, to reduce himself to the level of the judges." Lord Denman, who had no love of Wilkins, crested up instantly. His voice trembled with indignation as he uttered the words : "Where is the report, sir? where is it?" There was a death-like silence. Wilkins calmly turned round to the judge, and said : "It was burnt, my lord, in the Temple fire." The effect may be better understood than described, and it was a long time before order could be restored, but Lord Denman was one of the first to acknowledge the wit of the answer.

LASCIATE OGNI SPERANZA VOI CHE 'NTRATE.

FUSELI, seeing a portrait of Lord Chancellor Eldon in Sir Thomas Lawrence's studio, which Sir Thomas had painted for Sir Robert Peel, asked him who it was. Sir Thomas told him it was the chancellor. "Then," exclaimed Fuseli, "give me a bit of chalk ;" it was given him, when, in allusion to the interminable nature of all suits once getting into the chancellor's den, he wrote on the back of the portrait the following quotation :—

> " Olim quod vulpes ægroto cauta leoni
> Respondit, referam : quia me vestigia terrent
> Omnia te adversum spectantia, nulla retrorsum."
> Horace, *Epist.* I. 73.

In his speech in the House of Commons, on the Education of the Poor Bill, May 8, 1818, Lord Brougham thus spoke about the Court of Chancery : "Is not the Court of Chancery open? Come all ye who labour under the burden of fraud or oppression, enter the eternal gates of the Court of Chancery. True, you are the poor of the land—the grievance you complain of has robbed you of everything ; but, penniless though you are, you are not remediless—you have only to file a bill in Equity, and the matter will take its course ! Why, if there were nothing in the reality, there is something in the name of the Court of Chancery, that appals the imagination, and strikes terror into the unlearned mind. I recollect a saying of a very great man in the Court of King's Bench ; the judge having said of his client, ' Let him go into a Court of Equity,' Mr. Erskine answered in an artless tone of voice, which made Westminster Hall ring with laughter—' Would your lordship send a fellow-creature there ? ' "

NATURAL SEQUENCE.

RED Lion Square, in the days of George III. was a locality greatly in favour with lawyers : almost every house in the square harboured one. Soon after the first quarter of this century, however, the lawyers, following the tide of fashion, began to drift westwards, and a house in Red Lion Square, after having been occupied by a man of high eminence in the legal profession, was let to an ironmonger. Upon this Erskine wrote the following epigram :—

> " The house where once a lawyer dwelt,
> Now to a smith doth pass ;
> How rapidly the iron age,
> Succeeds the age of brass."

FOR ONE PENNY.

ONE William Dalhiot, little more than a hundred years ago, was convicted at the Salisbury Quarter Sessions of petty larceny, for stealing one penny. In consequence of this, his effects, consisting of bank-notes to the amount of £180 and twenty guineas in money, were forfeited to the bishop as lord of the manor. It so happened that the bishop had a conscience, and gave all the money back to the family, in this form, viz., £100 to the felon's father, the same to his daughter, keeping the remaining twenty shillings for himself.

POWERFUL EXORCISM.

ON one occasion a heavy shower had driven a party of the Westminster volunteers, the potential defenders of our shores from the invasions of Napoleon I., to take refuge in Westminster Hall. Hearing the clatter of the muskets, Lord Ellenborough, who was then sitting, called out, "Usher, what noise is that?" "Oh, my *lud,*" said the usher, "it's only the volunteers *exorcising,* my *lud!*" "Exorcising! are they? Well, sir, we will see who is best at that. Tell the volunteers if they do not depart instantly, I shall commit them to the custody of the tipstaff."

A STARTLING LEGACY.

IN the confession of Edward Clarke, who was executed at Chelmsford in the end of the last century, is the following curious article: "I, Edward Clarke, now in a few hours expecting to die, do sincerely wish, as my last request, that three of my fingers be taken from my hands to be given to my three children, as a warning to them, as my fingers were the cause of bringing myself to the gallows, and my children to poverty. And I also request that E. Brown and two brother prisoners will be so kind as to see it done— they knowing which fingers they are, by their marking them at my wish with ink." This request was complied with.

COMPARISON.

"AN attorney," says Sterne, "is the same thing to a barrister that an apothecary is to a physician, with this difference—that your man of law does not deal in scruples."

COURTESY AND ECONOMY.

IR JOHN TREVOR was of most penurious habits. When he was Master of the Rolls, he resided, for the sake of economy, at the Rolls House in Chancery Lane. One day, when quietly enjoying his wine after dinner by himself, his cousin, Roderic Lloyd, was unexpectedly introduced to him by a side door. "You rascal," said Trevor to his servant, "how dare you bring my cousin, Roderic Lloyd, Esquire, Prothonotary of North Wales, Marshal to Baron Price, and so forth and so forth, up my back stairs? Take my cousin, Roderic Lloyd, Esquire, Prothonotary of North Wales, Marshal to Baron Price, and so forth, you rascal, take him instantly down my back stairs, and bring him up my front stairs." Roderic in vain remonstrated, and whilst he was conducted down one and up the other pair of stairs, Sir John Trevor removed the bottles and glasses.

A REMARKABLE PRECEDENT.

T is one of the principles of eternal justice, that no one is to be punished or deprived of his property in any judicial proceeding unless he has had an opportunity of being heard. Justice Foster refers to a very old precedent in support of this doctrine. (Foster, 202.) "I have heard it observed by a very learned man," says he, "that even God himself did not pass sentence upon Adam before he was called upon to make his defence. 'Adam,' says God, 'where art thou? Hast thou not eaten of the tree whereof I commanded thee that thou shouldst not eat?' And the same question was put to Eve also." In a case in 1850 (Abley *v.* Dale) this passage was cited in his judgment by the late Mr. Justice Maule.

BRAIN-LAW *v.* STATUTE LAW.

BACON advises judges to draw their law "out of their books, not out of their brain." Hermand, a Scottish judge of the last century, generally did neither. He was very apt to say, "My laards, I *feel* my law—*here*, my laards," striking the left side of his waistcoat. Hence he sometimes made little ceremony in disdaining the authority of an act of parliament when he and it happened to differ. He once got rid of one which the first Lord Meadowbank, whom he did not particularly like, was for enforcing because the legislature had made it law, by saying, in his snorting contemptuous way, and with an emphasis on every syllable, "But then we're told that there's a statute against all this. A statute! What's a statute? Words: mere words! And am *I* to be tied down by words? No, my laards: I go by the laws of *right reason.*" Lord Holland noticed this in the House of Peers as a strange speech for a judge.

CURRAN'S SARCASM.

JUDGE ROBINSON, of the King's Bench, Ireland, once sneered at Curran's poverty, by telling him he suspected "his law library was rather contracted"—a remark which drew from the great Irish orator one of the severest, as it certainly was one of the most unpremeditated, rebukes ever administered to a judge,—all the more cutting as Robinson was known to be the author of many stupid, slavish, and scurrilous political pamphlets, and by his demerits had been raised to the eminence which he thus disgraced :—

"It is very true, my lord, that I am poor, and the circumstance has certainly somewhat curtailed my library. My books are not numerous, but they are select, and I hope they have been perused with proper dispositions. I have prepared myself for this high profession rather by the study of a few good works than by the composition of a great many bad ones. I am not ashamed of my poverty; but I should be ashamed of my wealth could I have stooped to acquire it by servility and corruption. If I rise not to rank, I shall at least be honest; and should I ever cease to be so, many an example shows me that an ill-gained elevation, by making me the more conspicuous, would only make me the more universally and the more notoriously contemptible." "Sir," exclaimed the judge, "you are forgetting the respect which you owe to the dignity of the judicial character." "Dignity!" replied Curran. "My lord, upon that point I shall cite you a case from a book of some authority with which you are, perhaps, not unacquainted." He then briefly related the story of Strap in *Roderick Random*, who, having stripped off his coat to fight, entrusted it to a bystander. When the battle was over, and he was well beaten, he turned to resume his garment, but the man had carried it off. Curran thus applied the tale: "So, my lord, when the person entrusted with the dignity of the judgment-seat lays it aside to enter into a disgraceful personal contest, it is in vain, when he has been worsted in the encounter, that he seeks to resume it—it is in vain that he tries to shelter himself behind an authority which he has abandoned." "If you say another word I'll commit you," replied the angry judge; to which Curran retorted: "If your lordship shall do so, we shall both of us have the consolation of reflecting that I am not the worst thing your lordship has committed."

CONCERNED.

SERGEANT DAVY was once engaged at the Old Bailey, and a very strong case having been made out, Judge Gould asked who was concerned for the prisoner; upon which Davy said, "My lord, I am concerned for him, and *very much concerned* after what I have heard."

¡THE WILL FOR THE DEED.

NE of the judges of the King's Bench, in an argument on the construction of a will, sagely declared, " It appears to me that the testator meant to keep ι life-interest in the estate to himself." "Very true, my lord." answered Curran, gravely; "testators generally do secure a life-interest for themselves, but in this case I rather think your lordship takes *the will for the deed.*"

A SCRIPTURE RIDDLE.

R. BETHELL'S (subsequently Lord Westbury) reputation as a lawyer gave him a great influence over the minds of those judges before whom he appeared as counsel. This was said to have been particularly the case with the late Vice-Chancellor of England, Sir Launcelot Shadwell, and which led to a riddle being propounded, that for the time had great popularity among the bar practising in the courts of that very estimable and amiable as well as able judge. "Why is Shadwell like King Jeroboam? Because he has set up an idol in Bethell."

This puts me in mind of another riddle solved by a barrister, the witty Jonathan Henn, Q.C. Some one at the Munster bar mess proposed the riddle, "Why should the captain of a ship never be at a loss for an egg?" The riddle was a new one to all present, and Henn was the only person who solved it. "Because he can always *lay-to.*" Being asked how ever he came to guess it, he promptly replied, " Because it was a proper question to solve for a *Henn.*"

DIFFICULTIES OF THE VERNACULAR

OF the difficulties experienced at times by judges and counsel, in making out the evidences of the Northumbrian witnesses, the following is a good illustration : On one occasion William Russell, deputy-surveyor of Newcastle, said from the witness-box, " As I was going along I saw a hubbleshew coming out of a chairfoot." His lordship was amazed. " What on earth is a ' hubbleshew,' that it could come out of a chair-foot ? " " My lord," explained a barrister, learned in the dialect of the natives, " a ' chairfoot ' is the end of a narrow lane or alley, and ' hubbleshew ' is a term signifying a riotous concourse of disorderly people." *

CONTEMPT OF PROSODY.

A LEARNED counsel in the Exchequer, applying for a *nolle prosequi*, pronounced the penultimate syllable long. " Consider, sir," said Baron Alderson, " that this is the last day of term, and don't make things unnecessarily long."

A STRIKE OF LAWYERS.

IN 1670, a commission, of which the celebrated Lord Stair was a member, was nominated to consider the whole matter of the Supreme Courts of Scotland—the Sessions, Justiciary, and Exchequer. The commissioners reported certain rules which they recommended for adoption, and the king ratified their report, and ordered the rules to be observed, and the lawyers to swear to them. Amongst the rules was one imposing the limits of advocates' fees, which created the greatest dissatisfaction among that body. The regulations to which the

* Like many provincial words, hubbleshew is slightly deteriorated Archaic English. In Shelton's *Doctor Double Ale*, we read :—

" With that all was in a hubbleshubble,
There was drawing and dragging," etc.

advocates specially objected were : No more than three advocates were to be employed in any cause for a single party, and
only two were to be allowed to speak in the Inner House, one
after another, upon the same side. The chancellor or president
was to keep the advocates close to the point, and their speeches
were limited to half an hour. The fees were to be according to
the quality of the client. The maximum for consultation,
pleading, and drawing bills upon any interlocutor, was fixed for
a nobleman at £18, a knight or baron at £15, a gentleman or
chief burgess at £12, and for other persons at £9. For infor-
mations after dispute (*i.e.* after the case had been debated),
half fees, and that only to one advocate, were allowed. The
parties were to give in a declaration, as they would answer to
God, that they had not given larger fees, and every advocate at
his admission was to swear that he would not receive larger fees.

To these regulations the advocates refused to swear, and
they tried to carry their point by a strike. They withdrew for
two whole months, viz., from November 10th till January, having
represented to the lords in a long speech that those regulations
were impracticable, and that it was impossible to observe them
without the inevitable hazard of perjury. Like many other
strikes, this attempt failed through want of union. The Dean
of the Faculty, Sinclair, on his return from London, where he
had been engaged in the negotiations as to the Treaty of Union,
took the oath ; a few other advocates followed his example, and
the majority, who, as usually happens in small as in great revo-
lutions, had divided themselves into parties—a more and a less
violent one,—were finally compelled to give in.

THE FIRST REPORTER.

WHO was the first reporter? This question is settled by
Sir Edward Coke, in VI. *Reports*, p. xv. It was Moses,
for he reported the divine laws promulgated on Mount
Sinai (Exodus xx.–xxiii.). Saith Sir Edward : "And God hath left

a precedent of a judge, who was also the first reporter of law ; " and in a marginal note it is explained that Moses is meant.

ON THE SICK-LIST.

WHEN Mr. (afterwards Lord) Campbell married Miss Scarlett, and departed on his wedding trip, Mr. Justice Abbott observed, on a cause being called on in the bench, " I thought, Mr. Brougham, that Mr. Campbell was in this case ? " " Yes, my lord," replied Brougham ; " but I understand he is ill, suffering from Scarlett fever."

STANDING ON ETIQUETTE.

CRADOCK, in his *Memoirs*, tells an amusing story of an encounter between a judge on circuit and a high sheriff. The world was then not so highly refined as at present, and after the usual common topics, such as the state of the roads and the weather, the high sheriff began to feel himself a little more emboldened, and ventured to ask his lordship whether at the last place he had gone to see the elephant. The judge, with great good humour, replied, " Why, no, Mr. High Sheriff, I cannot say that I did, for a little difficulty occurred. We both came into the town in form, with the trumpet sounding before us, and there was a point of ceremony to be settled, which should visit first."

IN-SUP-PORT-ABLE.

SOON after being called to the bar, Mr. Erskine went a circuit in the train of the celebrated Lord Kaimes. His lordship, though a man of a very enlarged mind, fell sometimes into the sin of parsimoniousness. On no occasion was he more apt to be stingy, than when he travelled and feasted at the public expense, and there was a possibility of saving something to himself out of the sum regularly allotted in Scotland to judges in their official county excursions. On the rising of the court one day Lord Kaimes invited Mr. Erskine, with some other young barristers, to dine with him. When the cloth was withdrawn, the company found that port alone was to be the order of the day. Hint after hint was given to his lordship that, since the public were to pay, something better might be afforded. His lordship allowed every allusion of the kind to pass unnoticed. When at last the flank attack seemed verging upon a more direct front movement, Lord Kaimes turned towards Mr. Erskine, and, with the view of changing the subject, asked him very gravely, "What could have become of the Dutch?" who had a short time before been defeated at the Doggersbank by Admiral Parker. No shift could have been more unfortunate for his lordship. Mr. Erskine, with a smile, replied, "I suppose, my lord, they are, like us, confined to port." Lord Kaimes, who with all his niggardliness had a mind sensibly alive to the sallies of wit, immediately ordered a supply of the best claret in the house to be placed on the table.

READING BRIEFS.

URRAN'S notions of industry were somewhat ludicrous, An hour to him was a day to another man, and in his natural capabilities his idleness found a powerful auxiliary. A single glance made him master of the subject; and though imagination could not supply him facts, still it very often became a successful substitute for authorities. He once said, in serious refutation of what he called the professional calumnies on this subject, that he was quite as laborious as was necessary for any *Nisi Prius* advocate to be. "For," said he, with the utmost simplicity, "I always perused my briefs carefully when I was concerned for the plaintiff; and it was not necessary to do it for the defendant, because you know I could pick up the facts from the opposite counsel's statement." This was what Curran considered being laborious : it was at best but an industrious idleness.

It would be a great mistake, however, to suppose that Curran was altogether indolent. It is quite impossible that any man who had not, at some time or other, devoted himself seriously to study, could have attained his acquisitions and his accomplishments. He was a most admirable classic scholar ; with the whole range of English literature he was perfectly acquainted ; he not only spoke French like a native, but was familiar with every eminent author in that language. Besides all these accomplishments, he had acquired a knowledge of music (the violin and violoncello) that entitled him rather to be considered a master than a mere proficient.

CODIFICATION.

THE famous code of Justinian was perfected in less than four years, fourteen months of which were spent in winnowing the chaff out of the legal grain, accumulated in a thousand years. Trebonian, aided by a staff of seventeen lawyers, in three years reduced three million sentences to one hundred and fifty thousand ; so perfecting the pandects and institutes. For the framing of the *Code Napoleon,* a commission of jurists was appointed on the twelfth of August, in the year 1800. In four months it delivered its report, which was then open to criticism. The Council of State afterwards completed the discussion of it in 102 sittings.

BURGLAR.

THE word burglar is derived from the Norman French *bourglaire,* which is a corruption of *burgilatro, i.e.* one who steals in a closed dwelling, *burgum.* Sir Edward Coke adheres closely to this etymology when he defines a burglar as "he that by night breaketh or entereth into a

mansion house, with intent to commit a felony." Anciently there
used to be—probably there are still—a great many delicacies in
the laws having reference to homicide and burglary : but in Sir
Matthew Hale's time, the knotty question of what was passable
Latin for *burglarious* and *burglar,* in the framing of indictments,
was THE delicacy of the season. More offenders escaped by
the writing of *burgariter* or *burgenter,* for *burglariter,* than
by proof of innocence. But, although these errors were common
and fatal flaws in an indictment, it was ruled that *burgulariter*
was sufficiently good Latin to serve the purposes of the law.

IMMORTAL WITHOUT A SOUL.

A CORPORATION has been defined as a thing having
neither a body to be kicked, nor a soul to be damned.
It would seem that no argument is necessary to prove
the latter part of this legal action. Chief Baron Manwood,
however, established the fact by a syllogism, in which it is not
easy to detect any false reasoning : " The opinion of Manwood, C.B., was this as touching corporations, that they were
invisible, immortal, and that they had no soul, and therefore no
subpœna lieth against them, because they have no conscience
or soul. A corporation is a body aggregate ; none can create
souls but God ; but the king creates corporations, and therefore
they have no souls. And this was the opinion of Manwood,
chief baron, touching corporations."

CAUSE OF DEATH.

A CERTAIN solicitor made a series of statements before
Lord Thurlow, in a vain endeavour to prove a person's
death. "Really, my lord," at last the solicitor exclaimed, goaded into fury by Thurlow's repeated ejaculations of
" That's no proof of the man's death,"—" Really, my lord, it is
very hard, and it is not right that you won't believe me. I saw

the man dead in his coffin. My lord, I tell you he was my client, and he *is* dead." "No wonder," retorted the uncourteous chancellor, with a grunt and a sneer, "since he was your client. Why did you not tell me that sooner? It would kill me to have such a fellow as you for my attorney."

TYING THE KNOT.

IN Tremaine's *Placitæ Coronæ* is a precedent of an indictment against Sir John Johnston, a Scotch knight, for stealing and marrying one Mary Wharton, an heiress, "to the great displeasure of Almighty God, to the great disparagement of the said Mary, and to the utter sorrow and affliction of her friends." Tremaine adds in a note, "Sir John Johnston was a stranger to the English laws, and when he was called to judgment was much surprised, and asked if it was a hanging matter; but, nevertheless, sentence was given against him, and he was executed on a gibbet before the lady's door in Great Queen Street."

LEADING QUESTION.

DURING an examination which Sergeant Whitaker conducted at the bar of the House of Lords, he put a question to a witness, to the legality of which some objection was taken. Counsel were ordered to withdraw, and a debate of two hours ensued, respecting the admissibility of the question, resulting in favour of the sergeant. When he was re-admitted, Whitaker was requested to put the question over again; but he merely replied: "Upon my word, my lords, it is so long since I first put that question, that I entirely forget it; but, with your leave, I'll now put another." This anecdote is also fathered upon Sergeant Davy, the locale being the bar of the House of Commons.

WHITELOCK'S CORANTO.

T cannot be said that there is no music in the souls of lawyers, for a number of most eminent men of law have been notable musicians. Such were Sir Thomas More and Lord Bacon. Chief Justice Dyer, in the time of Queen Elizabeth, found great solace in "musique sweete." Lord Keeper Guilford was a writer on music as well as a performer ; his biographer Roger North, was a proficient on many instruments. Lord Jeffrey, in direct contradiction with the well-known Latin proverb about the effects of music, was an occasional vocalist and a distinguished critic. Lord Camden was an operatic composer, and Lord Thurlow studied thorough bass with considerable success. But Bulstrode Whitelock, Cromwell's first commissioner of the great seal, appears to have achieved most popularity by his music. In his memoirs he relates that, *with the assistance of Mr. Ives* (a well-known composer of that day), he composed an air and called it " Whitelocke's Coranto," which was first played publicly by the Black Friars' orchestra, then esteemed the best in London. That whenever he went to the playhouse there, the musicians would immediately upon his coming in play it. That the Queen, Henriette Maria, hearing it, would scarce believe it was composed by an Englishman, because, as she said, it was fuller of life and spirit than the English airs, but that she honoured the "Coranto" and the maker of it with her royal commendation. And, lastly, that it grew to that request, that all the common musicians in London, and all over the kingdom, got the composition (the score) of it, and played it publicly for about thirty years after. As this is probably the only piece of music now in existence written by a grave lawyer, who subsequently became first commissioner of the great seal, it may interest some of my readers to know that this once popular dance-tune may be found in Hawkins' *History of Music*, Vol. IV. p. 51.

BARRISTERS' HOODS.

THE lapel which hangs from the back of the barrister's gown, is the part of his costume the origin of which dates furthest back. It is, in fact, the lineal descendant of the early mediæval hood, the tippet or liripipium of which—an important part of it, since its length indicates the rank of the wearer—hangs down in front of the left shoulder. In the Middle Ages the learned professions, and even the priesthood, followed secular fashions ; but by the end of the fifteenth century they became conservative, and rose above the follies and vagaries of fashion. Down to that period the hood was a head-dress worn by all classes ; then the fashion gradually passed away from the general public. But jurisconsults, magistrates, doctors, and M.A.'s continued to adhere to it. It was, however, no longer worn by them as a covering of the head, but as a symbol of their profession suspended over the shoulder. Thus the liripoop, being distinctive of the learned professions, the word came to be used as synonymous for knowledge and astuteness : "There's a girl who knows her lirripoop " (Lylly, *Mother Bombie*, i. 3). "Thou must be skilled in thy logic, but not in thy lerypoope " (Idem. *Sapho and Phaon*, i. 3). And Cotgrave translates the words, " qui sçait bien son roulet," by " one that knows his liripoope." For the same reason, in Rabelais' mock library the treatise of Magister Lupold, *Lyripipii Sorbonicæ Moralizationes*, explained all the learning connected with the hood and scarf of the Sorbonne.

ILLEGAL ACTIONS AFTER 9 P.M.

IN the " Statutes of the Streets," printed in 1598, it is ordered that " no man . . . . shall whistle after the houre of nyne of the clocke in the night," or " keep any rule whereby any such suddaine outcry be made in the still of the night, as making an affray, or beating his wife or servant."

D

RARA AVIS IN TERRIS.

N the epitaph of Georg Conrad Schusterus, a famous
lawyer and counsellor, who died at Heidelberg, A.D.
1672, occur the words—

> "Morti proximus vocem emisit
> Nihil se unquam suasse consilio
> Cujus jamjam moriturus poeniteret."

"When at the point of death, he declared that he had never
purposely given counsel for which at that moment he was
sorry." A lawyer who can go out of the world with such a
confession, would be a greater blessing than can be expected in
this wicked world.

CONJUGAL DUELS.

N the Royal Library at Munich there is a manuscript
book dated A.D. 1400, containing a collection of drawings on vellum, executed by the order of one Paulus
Kall, who filled the office of Master of Defence to the then
reigning Duke of Bavaria. Among other curious matter concerning the conduct of judicial combats, there is proof that a duel
of this kind was considered at that time to be a fitting mode
of settling differences between husband and wife. The rule
under which these strange means of adjusting grievances took
place, is expressed as follows : " The woman must be so prepared that a sleeve of her chemise extend a small ell beyond
her hand, like a little bag ; therein is put a stone weighing three
pounds ; and she has nothing else on but her chemise, and that
is bound between the legs with a string. Then the man makes
himself ready in a pit opposite his wife. He is buried therein
up to the girdle, and one of his hands is bound at the elbow to
his side." A drawing which illustrates these instructions shows
the man armed with a short stick, and up to his waist in a

cylindrical pit, in which there is only room to turn round, but not for any other movement. That such duels really took place cannot be doubted, since in 1200 a man and his wife are stated to have fought, under the sanction of the civic authorities of Bâle. It seems, however, that these combats were not always conducted precisely after the same fashion in every part of Germany. Thus in a book of drawings in the same library at Munich, executed more than a century after those in Kall's work, there is a representation of a duel between man and wife, where the former, instead of being placed in a pit, is standing, or more probably kneeling, in a sort of tub. The woman in this instance is represented in her usual clothing, and armed with a piece of cloth in which a stone is tied—not in her sleeve, as in the older work. Possibly the combat in this collection was described merely from tradition, as the book professes to describe every practicable species of combat; for one may fairly suppose that matrimonial spectacles of this sort must have been extremely rare, if not altogether obsolete, at the time when the latter work was compiled. However, it is quite certain that the man was sometimes placed in a tub, because there is an ancient drawing in the library of Gotha where he is so depicted. The artist has represented him as the conqueror of his wife, having pulled her head foremost into the tub, where she appears with her legs kicking up in the air. There is also one old drawing where the duel between man and wife is represented to have taken place with large knives. Both are naked down to the waist, and no advantage is given to the woman. The two combatants stand opposite each other, apparently fencing. The woman has a large gaping wound under her left breast, the man on his left arm. Such sanguinary duels, however, must have been of rare occurrence. The orthodox mode of fighting was, beyond all doubt, with stick and loaded sleeve; and as the man could easily parry the blows of the loaded sleeve and catch hold of his partner, the stick might be applied with less deadly effect than the knife, once he had got her into the position represented in one of the drawings above alluded to.

THE LAW OF IMPOSSIBILITIES.

THE English law will not lend its aid to enforce a condition which is impossible. An instance of this is given in *Coke upon Littleton*, 206 : "If a man be bound in an obligation, etc., with condition that if the obligor do go from the church of St. Peter, in Westminster, to the church of St. Peter, in Rome, within three hours, that then the obligation shall be void—the condition is void and impossible, and the obligation stands good."

PAINFULLY DECENT.

BEFORE the statute 30 Geo. III. women, from the remotest times, were sentenced to be burned alive for every species of treason. This Blackstone attributes to the regard of our ancestors for "the decency due to the sex."

MANNERS MAKYTH MAN.

JUSTICE GRAHAM was the most polite judge that ever adorned the bench. To one found guilty of burglary or some such offence, he would say : "My honest friend, you are found guilty of felony, for which it is my painful duty," etc., etc. On one occasion it was said he had by mistake condemned to transportation a man who had once before been capitally convicted. The Clerk of the Court set his lordship right in a whisper, who thereupon exclaimed very gravely, "Dear me ; I beg his pardon, I am sure ;" and, putting on the black cap, courteously apologized to the prisoner for his mistake, and consigned him to the gallows, to be hanged by the neck until he was dead.

THE LAND O' CAKES.

DR. JOHNSON once remarked that the finest view a Scotchman could see in his own country was the road leading to London. That the drifting southwards from the " land o' cakes " is a natural phenomenon, dating from ancient times, was triumphantly proved by the observations of Dean Buckland. This eminent geologist averred that, even in the slabs of the Old Red Sandstone, he had never seen one footprint of the Scottish antediluvian creatures, out of many hundreds, turned northwards. An amusing retort, based on this convergence of Scotchmen to the metropolis, was made on one occasion to Mr. Murray, afterwards Lord Mansfield.

When General Sabine was governor of Gibraltar, he endeavoured to extort a sum of money from a Barbary Jew, who lived in that place, but his efforts were unavailing. To punish the Jew for his contumacy, Sabine had him seized, put on board a vessel, and sent to Tetuan with a letter to the pasha, informing him he would receive therewith a pigeon to pluck. The pasha for some reason or other liberated the Jew, and gave up Sabine's letter, armed with which the Jew came to London, where he brought an action against the governor. When the action was tried, Murray, who was counsel for Sabine, affected to treat the matter very lightly. " Great stress had been laid," he said, " on the cruelty of the proceeding. The Jew, we have been told, was banished. True, he was banished ; but to where ? Why, to the place of his nativity ! Where is the cruelty, where the hardship, where the injustice, of banishing a man to his own country ? " Mr. Nowell, who appeared for the Jew, replied : " Since my learned friend thinks so lightly of this matter, I would just ask him to suppose the case his own. Would *he* like to be banished to *his* native land ? " The court rang with peals of laughter, in which Murray himself most heartily joined.

EVENHANDED JUSTICE.

WHEN one of Sir Thomas More's sons complained to him, that he received no advantage whatever from being so nearly connected with him, More answered that he favoured him as much as might be done in justice. "Howbeit, this one thing, son, I assure you on my faith—that if the parties will at my hands call for justice, then, were it my father stood on one side, and the devil on the other, his cause being good, the devil should have right." This reminds one of the oath of the Judges in the Isle of Man, as given in Wood's account of the isle : " By this book and the holy contents thereof, and by the wonderful works that God hath miraculously wrought in heaven above, and in earth beneath, in six days and seven nights, I do swear that I will without respect of favour or friendship, love or gain, consanguinity or affinity, envy or malice, execute the laws of this isle justly, betwixt our Sovereign Lord the King and his subjects within this isle, and betwixt party and party, as indifferently as the herring's backbone doth lie in the midst of the fish."

PATHOS AND BATHOS.

NOT many years ago, in Pennsylvania, Mr. Justice Lewis, opposing a condition in a will in restraint of marriage of a widow, soared into what Lord Ellenborough called " the high sentimental latitudes," and broke forth into the following epithalamium :—

" The principle of reproduction stands next in importance to its elder-born correlative self-preservation, and is equally a fundamental law of existence. It is the blessing which tempered with mercy the justice of expulsion from Paradise. It was impressed upon the human creation by a beneficent Providence, to multiply the images of Himself, and thus to promote His own glory, and the happiness of His creatures. Not man alone, but the whole animal and vegetable kingdom, are under an imperious necessity to obey its mandates. From the lord of the forest to the monster of the deep, from the subtlety of the serpent to the innocence of the dove, from the celastic embrace of the mountain kalmia to the descending fructification of the lily of the plain, all Nature bows submissively to this primeval law. Even the flowers which perfume the air with their fragranee and decorate the forests and fields with their hues, are but 'curtains of the nuptial bed.' The principles of morality, the policy of the nations, the doctrines of the common law, the law of nature and the law of God, unite in condemning as void the conditions attempted to be imposed upon this widow." This charming specimen of the "art of sinking" can only be paralleled by Colley Cibber's well-known parody on Pope's lines on Lord Mansfield :—

" Persuasion tips his tongue whene'er he talks,
And he has chambers in the King's Bench walk."

ENGLISH *V.* FRENCH TRIBUNALS.

" SEVERAL times attended French courts of justice," says H. Crabb Robinson in his *Reminiscences*, "and heard both arguments before judges, and trials in criminal cases before juries. I have no remark to make on the arguments, for I never understood them sufficiently; and indeed I very imperfectly understood the examination of witnesses; but I did understand enough to enable me to come to this conclusion, that if I were guilty I should wish to be tried in England—if innocent, in France. Making this remark once to Southey, he changed the expression and said, "The English system seems to have for its object that no innocent person should be found guilty; the French system, that no criminal should escape." Now, if it be the fact that of the accused by far the greater number are guilty, it will follow that injustice is more frequent in the English than in the French courts.

" It is customary for the admirer of English law to boast of that feature of it which prohibits all attempts to make the prisoner convict himself, as if the State, represented in the court, had not a right to the truth, and as if a man who had violated the law were privileged through the violation. This surely betrays want of discrimination. It is right that no violence should be used to compel an answer, because that may as often produce falsehood as truth,—nor is any used in the French courts. But the prisoner is interrogated as well as the prosecutor and witnesses, and the same means are used to detect falsehood in all. If he refuse to answer, he is made to understand the unfavourable inferences that will be drawn. And this interrogation taking place before the public, no great injustice can be done."

These observations still remain true in the main, but the French system has its drawbacks. Public opinion in France being by no means so sensitive, nor of so high a standard as in this country, a style of cross-examining is allowed which would not be tolerated here. Browbeating of witnesses is quite common, and irrelevant questions are proposed merely to the effect of damning character. On the other hand, the French juries, in late cases, have been especially remarkable for flagrant injustice prompted by morbid sentimentality and romantic feeling.

LORD KENYON'S PARSIMONY.

THE hatchment put up over Lord Kenyon's house in Lincoln's Inn Fields, at his lordship's demise, bore the motto, *Mors Janua Vita*. When this mistake was mentioned to Lord Ellenborough, he exclaimed, " Mistake ! it is no mistake at all. The considerate testator left particular directions in his will that the estate should not be burdened with the expense of a diphthong."

QUALIFYING FOR BAIL.

GENTLEMAN once appeared in the Court of King's Bench to give bail in the sum of £3000. Serjeant Davy, eager to display his wit, asked him sternly, "And pray, sir, how do you make out that you are worth £3000?" The gentleman stated the particulars of his property, up to £2940. "That's all very good," said the serjeant, "but you want £60 more to be worth £3000." "For that sum," replied the gentleman, in no ways disconcerted, "I have the note of hand of one Mr. Serjeant Davy, and I hope he will have the honesty soon to settle it." The serjeant looked abashed, and Lord Mansfield observed, in his usual urbane tone, "Well, brother Davy, I *think* we may accept the bail."

JUSTICE TEMPERED WITH MERCY.

PEAKING about non-capital punishment William Lambard, the eminent lawyer and antiquary, in his *Eirenarchia, or Office of the Justice of Peace*, 1581, observes: "Of this kind of punishment our old law, *making pretious estimation of the lives of men*, had more sortes than we now have, as pulling out the tongue for false rumours, cutting of the nose for adultery, emasculating for counterfeiting money," etc. To these may be added pulling out of eyes, and cutting off hands or feet, "according to the greatness of the offence." Instances of these merciful punishments occur more frequently than is quite pleasant in old chronicles. Florence of Worcester, for instance, in his annals A.D. 1098, makes mention of some unfortunate Welshmen, who, for petty treason, had their hands and feet cut off, and their eyes pulled out, etc. "Rapinas Curialium," says William of Malmesbury, "stupra, edicto compescuit, deprehensis oculos cum testiculis evelli præcipiens." And in Fox's *Book of Martyrs* a miracle is reported in relation to this punishment. One Elivard, of Weston Regis, in Bedfordshire, being convicted in the reign of King Henry II., for stealing a pair of hedging-gloves and a whetstone, for the same crime lost his eyes and was otherwise mutilated. Through his devout prayers, made at the shrine of St. Thomas of Canterbury, however, the parts of his body he had been deprived of were again miraculously restored.

A HIGHWAYMAN'S CHANCERY SUIT.

IN 1725, a bill was brought in the Exchequer by a highwayman, named John Everett, against his companion, Joseph Williams, to compel him to account for a moiety of the partnership effects, the proceeds of their joint robberies. It did not state the unlawful employment in direct terms, but, notwithstanding that, the court would not entertain the application. The bill stated that the plaintiff, John Everett, of the parish of St. James's, Clerkenwell, gentleman, was skilled in dealing in several commodities, such as plate, rings, watches, etc.; that the defendant, Joseph Williams, gentleman, applied to him to become a partner; that they entered into partnership, and it was agreed that they should equally provide all sorts of necessaries, such as horses, saddles, bridles, and equally bear all expenses on the roads, and at inns, taverns, or alehouses, or at markets or fairs. "And your orator and the said Joseph Williams proceeded jointly with good success in the said business, on Hounslow Heath, where they dealt with a gentleman for a gold watch, and afterwards the said Joseph Williams told your orator, that Finchley, in the county of Middlesex, was a good and convenient place to deal in, and that commodities were very plentiful at Finchley aforesaid, and it would be almost all clear gain to them. That they went accordingly, and dealt with several gentlemen for divers watches, rings, swords, canes, hats, cloaks, horses, bridles, saddles, and other things; that about a month afterwards the said Joseph Williams informed your orator that there was a gentleman at Blackheath who had a good horse, saddle, bridle, watch, sword, cane, and other things to dispose of, which he believed might be had for little or no money; that they accordingly went, and met with the aforesaid gentleman, and, after some small discourse, they dealt for the said horse, etc. That your orator, and the said Joseph Williams, continued their joint dealings together in several places : viz., at Bagshot, in Surrey; Salisbury, in Wiltshire; Hampstead, in Middlesex; and elsewhere to the amount of £2000 and upwards." The rest of the bill was in the ordinary form of a partnership account. The parties concerned did not, however, gain much by this proceeding. The bill was referred for scandal and impertinence. The solicitors were attached and fined, and the counsel who signed the bill was directed to pay the costs. The plaintiff John Everett, gentleman, was executed at Tyburn, in 1730,* Joseph Williams at Maidstone in 1727 ; and one of the solicitors, William Wrenthock, was in 1735 sentenced to death for robbing Dr. Lancaster, but was reprieved and transported.

The whole bill filed in the court is given in the *European Magazine* for May, 1787, Vol. I., p. 360. The case was sufficiently notorious to have been referred to by Lord Kenyon, in *Ridley and Morse, Append. Cliff. Rep. of Southw. Elec.*

A somewhat similar instance is mentioned by the very learned annotator of *Saunders' Reports*, in which the courts refused to countenance a defence which strongly resembled the above case in its illegal nature. It was a prescription for a right of robbery on Gadshill.

---

* This gentleman left an autobiography, entitled " Genuine Narrative of the Memorable Life and Actions of John Everett, who formerly kept the Cock Alehouse in the Old Bailey, and lately the Tap in the Fleet Prison. Executed at Tyburn, on Friday the 20th day of February, 1729-30. Written by himself when under condemnation, and in his cell in Newgate, and published at his own request. London, 1730."

PERPLEXITIES OF THE LAW.

"LAW," said Dr. Johnson, "is the science in which the greatest powers of the understanding are applied to the greatest number of facts." No one who is acquainted with the variety and multiplicity of the subjects of jurisprudence, and with the prodigious powers of discrimination employed upon them, can doubt the truth of this observation.

BACON AND HOG.

IN the good old times the lightest heed was taken of the punishment of death. It was not, as now, a rare and solemn sentence, but staple judicial routine, that might be enlivened with a joke, when possible, to colour its monotony. Thus Lord Bacon tells of his father, Sir Nicholas, that when appointed a judge on the Northern Circuit, "he was by one of the malefactors mightily importuned for to save his life, which, when nothing he had said did avail, he at length desired his mercy on account of kindred. "Prithee," said my lord judge, "how came that in?" "Why, if it please you, my lord, your name is Bacon, and mine is Hog; and in all ages Hog and Bacon have been so near kindred that they are not to be separated." "Ay; but," replied Judge Bacon, "you and I cannot be kindred except you be hanged; for Hog is not Bacon until it be well hanged."

LORD KENYON'S TEMPER.

LORD KENYON was a man of a violent and petulant temper. Whilst at the bar he was engaged in perpetual wrangles with his colleagues. Once, having conducted himself with much irritation of manner, the judge said to him, "Pray, Mr. Kenyon, keep your temper." "My lord," said Mr. Cowper, who was sitting by, "you had better recommend him to part with it as soon as possible."

He was once examined respecting the emoluments of his office before a committee of the House of Commons, over which Mr. Abbot, who then held a subordinate post in the King's Bench, presided. Lord Kenyon, declining to reply to some question put to him, the chairman, with characteristic pomposity, informed him that he was "armed with the authority of the Commons' House of Parliament." "Sir," replied the irascible chief justice, "I have not come here to be yelped at by my own turnspit."

DURATION OF CRIMINAL TRIALS.

N ancient times trials never lasted beyond a day. Burke said trial by jury was unfit for cases which did not lie within the compass of one day, and it was not until modern times that they lasted longer. In the case of Lord George Gordon, in 1781, Lord Mansfield sat from eight in the morning until five next morning ; and as he and the jury were *able* to sit, he felt himself bound in law to do so. But when trials came to last several days it became physically impossible. In the case of Elizabeth Canning, tried for perjury in the middle of the last century, which excited immense interest, the trial lasted fifteen days. In the State trials for treason, in 1794, Thelwall's lasted four days, Horne Tooke's, six, and Handy's, nine days. Of course, in such cases it was physically impossible to sit on without intermission, and, accordingly, Lord Kenyon and the judges resolved that they had power to adjourn, but only, as Lord Kenyon stated, on the ground of actual physical *necessity*. This was laid down in 1796, and in 1819 Lord Tenterden applied the same rule to trials for misdemeanour. Until the Tichborne case, no one had ever conceived that there was power to adjourn a criminal trial for any other cause : and a long train of learned judges—Gurney,

Cresswell, Wightman, Willes, and Watson—held that it was inadmissible to adjourn for purposes of evidence, though it might be admissible to suspend the trial for a short time for the attendance of witnesses in consequence of some unavoidable accident. Even in civil cases adjournment is only allowed by a statute passed in 1854, and that statute does not apply to criminal cases. The adjournments in the Tichborne case for purposes of evidence were unprecedented, especially the first adjournment, which was not for the attendance of witnesses, but for the discovery of new evidence.

CAPITAL JOKING.

THE conduct on the bench of Lord Braxfield, a Scotch judge of the last century, was a disgrace to the age. A dexterous and practical trier of ordinary cases, he was harsh to prisoners even in his jocularity. It may be doubted if he was ever so much in his element as when tauntingly repelling the last despairing claim of a wretched culprit, and sending him to Botany Bay or to the gallows with an insulting jest—over which he would chuckle the more from observing that correct people were shocked. "You're a vera clever chiel, mon," he remarked once to a very argumentative culprit at the bar ; "but I'm thinking ye wad be nane the waur of a hanging." Yet this was not from cruelty, for which he was too strong and too jovial, but from cherished coarseness. He was the Jeffreys of Scotland during the political trials of 1793 and 1794. "Let them bring me prisoners, and I'll find them law," used to be openly stated as his suggestion when an intended political prosecution was marred by anticipated difficulties. Mr. Horner, who was one of the jurors in Muir's case, told Lord Cockburn that, when he was passing, as was then often done, behind the bench to get into the box, Braxfield, who knew him, whispered, " Come awa, Maister Horner, come awa, and help us to hang one o' thae daamned scoundrels." The reporter of Gerald's case could not venture to make the prisoner say more than that "Christianity was an innovation." "But the full truth is," says Lord Cockburn, "that in stating this view he added that all great men had been reformers, even our Saviour Himself." "Muckle he made o' that," chuckled the profane Braxfield, in an undertone; "He was hanget." Before Hume's Commentaries had made our criminal record intelligible, the forms and precedents were a mystery understood by the initiated alone, and by nobody so much as by Mr. Joseph Norris, the ancient clerk. Braxfield used to quash anticipated doubts by saying, "Hoot l just gie me Josie Norris and a gude jury, an' I'll doo for the fallow." This disgrace to the bench died in 1799, in his seventy-ninth year.

SUIVEZ RAISON.

SOME years ago a suitor in the Dublin Court of Exchequer complained in person to Lord Yelverton that he was quite *ruinated*, and could go on no further. "Then," said the chief baron, "you had better leave the matter to be decided by reference." "To be sure I will, my lord," said the plaintiff; "I've been now at law thirteen years, and can't get on at all ! I'm willing, please your lordship, to leave it all either to *one honest man* or two *attorneys*, whichever your lordship pleases." "You had better toss up for that," said Lord Yelverton, laughing. Two attorneys were, however, appointed, and in less than a *year* reported that they could not agree. The litigant parties then declared they would leave the matter to a very honest farmer, a neighbour of theirs. They did so, and in about a *week* came hand-in-hand to the court, thanked his lordship, and told him their neighbour had settled the whole affair square and straight to their entire satisfaction. Lord Yelverton used to tell this anecdote with great glee.

A SPORTIVE LAW.

THE idle subtleties that have been spent by criminal lawyers upon the subject of theft could scarcely be seen to more advantage than in the consideration of that element of thieving, which consists in carrying the stolen thing away, or, as the books called it, the "*asportavit.*" Thus it was held that if a prisoner removed a package from the head to the tail of a waggon the "asportavit" was complete. But if he removed it only by lifting it up where it lay and standing it on end, for the purpose of ripping it open, the "asportavit" was not complete, because every part of the package was not shown to be moved. The central point of it might be exactly where it was before. This was understood by the poet, who declared the "asportavit" to be complete, when—

> " The king of hearts
> He stole some tarts
> And took them quite away."

A SINGULAR PLURAL CASE.

MOST amusing instance of identification of counsel with client is related. It occurred in the case of a counsel for a female prisoner, who was convicted on a capital charge, and on her being asked what she had to say why sentence of death should not be passed upon her, he rose and said, "If you please, my lord, *we* are with child." This anecdote has an air of manufacture about it. Counsel would have known that pregnancy cannot be taken advantage of in arrest of judgment, but only in stay of execution. The hackneyed quotation, however, is applicable : "Se non è vero, è ben trovato."

THE BETTER HALF OF A PAUPER.

ON the 7th of December, 1815, a case came before the Clerkenwell Sessions, ludicrous from the minuteness required in the examination. Was a certain pauper settled in the parish A or B ? The house he occupied was in both parishes, and models, both of the house and the bed in which the pauper slept, were laid before the court, that it might be ascertained how much of his body lay in each parish. The court held the pauper to be settled where his head lay (being the nobler part) though one of his legs and the greater part of his body lay in the next parish.

A NICE POINT.

GRAINGER says that Sir Edmund Anderson, subsequently Lord Chief Justice, sat in judgment upon Mary Queen of Scots, in October, 1586, and the next year he presided at the trial of Secretary Davison, in the Star Chamber, for signing the warrant for the execution of that princess. His decision in that nice point was that he had done *justum non juste*. He had done what was right in an unlawful manner, otherwise he thought him no bad man. "This," adds Noble, "was excellent logic for finding an innocent man guilty."

Lord Chief Justice Anderson was an able lawyer, but adhered rigorously to the statutes. In the trial of Henry Cuffe, secretary to Queen Elizabeth's Earl of Essex, when the attorney-general argued the case on general principles, the chief justice said, "I sit here to judge of law, and not of logic."

TALKING METAPHOR.

MR. (afterwards Sir) R. Dallas, who was junior counsel for Warren Hastings, is reported to have said in one of his speeches :—"Now we are advancing from the starlight of circumstantial evidence to the daylight of discovery ; the sun

E

of certainty has melted the darkness, and we have arrived at the facts admitted by both parties."

"When I cannot talk sense, I talk metaphor," said Curran, very shrewdly.

MANNERS AT OXFORD IN 1625.

ONE of the cases in Littleton would present but a bad idea of the manners at Oxford in 1625. We find at least the principal of St. Mary's Hall libelling one of the masters of art, and a commoner of the same hall, calling him "red-nose," "mamsey" (*i.e.*, malmsey, a sort of wine), "nose," "copper-nose knave," "rascal," "base fellow," and other names. Another case speaks as ill of the behaviour of communicants in those days of Archbishop Laud. The Rev. Mr. Burnet sues one Symons in the High Commission Court, because he has called him fool in the church, and addressed him as "Sirrah! sirrah!" and because moreover, he, Burnet, being vicar there, Symons, at Whitsuntide, after the Communion was ended, took the cup and drank all the wine that was left; and that when Mr. Burnet took the cup from him, Symons violently tore it from his hands, in the presence of many parishioners who had not yet left the church. It is curious, and perhaps worth noting, that the court decided that all the wine that was left after the Communion belonged to the parson. The same declaration will be found, I believe, in the rubric to the Book of Common Prayer, printed in the time of Charles II. It shows the doctrine of that day, though at present a special and more reverent provision is made for the case.

A TRAVELLING OPINION.

SERJEANT Fazakerley, an eminent Chancery barrister in the time of Lord Hardwicke, being on a visit in the country during the long vacation, was one day riding out with a rich squire who happened at that time to be about engaging in a lawsuit, and thought it a good opportunity to pump an opinion out of the counsellor gratis. The serjeant gave his opinion in such a way that the squire was encouraged to go on with the suit, which, however, he lost, after expending considerable sums. Irritated by his disappointment he waited upon the serjeant at his chambers, and exclaimed, "Zounds, Mr. Serjeant, here I have lost £3000 by your advice." "By my advice," said Fazakerley, "how can that be? I don't remember giving you my advice; but let me look over my book." "Book!" exclaimed the squire, "there is no occasion to look at your book. It was when we were riding together last autumn near Pembridge, in Herefordshire." "Oh!" exclaimed the serjeant, "now I remember something of it; but, neighbour, that was only my travelling opinion, and my opinion is never to be relied on except it is registered in my fee-book."

THE BLIND GODDESS.

JUDGE BURNETT being applied to by an old farmer for his advice in a lawsuit, heard his case with great patience, and then asked him "if he had ever put in a lottery." "No, sir," said the farmer, "I hope I have too much prudence to run such risks." "Then, take my advice, my good friend, and suffer any inconvenience rather than go to law, as the chances are more against you there than in any lottery."

PLAIN ENGLISH.

A BOLD, familiar, and forcible manner, conveying to the minds of all present a belief that the speaker is in earnest, is the most effective style for addressing a jury. An editor of a newspaper brought an action against three gentlemen, who had been attacked in his paper, and who had taken the law in their own hands, by inflicting a severe cor-

poreal chastisement on the editor. Mr. Charles Phillips, who
was of counsel for the complainant, made a splendid speech,
depicting with great eloquence the cruelty with which his client
had been treated, and managed very evidently to carry the jury
along with him. Mr. (afterwards Justice) Taunton, who appeared for the defendants, quickly obliterated the impression
his opponent had made, by saying in a powerful, but familiar
tone, " My friend's eloquent complaint in plain English
amounts to this—that his client has received a good horse-
whipping ; and mine is as short—*that he richly deserved it.*"

PUNNING TRIALS.

IT was said by Cicero, on the authority of Ennius, that
a wise man sooner could keep a red-hot coal in his
mouth, than not to give utterance to a joke which
struck him. " Dicere enim aiunt Ennium : flammam a sapiente
facilius ore in ardente opprimi, quam bona dicta teneat, hæc
sic licet bona quæ salsa sunt" (*Cic. de Orat.* II., 54).   The
same luminary of the Roman bar, in his treatise concerning
oratory, allows the admissibility of puns, and goes to the trouble
of laying down certain rules for the licence allowed in that
respect, but the specimens of puns he gives are very poor, and
would even be rejected by the illustrated comical papers of the
present day.   Dr. Johnson's opinion that punning was akin to
petty larceny was never admitted in court.   It is even said that
when somebody observed to Lord Eldon that punning was a
very low sort of wit, he answered, " You are right, sir, for it is
the foundation of all wit."   His lordship certainly was very
fond of enlivening the dullness of a case with wit of that kind.

The punning bout between him and Sir Samuel Romilly, in
Re Fax *v.* Metcalfe, a question of the infringement of a patent
for hairbrushes, has been too often in print to find a place here.
A similar strain of so-called wit is less generally known.   It
was displayed in the trial of a cause in 1824, in which one How

was plaintiff, and one Much defendant. Serjeant Pell, who was concerned in the case, punned on the parties' names all through his speech. After putting *How* through all the changes that it could undergo, he observed that he "had still a difficult task to perform, for *Much* remained to be *done*." He then went on and assured the jury, that although the case was one of the greatest importance, and the proof was very brief indeed, yet, if they gave the verdict, which he earnestly trusted they would, the reflection would at least be theirs, that they had *done Much*." He then went on to speak of these two unhappy names together, and How-Much was presented in all its combinations ; but, with all his wit, the learned serjeant did not succeed in punning the jury out of a verdict.

OBSOLETE LAWS.

RAKED from the ashes where still "live their wonted fires," may be found, as chance offers, the remains of "strict statutes and most biting laws." Not many years since a Dorsetshire labourer made a disturbance in a church. The offence was becoming common, and the law on the subject was intricate. But industry discovered an old Act of Parliament, not passed in Protestant times, but in the reign of Mary, nicknamed "Bloody." Under this law he was committed for nearly six days, then sent to prison by two justices for three months, and beyond that to the Quarter Sessions. There he was to express his sense of repentance, and to find a surety for one year for his good behaviour. And if he refused to repent, he was to remain in gaol. But the Dorsetshire labourer did repent, after having been in prison for some months. Another statute, of which Lord Wensleydale had the care, prescribes an easy and mitigated remedy for these unholy brawls ; " but we are much mistaken, says Serjeant Woolrych " (*Lives of Eminent Serjeants*, Vol. II. p. 836), "if the old Act of Queen Mary is not still on the Statute Book."

Some twenty years since, a pawnbroker gave a magistrate in London considerable trouble respecting the return of certain pledges, in compensation for some misconduct. There was a legal remedy, but the broker was disposed to defy the bench. The magistrate thought awhile, and directed the clerk to hand a volume of the Acts of Parliament to him. It was there found that the offence charged upon the defendant was punishable with a public whipping. Fearfully crestfallen, the pawnbroker yielded at once. The punishment was such as the bench could hardly award at that time of day. But *there* was the *statute*.

Swift had a notion which partook of fear as to these old laws. He somewhere remarks, " What if there be an old dormant statute or two against him, are they not now obsolete ? " The extraordinary modern discovery of the severe penalty against the Rapparees, and lately in Ireland the use of those made against the White Boys, must be familiar to all readers.

PROGNOSTICATION.

JUSTICE WILLES had an unpleasant habit of inter-rupting the counsel. On one such occasion Serjeant Gurney said to him, " Your lordship is even a greater man than your father. The chief baron used to understand me after I had done, but your lordship understands me before I begin."

MEMINISSE JUVABIT.

SERJEANT WILLIAM DAVY, like a well-known chief justice in the reign of Charles II., learnt what he knew in the King's Bench Prison. He was a druggist or grocer at Exeter, and became a bankrupt. But by force of a strong natural understanding, he became eminent at *Nisi Prius*, which such a man may be without knowing much law. He usually went by the name of " Bull Davy," on account of his manners. Being once on the Western Circuit, he cross-examined an old woman very rigorously respecting a circumstance that had happened within her observation some years before, " And pray, good woman," said the serjeant, " how is it that you should be so particular as to remember that this affair happened on a market day ? " " Why, sir," replied the woman, " by ths token—that all the cry of the city went that Mr. Davy, the drugster, had that morning shut up shop and run away." " I think, brother," said the judge, " that you want no further proof of the witness's memory."

THE LANGUAGE OF COMMON SENSE.

ORD CHANCELLOR ELDON, although born close to the Scottish border, affected not to understand the Scottish dialect and pronunciation. He was once hearing appeals in the House of Lords, and Mr. Clerk, an eminent Edinburgh lawyer (subsequently a judge and styled Lord Eldin), having said in his broadest accent, " In plain English, my lords,' was interrupted, half seriously, by Lord Eldon, with— " In plain Scotch, I suppose you mean ? " " Nae matter," rejoined Clerk, " in plain common sense, my lord ; and that's the same n all languages, ye'll ken, if you understand it."

A CANDID CONFESSION.

IR FLETCHER NORTON was noted for his want of courtesy. When pleading before Lord Mansfield on some question of manorial rights, he chanced unfortunately to say, " My lord, I can illustrate this point in an instant in my own person : I myself have two little manors." The judge immediately interposed with one of his blandest smiles, " We all know it, Sir Fletcher."

THE GREAT SEAL LOST.

LORD ELDON, when lord chancellor, never went to bed a single night without having the Great Seal of England in his chamber. In the night of the 18th of September, 1812, a fire broke out at Encombe, his seat, by which one wing of the house was destroyed. Speaking about this event towards the close of his life, with his niece Mrs. Forster, he said, "It really was a very pretty sight, for all the maids turned out of their beds, and they formed a line from the water to the fire-engine, handing the buckets ; they looked very pretty, all in their shifts. My first care was the Great Seal ; so, by way of securing it during the confusion, I buried it. The next morning, when I came to reflect, I could not remember the spot where I had put it : you never saw anything so ridiculous, as seeing the whole family down that walk, probing and digging till we found it."

ERRARE HUMANUM EST.

IN the last century many persons who, like Shallow, could write themselves "in any bill, warrant, quittance or obligation armigero," were made magistrates in Ireland without any qualification for that office. The vade-meum of such J.P.'s, under which they dispensed law very indifferently, was Mac Nally's *Justice of the Peace in Ireland*, which has long been to magistrates in Ireland what Burn's *Justice* is to those of this country. As originally published however Mac Nally was full of errors, and those who acted on it often found themselves drawn into lawsuits as defendants. "What could make you act so?" Mac Nally would ask. "Faith, sir, I acted on the advice of your own book." Not much taken aback, for such scenes were frequent, Mac Nally would say, "As a human work the book has errors, no doubt ; but I shall correct them when it comes to a second edition."

Mac Nally was the author of the well-known song, *The Lass of Richmond Hill*, which he wrote in honour of a Miss Janson. She sympathized with him in scribbling verses and not washing her hands. They were married, lived happily, and to the last were economic in the use of soap.

SHAKESPEARE'S KNOWLEDGE OF THE LAW.

"THE first thing we do," says Dick, the butcher of Ashford in *Henry VI.*, "let's kill all the lawyers;" and Jack Cade, "Now go some and pull down the Inns of Court ; down with them all." And in *Richard III.*, iv. 4, the poet talks of "windy attorners to their clients' woes." Evil-disposed persons might perhaps adduce these passages as proofs of Shakespeare's thorough acquaintance with the professors of the law. But that is a matter of opinion.

That Shakespeare was a universal genius is a truism : there is not a subject within the range of the human mind which seems to have been unfamiliar to him. Still his knowledge of law terms is remarkable. Charles and Mary Cowden Clarke, in their *Shakespeare Key*, give no less than 114 quotations from his works in which legal terms are used, and no doubt a professional jurist would find still more evidences of his intimate acquaintance with the law. It is true in many instances Shakespeare uses legal terms pretty generally known, such as vouchers, free farm, fee simple, fine and recovery, and in Hamlet's beautiful speculations about the skull : "Why ! may not that be the skull of a lawyer? Where be his *quiddits* now, his *quillets*, his *cases*, his *tenures*, and his tricks? Why does he suffer this rude knave now to knock him about the sconce with a dirty shovel, and will not tell him of his *action of battery?* H'm ! This fellow might be in 's time a great buyer of land, with his *statutes*, his *recognizances*, his *fines*, his *double vouchers*, his *recoveries :* is this the fine of his *fines* and the recovery of his *recoveries*, to have his fine pate full of fine dirt ? Will his *vouchers* vouch him no more of his *purchases*, and *double* ones too, than the length and breadth of a pair of *indentures ?* The very *conveyances* of his land will hardly lie in this box ; and must the *inheritor* himself have no more? " All the terms here used are familiar to most men,* but there occur others in Shakespeare's works which betray a more intimate acquaintance with the law than generally falls to the share of outsiders ; such as : " She hath enfranchised them upon some other pawn for fealty," *Two Gentlemen of Verona*, ii. 4 ; " Let her except before excepted," *Twelfth Night*, i. 3 ; " He came but . . . . . to sue his livery," 1 *Henry IV.*, iv. 3 ; " I was taken with the manner," *Love's Labour Lost*, i. 1 ; " Those precepts cannot be served," 2 *Henry IV.*, v. 1 ; " It shall be bootless that longer you desire the court," *Henry VIII.*, ii. 4 ; "·An act has three branches," *Hamlet*, v. 1 ; " To pray in aid," *Antony and Cleopatra*, v. 2 ; " To 'cide this title is impannelled a quest of thoughts," *Sonnet XLVI.* ; "Men shall hold of me *in capite*," *Henry VIII.*, iii. 2 ; etc. The learned compilers account for these terms by Shakespeare's familiarity with the attorneys Thomas Greenes, father and son, at Stratford-on-Avon, and with the law-students and lawyers with whom the poet associated in London. To a mind like Shakespeare's the acquisition of knowledge of all sorts was like inhaling the air he breathed, a strong vital necessity. He could no more help the one than the other, and both he turned to best account. Still the accurate use remains astonishing, and since nothing of Shakespeare's youth is known to the contrary, it is not impossible that he commenced life as a lawyer's clerk. There is nothing improbable in the supposition that his parents, perceiving the wonderful parts of the " divine William," should have devoted him to that profession in which they thought, from brilliant instances within their recollection, that most chances of success seemed to await him.

* Nowadays, thanks in a great measure to the newspapers, but would not be quite so familiar to Shakespeare's contemporaries.

LORD CAMPBELL ON DICKENS.

IN the Court of Queen's Bench, the name of Mr. Charles Dickens having been called, Lord Campbell said, "The name of the illustrious Charles Dickens has been called on the jury, but he has not answered. If his great chancery suit, Jarndyce *v.* Jarndyce, had been still going on, I certainly would have excused him, but, as that is over, he might have done us the honour of attending here, that he might have seen how we went on at common law."

CONSANGUINITY.

AT the time when making a new serjeant was considered an important event, part of the ceremony was a procession which set out from the Temple westwards, up Surrey Street, in the Strand, and then, turning eastwards, went up Chancery Lane to Serjeants' Inn, where those who already held the rank were assembled in their hall to receive the new serjeant ; and on his approach the intimation was given, " I spy a brother." When Prime, noted for his interminable and prosy speeches, was called to the rank of serjeant, some one placed a stuffed owl at the first-floor window of a house in the Strand, directly facing Surrey Street, with a label round his neck, on which was written in large characters, " I spy a brother."

A CANDID WITNESS.

ONCE in the case of an action brought for the non-fulfilment of a contract on a large scale for shoes, before Lord Kenyon, the question mainly was, whether or not they were well and soundly made, and with the best materials. A number of witnesses were called. One of them, a first-rate master of the gentle craft, being closely questioned, returned contradictory answers, when the chief justice observed, pointing

to his own frequently re-soled shoes, which were regularly be-
stridden by the broad silver buckle of the day : "Were the
shoes anything like these?" "No, my lord," replied the evidence, "they were a good deal better and more genteeler."
The court was convulsed with laughter, in which the chief
justice heartily joined.

DRIVING IT HOME.

THE late James Fergusson, clerk of the sessions, a most
genial and amiable man, of whose periodical fits of
absence most edifying stories are still repeated by his
friends, was an excellent and eloquent speaker, but, in truth,
there was often more sound than matter in his orations. He
had a habit of lending emphasis to his arguments, by violently
thumping with his clenched hand the bar before which he
pleaded. Once when stating a case before Lord Polkemmet,
with great energy of action, his lordship interposed and exclaimed, "Maister Jemmy, dinna dunt ; ye think ye're duntin 't
into me, and ye're just duntin 't *out o' me.*"

THE WRATHFUL BARBER.

"AT Appleby Assizes," says Lord Eldon, "I cross-examined a barber rather too severely. He got into a
great passion. I desired him to moderate his anger,
and said that I should employ him to shave me as I passed
through Kendal to the Lancaster Assizes. He said with great
indignation, 'I would not advise you, lawyer, to think of that
or risk it.'"

A POETICAL CIRCUIT.

HE old South Wales Circuit, in the last century was an office of some emolument and honour, and no fatigue. The civil business was necessarily slight from the smallness of the counties, comprising a rural population and an insignificant amount of traffic. As to the criminal cases, the extent of them was best explained by a jocular serjeant, who went that barren round, and when asked if he expected much business on the circuit, replied off-hand, " Very little, as far as I collect. We read of three or four murders in the calendar ; but I understand the parties have met and made it up ; they are all compromised." Mr. Hardinge, one of the South Wales judges, prone to rhetorical effusions, was accustomed to vary his addresses to the grand juries in the following manner. " At Brecon, he would say, " Where, gentlemen, is my calendar ? It is not in my hand ; it is a perfect blank. There is not one prisoner for trial." When he got to Cardiff, he would say, " I cannot forbear to admire the eloquence of the gaoler and of his calendar. There I perceive three little words never to be sur-passed by Demosthenes himself, *None for Trial.* May those brilliant words record and perpetuate the honour of this county for ages to come." Arrived at the last circuit town, Presteign, the learned orator would thus ring a triple bob major over the paucity of crime : " I pass over the calendar with its pilfered watch, the single and petty offence brought before us, just as if no calendar had been put into my hands. We come to deliver, as it is called, an empty gaol." The increase of a manu-facturing population has tended to destroy this Arcadian sim-plicity, but in North Wales the same absence of felons still prevailed not forty years ago. When Lord Lyndhurst, then chief baron, first visited Dolgelly, he expressed his surprise to the high sheriff, that there should not be a single prisoner for trial. That worthy official seemed afraid that his lordship might be offended at such a state of things, and answered with much concern for the honour of Merionethshire, "I can assure you, my lord, the whole county has been in pursuit of a sheep-stealer." On another circuit one of the puisne barons, who was not disinclined to blend judicial gravity with wit, found in the assize town of Flintshire only one prisoner, charged with simple larceny, and is reported to have thus pithily harangued the grand jury, whose full number was complete, "Well, gentlemen, four-and-twenty of us to one poor duck."

PILLARS OF THE LAW.

ONE of the customs, which used to be observed so late as the reign of Charles I., in the creation of serjeants, was for the new dignitary to go in procession to St. Paul's, and there to choose his pillar. There they stood at their pillars, like merchants on change, and received their clients. "There is a tradition," says old Dugdale, in his *Origines Judiciales*, "that in times past there was one Inn of Court at Dowgate, called Johnson's Inn, another in Fetter Lane, and another in Paternoster Row; which last they would prove, because it was next to St. Paul's Church, where each lawyer and serjeant at his pillar heard his client's cause, and took notes thereof upon his knee, as they do in Guildhall at this day. And that after the serjeants' feast ended, they do still go to Paul's in their habits, and there choose their pillars, whereat to hear their client's cause (if any come) in memory of that old custom."

This ceremony is thus described in "The Manner or Order of making of New Serjeants created and made in Trinity Term, 13 Hen. VIII." (1522): "When the new serjeants have dined, then they go in sober manner with their officers and servants into London, on the east side of Cheapside, unto St. Thomas's of Acre, and there they offer, and then come down to the west side of Cheapside, to Paul's, and there offer at the rood of the north door, and at St. Erkenwald's shrine, and then go down into the body of the church, and they be appointed to their pillars by the steward and comptroller of the feast, who brought them thither with the other officers."

An anonymous " Resident in London " witnessed this ceremony in the next reign, when, Protestantism being then the order of the day, it was slightly but not very materially different from the Catholic days of Henry VIII. It is recorded in his " Diary" in the following words : " The xviij day of October (1552), was made vii serjeants of the coif, and after dinner they went unto Paul's, and so went up the steps and round the choir, and there they did their homage, and so to the north side of Paul's, and stood upon the steps, until iiij old serjeants came together, and fetched iiij [of the new ones], and brought them unto certain pillars, and left them, and there they fetched the residue unto the pillars." Nor was this custom solely connected with St. Paul's ; it was also observed in the Temple Church. " And for advice 'twixt him and us, he had made choice of a lawyer, a mercer, and a merchant, who that morning was appointed to meet him in the Temple " (Middleton, *Father Hubbard's Tales*, 1604). Indeed, it seems to have been customary in all churches, for when Laud consecrated the church of St. Catherine Cree, he particularly pronounced a curse upon " all who should make a law court of it."

Lord Campbell, in his *Lives of the Lord Chancellors*, speaking of this custom, observed that there was nothing discreditable in it, and that some provincial counsel are still said to " keep the market," in the towns where they reside. The practice of taking instructions directly from a client was followed by the most eminent members of the English Bar, up to a recent period. Not only young students, but even such men as Sir Edward Coke and Sir James Astham then were, took instructions from their clients in person. Be this as it may, the practice of taking instructions from any one but a solicitor or attorney, has been opposed to the etiquette of the profession for many years, and few nowadays are able to bear witness to any member of the bar holding " purvis " in any provincial town.

A LORD CHIEF JUSTICE AT THE BAR.

N the reign of William and Mary, the great sinecure of chief clerk of the Court of King's Bench, compensated by a pension of £9000 a year, falling vacant, Sir John Holt granted it to his brother Roland. Hereupon the question arose whether the patronage belonged to the chief justice or the king. This came to be tried by a trial at bar before three puisne judges and a jury. A chair was placed on the floor of the court for Lord Chief Justice Holt, on which he sat uncovered near his counsel. It was then proved that the chief justices of the King's Bench had appointed to the office from the earliest times, till a patent was granted irregularly by Charles II. to his natural son the Duke of Grafton. In consequence of this there was a verdict against the Crown, which was confirmed on appeal by the House of Lords.

"HEADS OR TAILS."

HALES and sturgeons are royal fish, and formerly, when either cast ashore or caught near the coast, belonged to the Crown. Blackstone notices a curious distinction made by the old legal authorities, which is that the whale is to be divided between the king and the queen, the king taking the head and the queen the tail ; the reason assigned being that the queen might have the whalebone for her wardrobe, although in fact the whalebone is found in the head and not in the tail. (Forsyth, *Cases and Opinions on Constitutional Law*, p. 178.)

THE "GLORIOUS UNCERTAINTY."

URING the debate on the reform of criminal law, in 1811, the following statement was made, illustrative of the faultiness of the then state of the law. Not many years previously, on the Norfolk Circuit, a larceny was com-

mitted by two men in a poultry-yard, one of whom was appre-
hended. This man was tried at the next assizes, found guilty,
and sentenced by Lord Loughborough to a few months' imprisonment. When the accomplice heard of this he surrendered,
and was tried at the following assizes. Unfortunately for him
the presiding judge was Mr. Justice Gould, who had observed
or fancied that a man who sets out with stealing fowls generally
ends in committing atrocious crimes. On this ground he sentenced the criminal to transportation, proving the truth of the
lines—

> " 'Tis with our *judgments* as our watches, none
> Go just alike, yet each believes his own."

A GRAND POULTRY CASE.

AT the Cork Summer Assizes in 1833, a prisoner was indicted for stealing some cocks and hens from a poor
woman. The trial took place before Baron Pennefather. The case of the prosecution was conducted by Mr.
Garrett Standish Barry, member of parliament for the county,
barrister-at-law ; and the prisoner was defended by Mr. Fergus
O'Connor, member of parliament for the county, barrister-
at-law. Two knights of the shire arguing points of law in a
cock and hen case had probably never before appeared in a
court of justice, and the presiding judge's sense of the ludicrous
was irresistibly tickled. On reference being made to him upon
a disputed point, he declared that he would leave it all to "the
two legislators" to settle as they pleased. Mr. Barry was
distinguished by overgrown black whiskers ; and Fergus was
equally conspicuous for a red head of hair. Upon the judge
expressing the above opinion, a droll attorney rose, and convulsed the court with laughter by exclaiming, " In that case, my
lord, I'll back *red ginger* [meaning Fergus] at any time against
the *black cock.*"

F

TYBURN TICKETS.

Y virtue of the Act 10 and 11 Will. III. c. 23, s. 2 (1689), a certificate was given to the prosecutor on the capital conviction of a criminal, which exempted the prosecutor from all manner of parish and ward offices within the parish where such felony was committed. Such a certificate was called a **Tyburn ticket,** of which the following is an example :—

"THESE ARE TO CERTIFY that at the Session of General Gaol Delivery of Newgate, holden for the County of Middlesex, at Justice Hall, in the Old Bailey, in the Suburbs of the City of London, on Wednesday the thirteenth Day of January last, before us whose names are hereunto subscribed, and others his Majesty's Justices assigned to deliver the said Gaol of the prisoners therein being. John Spicer was tried and convicted of feloniously and burglariously breaking and entering in the night-time of the Thirtieth Day of December last, the Dwelling-House of the Reverend John Ousby, Clerk, at the Parish of St. Luke, Chelsea, in the said County of Middlesex, and stealing therein Goods of the value of Six Pounds and Fourteen Shillings, his property. And it is hereby further certified, that the said Reverend John Ousby was the person that did apprehend and take the said John Spicer, and did prosecute him until he was convicted of the said burglary. And pursuant to an Act of Parliament, made and passed in the tenth and eleventh year of the reign of his Majesty King William the Third, entituled An Act for the better Apprehending, Prosecuting, and Punishing of Felons that commit Burglary, House-breaking, or Robbery in Shops, Warehouses, Coach-houses, or Stables, or that steal Horses, he, the said JOHN OUSBY, ought to be, and is hereby discharged of and from all, and all manner Parish and Ward Offices, within the said parish of St. Luke, Chelsea, in the County of Middlesex aforesaid, wherein the said burglary was committed. And this we do certify in order to His being Discharged accordingly. Dated the seventeenth Day of February, in the Fifty-third year of the Reign of Our Sovereign Lord George the Third, by the Grace of God of the United Kingdom of Great Britain and Ireland, King, Defender of the Faith, And in the year of Our Lord One Thousand Eight hundred and thirteen.

GEO. SCHOLEY, *Mayor.*
JOHN SILVESTER, *Recorder.*"

Such tickets could be transferred once, under the following form :—

" Know all Men by these presents That I, the within-named C. D. of the Parish of   in the County of in pursuance of the power given me by the Act of Parliament within mentioned, and in consideration of the Sum of ǀ of lawful Money of Great Britain, to me in hand paid by of the same Parish and County, the Receipt whereof I do hereby acknowledge, have bargained, sold assigned, and transferred, and by these presents do hereby Bargain, Sell, Assign and Transfer unto the said   , as well the Certificate within written, as all Rights, Interests, and Demands of me, the said C. D., thereto, and all Exemptions, Benefit, and Advantage that may be had and made thereof, by virtue of the said Act of Parliament, as fully as I myself might or could have had if these presents had not been made. And, I, the said C. D., by these presents do hereby Covenant to and with the said   that I have not Assigned the said Certificate, other than by these presents, nor have made use thereof myself, nor have done, nor shall hereafter do any act, whereby the said   shall or may be deprived of the benefit or advantage which he is entitled to thereby, and by virtue of the said Act of Parliament. In Witness whereof I have hereunto set my Hand and Seal, this   Day of in the   year of the Reign of Our Sovereign Lord, George the Third, by the Grace of God of the United Kingdom of Great Britain and Ireland, King, Defender of the Faith, and in the year of Our Lord,

Signed, Sealed and Delivered by   C. D. (L. S.)"
the above-named C. D. (being
first duly stamped) in the
presence of

The act concerning the granting of Tyburn Tickets was repealed by 58 Geo. III. c. 70, passed June 3, 1818. Mr. George Philips, late of Charlotte Street, Bloomsbury, and now residing in Kingsgate Street, Theobald's Road, was the last individual who received one, for the conviction of two burglars who had broken into his premises. As late as the autumn of 1856, however, Mr. Pratt, armourer of New Bond Street, claimed and obtained exemption from serving on the jury, by reason of his possession of a Tyburn Ticket. Probably the judge did not remember that they had been abolished.

The usual price for the transfer of a Tyburn Ticket appears to have been ten pounds. Some peculiar interest must have been attached, therefore, to the ticket, which, according to the *Stamford Mercury* of March 27, 1818, was sold at that time in Manchester for the exorbitant sum of £280.

OPPOSING AN EJECTMENT.

N a motion once before Lord Norbury, a sheriff's officer who had the hardihood to serve a process in Connemara, Dick Martin's territory, where the king's writ *did not run*, swore that the natives made him eat and swallow both copy and original. The only consolation the unfortunate "limb of the law" received from his lordship, was the exclamation, with a great affectation of disgust, " Jackson, Jackson, I hope it is not made returnable in this court ! "

THE RULING PASSION.

SERJEANT Sir John Maynard, the best old book lawyer of his time, used to say that the law was *ars bablativa.* Notwithstanding this disparaging statement, Sir John delighted so much in his profession that he always carried one of the year-books in his coach for his diversion, saying that it was as good to him as a comedy. His passion for law ruled him to such a degree, that he left a will purposely worded so as to cause litigation, in order that sundry questions, which had been "moot points" in his lifetime, might be settled for the benefit of posterity.

SHARP PRACTICE.

THE following instance of sharp practice is related in the *London Chronicle,* Jan. 11–13, 1783 :—

"An attorney in Dublin, having dined by invitation with his client several days pending a suit, charged 6s. 8d. for each attendance, which was allowed by the master on taxing costs. In return for this the client furnished the master-attorney with a bill of his eating and drinking ; which the attorney refusing to pay, the client brought his action and recovered the amount of his charge. But he did not long exult in his victory ; for in a few days after the attorney lodged an information against him before the commissioner of excise for retailing wine without a licence ; and not being able to controvert the fact, to avoid an increase of costs, he submitted by advice of counsel to pay the penalty, a great part of which went to the attorney as informer."

LEGAL HAIRSPLITTING.

HE late Sir William Maule, perhaps the ablest judge of his time, was distinguished by his mathematical powers. It was the opinion of Mr. Babbage that if Sir William had given himself up to that science he might have been the first mathematician in Europe. There can be no doubt that his judgments fully corroborate this estimate. They unite force and subtlety in a manner characteristically English. His mind was like a Nasmyth's hammer, which can forge an anchor, or crack a nut with equal facility. There was no one who could split straws with such miraculous nicety, of which an instance is related in the *Law Review,* connected with the scandal—now happily done away with—of special demurrers. A man was described in a plea as " I Jones," and the pleader, probably not knowing his name, referred in another part of the plea to " I " as an initial. The plaintiff demurred, because " I " was not a name. Sir William Maule said that there was no reason why a man might not be christened " I " as well as Isaac, inasmuch as either could be pronounced separately. The counsel for the plaintiff then objected that the plea admitted that " I " was not a name by describing it as an initial. " Yes," retorted Sir William, "but it does not aver that it is not a *final* as well as an *initial* letter."

This is not unlike Lord Brougham's celebrated decision, that a will in which property was left to " the second, third, fourth, *and other sons* severally and in succession, according to their priority of birth "—the limitation of the first son having been omitted by an oversight of the copying clerk—gave the property to the elder son, because though neither second, third, nor fourth, he was *another son.*

TYRE AND TIRE.

THE arms of the body of serjeants are or, an ibis proper, to which Jekyll *might* have added for motto " *Medio tutissimus.*" The same learned punster made an epigram upon the oratory and scarlet robes of his brethren, which may be here repeated without offence, as the serjeants have had among them some of the best, as well as some of the most tiresome of speakers :—

> "The serjeants are a grateful race ;
> Their dress and language show it :
> Their purple robes from Tyre we trace,
> Their arguments *go to it.*"

COMMON SENSE.

SHORTLY after Lord Mansfield became chief justice, a learned counsel took up much of the time of the court in citing several black-letter cases to show the true construction to be put on an old woman's will. Lord Mansfield heard him to the close of his argument, and then addressed him gravely :—" Pray, sir, do you think it is anyways likely that this old woman ever heard of these cases ? And if not, what construction do you think common sense points to ?" He then decided for common sense.

THE STABLES OF AUGEAS.

THE English laws lie deeply buried in three mines yclept the statutes at large, the law reports, and the text-books.

The statute law is *par excellence* the written law of England, and is comprised in some hundred octavo volumes, containing more than eighteen thousand Acts of Parliament. These statutes are placed in chronological order without any systematic arrangement. A considerable portion of this mass

of law is obsolete, another portion relates to local and private
matters, while the subject matter of the effective legislation is
as varied and extensive as the social and mercantile life of
England.

The reports contain the decisions of judges on important cases
brought before them for a period of 573 years.   According to the
statistical memorandum prepared by the Society for the Digest
of the Law Commission, they consisted in 1866 of 1308 volumes,
and it may be reckoned that they increase at the rate of twenty-
five to thirty volumes a year.   In 1866 the reported common law
cases amounted to more than sixty thousand, and the equity
cases to more than twenty-eight thousand.   The series begins
with the year-books, written in law French, and extend over a
period of about two hundred years—from the beginning of the
reign of Edward II. in 1307, to the latter years of the reign of
Henry VIII.—and it ends with the last number of the *Weekly
Notes,* to be continued *ab libitum.*

> Rusticus exspectat dum defluat amnis, at ille
> Labitur et labetur in omne volubilis ævum.

The text-books consist, as their name imports, of treatises and
compilations extending over the whole area of law.   To the law
reformer they are only of interest, in so far as they contain the
ἀναγράφα νόμιμα of English law, that is to say the maxims of the
common law and the unwritten laws of the Courts of Equity.
The common law furnishes the axioms, so to speak, of law.
Take the law of inheritance.   Every man, woman, and child is
supposed to know that in England the eldest son inherits the
father's land ; yet this rule is laid down in no statute, and is,
without proof, assumed to be law.   Similarly common law
definitions of murder, larceny, and other crimes, lie at the root
of our criminal law.   In fact, there is scarcely a chapter in the
great book of law which would not properly begin with some
maxim of the common law.

"There be in the common law," said James I. to his Parliament, "divers contrary reports and precedents ; and this corruption doth likewise concern the statutes and Acts of Parliament, in respect that there are divers cross and cuffing statutes, and some so penned as they may be taken in divers, yea, contrary senses. And therefore would I wish both those statutes and reports, as well in the parliament as common law, to be at once maturely reviewed and reconciled ; and that not only all contrarieties should be scraped out of our books, but even that such penal statutes as were made but for the use of the time, which do not agree with the condition of this our time, ought likewise to be left out of our books. And this reformation might methinks be made a worthy work, and well deserves a parliament to be sat of purpose for doing it." For two centuries and a half after James spoke these words, heap to heap continued confusedly to be added, mingling living laws with the dead. It could no longer be borne, and at last, in 1878, Government appointed a Royal Commission to draft a criminal code, which seems to have been effectually shunted for some time to come off the main parliamentary lines.

A TENDER QUESTION.

IN a cause heard at Exeter assizes, Serjeant Garrow severely cross-questioned an old woman, trying to elicit from her that a tender had been made for some premises in dispute. Upon this Jekyll threw a scrap of paper across the table to him, containing these lines :—

> Garrow, forbear ! that tough old jade
> Can never prove a *tender made.*

REVERSING THE LAW OF NATURE.

JERRY KELLER was one of the best lawyers on the Munster Circuit when this present century was in its teens—unfortunately he sacrificed his fame and fortune to the love of society. There were times, however, when he repented of the way in which he had passed his time. He gave utterance to this feeling on the first day when Judge Mayne took his seat upon the bench. Mayne was a formal coxcomb—a thing of solemn, artificial legal foppery, with a manner of intense gravity, and a well got up look of profundity. He had passed himself off on the public as a deep lawyer, and was never found out by the same discerning public until he was made a judge. "Ah ! Mayne," said Keller, in a voice half audible, " my levity keeps me down here, while your gravity has raised you up there."

A QUEER PET.

LORD GARDENSTONE, an Edinburgh judge of the last age, had a predilection for pigs. One of these animals, in its juvenile years, took a particular fancy for his lordship, and followed him like a dog wherever he went, reposing even in the same bed. When it attained the mature years and size of swinehood, this of course was inconvenient. However, his lordship, unwilling to part with his friend, continued to let it sleep at least in the same room, and when he undressed, laid his clothes upon the floor for it. He said that he liked it, for it kept his clothes warm till the morning. Lord Gardenstone in his mode of living was full of strange eccentric fancies, which he seemed to adopt chiefly with a view to his health, which was always that of a valetudinarian.

SAVED FROM THE GALLOWS.

HE following note occurs in a newspaper of 1740 :— "24 Nov. William Dewell, convicted of a capital offence, was carried to the Surgeon's Hall in order to be dissected, when he came to himself again, and was last night committed to Newgate." Soon after the same journal states : " His Majesty (George II.) has been pleased to order William Dewell, who, after his being hanged on Monday se'nnight, is still alive and perfectly recovered, to be transported for life."

A still more wonderful occurrence is related in Plott's *History of Staffordshire*, viz., "That one Judith of Balsham, was condemned in the reign of Henry III. for receiving and concealing thieves, and hanged from nine o'clock on the Monday morning till after sunrise on the Tuesday following, and yet escaped with life." In evidence of this miracle, Plott recites verbatim a royal pardon granted to the woman, in which the fact is circumstantially recorded :—" Quia Inetta de Balsham, pro receptamento latronum ei imposito nuper, per considera-tionem curie nostre suspendio adjudicata, et ab hora nona diei lune usque post ortum solis diei Martis sequentis suspensa, viva evasit sicut ex testimoniis fide dignorum accepimus, etc."

In the account of Oxfordshire by the same author, we find a remarkable notice of a woman named Anne Greene, who, after being hanged for felony, December 14, 1650, was recovered by Sir William Petty, the celebrated political arithmetician. The time of suspension, however, was not quite so long as that of Judith of Balsham—she hung only about half an hour. "What was most remarkable," says Plott, "and distinguished the hand of Providence in her recovery, is that she was found to be innocent of the crime for which she suffered." This case is alluded to by Evelyn, in his diary, under date March 22, 1675, where he says that Sir William Petty "became famous for his recovering a poor wench that was hanged for felony, and her body having been begged (as the custom is) for the anatomical lectures, he bled her, put her to bed to a warm woman, and with spirits and other means restored her to life. The young scholars joined, gave her a little portion, and married her to a man who had several children by her, she living fifteen years after, as I have been assured." A full account of this remarkable event was published in a pamphlet, entitled "Newes from the Dead, or a True and Exact Narrative of the Miraculous Deliverance of Anne Greene." Added to the narrative were several copies of verses in English, Latin, and French; among others, one by Cristopher Wren, then of Wadham College, and another by Joseph Williamson, subsequently Secretary of State.

CROCODILE TEARS.

MR. LOCKHART was a very celebrated pleader at the Scottish bar, who bore away all the laurels and all the emoluments of the profession. He appears to have excelled chiefly in the pathetic, and it was jocularly remarked of him that the amount of his honorarium could be easily discovered in his countenance; for if it had been liberal he appeared deeply affected at the justice of his client's case; but if it turned out unexpectedly large, he regularly melted into tears. It was owing to a sarcasm by Mr. Wedderburn on this lachrymose propensity of Lockhart, that Wedderburn was driven from the Scottish bar to reap that harvest of renown which awaited him in England. Replying on one occasion to a very powerful speech of Lockhart's, Wedderburn drew a ludicrous picture of his opponent's eloquence, and summed up by saying, " Nay, my lords, if tears could have moved your lordships, tears I am sure would not have been wanting." The lord president immediately interrupted him, saying that such observations did not befit the dignitary of the court. Wedderburn, unabashed at the reproof, declared that he had not said anything he was not entitled to say, and that he should not shrink from saying it again. To this the president rejoined in such a manner as to extort from the young advocate the observation that his lordship had "said that as judge, which he durst not maintain as a man." The president immediately appealed to the court for protection, and Wedderburn was desired to make most humble apology upon pain of deprivation. This he resolutely refused to do, and tearing his gown from his shoulders, declared that "he would never again enter a court as an advocate, where freedom of speech was forbidden him." Wedderburn left the Scotch for the English bar, and in course of time became Lord Loughborough. Thus what every one thought then to be his ruin, turned out to be the very best thing that could have happened to him.

A BOTTLE HOAX.

JEREMIAH KELLER, or, as he was commonly called, "Jerry" Keller, was a barrister who held a foremost place in the social circle of Dublin. He had a singular twist of countenance which of itself provoked mirth, and his powers of drollery were admirable. A cousin of his, a wine merchant, supplied the cellars of the bar mess, upon which circumstance a supercilious junior thought to raise a laugh at the expense of Jerry. Addressing him at the bar mess, the young barrister observed, "It is very odd, Mr. Keller, but I have noticed the claret bottles growing smaller and smaller each assize since your cousin became our wine merchant, though I dare say there is no reduction in the price." "Whist," said Jerry, "don't be talking of what you know nothing about. Of course, 'tis natural the bottles should be growing smaller, because we all know *they shrink* in the washing." A general shout of laughter extinguished the luckless junior.

LAWYERS NOT LITIGANTS.

LAWYERS are, it is notorious, a class least anxious of any to go to law. Their antipathy to appearing before a court in any other shape than that of representatives of other individuals results, as we may fairly suppose, from the intimate knowledge they possess of what a lawsuit is. It has been related of Mr. Marryatt, the eminent king's counsel, that some time after he had retired from practice, being present at a conversation in which some one mentioned "the glorious uncertainty of the law," he observed with great earnestness, " If any man were to claim the coat on my back, and threaten my refusal with a lawsuit, I should certainly give it, lest in defending my coat I should find that I was deprived of my waistcoat also." Dunning is known to have dreaded above all things becoming involved in litigation. One day, in returning to his house near town, he was met in the front garden by the gardener, full of complaints about some audacious fellow whom he had found trespassing on a neighbouring field, Dunning's property. " Well, what did you say to him?" inquired Dunning. " Oh, sir, I told him if I found him there again you would be sure to prosecute him." "You may prosecute him yourself, John, if you like ; but I tell you what, he may walk about my fields till he is tired before I will prosecute him."

THE ESTABLISHED CHURCH.

HENRY CRABB ROBINSON records in his Diary that " at a dinner party at Messrs. Longman and Co.'s, in 1812, the only one who said anything worth repeating was Dr. Abraham Rees, the well-known Arian 'Encyclopædic Rees.' He related that when in 1788 Beaufoy made his famous attempt to obtain the repeal of the Corporation and Test Act, a deputation waited on the Lord Chancellor Thurlow to obtain his support. The deputies were Drs. Kippis, Palmer (of Hackney), and Rees. The chancellor heard them very civilly, and then said, '.Gentlemen, I'm against you, by G——. I am for the Established Church, demme! Not that I have any more regard for the Established Church than for any other church, but because *it is* established. And if you can get your d——d religion established I'll be for that too.' Rees told this story with great glee."

MAJESTY OF THE LAW.

N the year 1704 several persons, who claimed to be free-men of the borough of Aylesbury, were refused the privilege of voting at an election for a member of Parliament, and brought an action against the returning officer for the penalties which the law imposes in such cases. The House of Commons, conceiving this appeal to the courts to be an invasion of their privileges, passed an order declaring it to be penal in either judge, or counsel, or attorney, to assist at their trial. The Lord Chief Justice Holt and several lawyers were, notwithstanding, bold enough to disregard this order, and proceeded with this action in due course. The House, extremely offended at this contempt of their order, sent the serjeant-at-arms to command the judge to appear before them; but this resolute administrator of the laws refused to stir from his seat. On this the Commons sent a second message by their speaker, attended by a great many of their members. After the speaker had delivered his message, his lordship replied to him in the following memorable words, " Go back to your chair, Mr. Speaker, within these five minutes, or, you may depend on it, I will send you to Newgate. You speak of *your* authority! But I tell you I sit here as interpreter of the laws and a distributor of justice; and were the whole House of Commons in your belly I would not stir one foot." The speaker was prudent enough to withdraw, and the House, with equal prudence, let the matter drop.

FIAT JUSTITIA, RUAT COELUM.

HIS is not a classic quotation. In 1772 Lord Mansfield decided that there was no property in slaves, and in answer to the vast property, amounting to millions, at issue on the question, he uttered the above memorable maxim. In 1788, in an equally celebrated case (*The King* v. *Wilkes*), he made use of the same words again. Sir Thomas Browne has in his *Religio Medici* (p. ii., s. xi.), written in 1642, "Ruat coelum fiat voluntas tua." Bartlett, *Familiar Quotations*, p. 589, fifth edition, says that this celebrated apothegm occurs first in Nathaniel Ward's *Simple Cobbler of Aggawam in America*, the first edition of which was printed in 1647. His words are, "It is lesse to say 'statuatur veritas, ruat regnum,' than 'fiat justitia, ruat coelum.'" Ward was at one time pastor of the church at Ipswich, or Aggawam, subsequently minister of Shenfield, near Brentwood, Essex. Up to the present this is thought to be the oldest instance of the use of these remarkable words, but it is not known whether Ward merely quoted or actually composed this maxim.

"LADIES, J.P."

N Harleian MSS. 980, f. 153, is the following curious entry, taken from Mr. Attorney-General Noy's readings in Lincoln's Inn in 1632 :—

"The Countess of Richmond, mother to Henry VII., was a justice of the peace. Mr. Attorney said if it was so, it ought to have been by commission, for which he had made many an hour's search for the record, but could never find it; but he had seen many arbitraments made by her. Justice Joannes affirmed that he had often heard from his mother of the Lady Bartlet,* mother of the Lord Bartlet, that she was a justice of the peace,

---

* Berkeley? see *infra.*

and did sit usually on the bench with the other justi Gloucestershire; that she was made so by Queen Mary, upon her complaint to her of the injuries she sustained by some of that county, and desiring for redress thereof, that as she herself (the queen) was chief justice of all England, so this lady might be in her own county, which, accordingly, the queen granted." Another example was alleged of one —— Rowse, in Suffolk, who usually at the assizes and sessions there held sat upon the bench among the justices, " gladio cincta."

To these may be added the celebrated Ann, Countess of Pembroke, Dorset, and Montgomery, who had the office of hereditary sheriff of Westmoreland. At the assizes at Appleby she sat with the judges on the bench. *Vide* Butler, notes to Coke and Litt. : " A woman may be of homage in a customary court and even in a court baron, to present, etc. ; but she shall not sit as a judge to try issues" (2 Inst. 119, Gilbert's *Ten.*, by Walker, 475).

In France there are also instances on record of ladies personally presiding in their own courts, even over judicial combats. Such was Mahaut, Countess of Artois, who assisted at the trial of Robert of Flanders.

In the above instances the judicial capacity appears to have been vested in those ladies permanently ; in the following it was granted apparently temporarily (unless this be the above-named *Lady Bartlett*), and under such extraordinary circumstances that the complainant became judge in her own case :— In the reign of Henry VIII., Maurice Berkeley, Nicholas Poyntz, and a riotous company of their servants, entered the park of Lady Anne Berkeley, at Yate, killed the deer and set a hayrick on fire. The lady repaired to court, and made her complaint, when the king immediately granted her a special commission under the great seal to inquire, hear, and determine these riots and misdemeanours, and made her one of the commissioners of the quorum. She then returned to Gloucester, opened the commission, sat on the bench in the public Sessions

G

Hall, impannelled a jury, and received the evidencé, when
Maurice Berkeley, Nicolas Poyntz, and their followers were
found guilty of divers riots and disorders, and punished accordingly.   .

FREAKS OF THE JURY.

MR. JUSTICE GOULD, trying a cause at York, when
he had proceeded for about two hours, observed that
there were only eleven jurymen in the box. " Where is
the twelfth ? " he asked. " Please you, my lord," said one of the
eleven, "he is gone home about some business, but he has left
his verdict with me."

In the case of Foster *v.* Hawden, in the King's Bench, reported in Leving, " the jury not agreeing, cast lots for their
verdict, and gave it according to lot : for which, upon the
motion of Leving, the verdict was set aside, and the jury was
ordered to attend next term to be fined."

In an appeal of murder, reported in Coke, the fact, that is to
say the killing, was not denied by the defendant : but he rested
his defence upon a point of law, namely, that the deceased had
provoked him by mocking him, and he therefore contended
that it was not murder. The jury could not agree whether it
was murder or not ; but the major part of them were for finding
the defendant not guilty. They, however, at last came to an
agreement in this manner—that they should bring in and offer
their verdict "*not guilty;*" and if the court disliked thereof,
that then they should all change their verdict, and find him
"*guilty.*" In pursuance of this agreement the jury brought in
their verdict *not guilty*. The court disliking the verdict, sent
the jury back again, who, in pursuance of the agreement made,
returned and brought in their verdict *guilty*.

As good a story is related by Sir Francis Palgrave : " Within
memory, at the heat of a cause, in Merioneth, when the jury
were asked to give their verdict, the foreman answered : ' My

lord, we do not know who is plaintiff or who is defendant, but we find for whoever is Mr. ——'s man.' Mr. —— was a barrister who had been the successful candidate at a recent election, and the jury happened to belong to his colour."

A volume of most respectable dimensions might be filled with the freaks of the twelve good men and true of former and even of present days.

THE WAY OF PUTTING A QUESTION.

BARON WOOD was a judge remarkable for his popular feelings, and had a strong dislike to prosecutions or actions on the game laws. This led him to make use of a strong expedient to defeat two actions. A. and B. had gone out poaching together : the plaintiff brought two actions, and the action against B. called A. to prove the poaching by B., and meant to call B. to prove the case against A. This was apparent—indeed, avowed. But the baron interposed, when the witness objected to answer a question that *tended* to convict himself. A squabble arising between the counsel, the baron said to the witness, " I do not ask you whether you ever went out poaching with the defendant, because, if I did, you would very properly refuse to answer. But I ask you this : Except at a time when you might have been sporting with the defendant did you ever see him sport ? " " Certainly not, my lord." " Of course you did not." Then the baron laughed heartily, and nonsuited the plaintiff. No motion was made to set this nonsuit aside.

HANGABLE FOR 12¼*d.*

IT was no longer ago than the year 1808 that the offence of stealing from the person above the value of 12*d.* was punishable with death. So it was before the Conquest, only there was a ransom at that time, and he who could pay it saved his life. But in the reign of Henry I. it was made strictly capital, and in the reign of Elizabeth debarred the benefit of clergy, and then neither ransom nor learning would do. During many a reign, and after the value of 12*d*. was shrunk to insignificance, men continued to be executed according to those antediluvian comparisons of life against money. Sir Henry Spelman justly complained that whilst everything else was risen in its nominal value and become dearer, the life of man had continually grown cheaper. Still we adhered to the constitutions of Athelstane till Sir Samuel Romilly had the courage to make a stand against him, and obtained a repeal of his life-appraisement.

IRRIGATION OF THE LAW.

THAT the study of law is dry work is admitted on all hands, and may be considered an excuse for the quantities of liquor formerly absorbed by gentlemen in the legal profession. On their bibulous capacities, an order made by the authorities of Barnard's Inn, in November, 1706, throws some light. This order names two quarts as the allowance of wine to be given to each mess of four men, on going through the ceremony of "initiation." Of course, this amount of wine was an "extra" allowance, in addition to the ale and port wine allotted to members by the regular dietary of the house. Even Sheridan, who boasted he could drink any *given* quantity of wine, would have thought twice before he drank so large a given quantity in addition to the liberal allowance of stimulant. Anyhow, the quantity in this case was fixed—a fact that would have elicited an expression of approval from Baron Thomson, who, loving port wine wisely, though too well, expressed at the same time his concurrence with the words, and his dissent from the opinion of a barrister who observed, " I hold, my lord, that after a good dinner a certain quantity of wine does no harm." With a smile the chief baron rejoined, " True, sir, it is the uncertain quantity that does mischief."

RANK OF THE HANGMAN.

UNDER the Saxon kings the prelates sat in the Witenage-mote, but as time went on their position grew a little uncertain. They ranked with equivocal people, and as early as Canute there seems to have been some curious notions in matters of precedency. At that time that grim official, the carnifex, or hangman, was so highly accounted of that he ranked with the Archbishop of York, the highest earl, and the lord Steward. This curious fact is recorded in the chronicles of Florence of Worcester.

THE KIND OF J.P. FOR IRELAND.

AT the time of the Doneraile conspiracy, in 1829, Mr. Bond Low, a very active and zealous magistrate, was fired at on three different occasions. One day, at noontide, two strong and active peasants fired at him with muskets from behind a fence. Nothing daunted, although his mare was severely wounded, he jumped off and crossed the fence. The men fled before him, and he gave chase, but, being rather unwieldy, had little chance of catching them. He had pistols, one of which he had ineffectually discharged ; they had guns, which they reloaded. He was afraid to fire lest they were beyond his range, and when the men halted to fire again at him he calculated that by running in on them, even at the hazard of his life, he would still have a chance of capturing them. He did so ; one of the men fired, missed, and ran away. On rushed Mr. Low, and when the second ruffian had discharged his piece without effect, though he grazed the shoulder of his dauntless pursuer, Mr. Low, having lessened his distance, fired his remaining pistol, and mortally wounded the peasant. With assistance he captured his other assailant, and brought him to trial at the next assizes, when he was capitally convicted and executed.

CAPRICIOUS JUSTICE.

HE way in which the Jacobites were treated after the rebellion of 1715 is not a little curious, and it must be allowed that Justice in those days was the blind goddess with a vengeance. While men were put to death for little more than wishing King George back in Hanover, others were fined only a few marks for much worse offences. For instance, one Thomas Smout was fined five marks "for speaking traiterous and devilish words of his most excellent Majesty, namely, devoting that sacred Majesty to the nethermost hell, and protesting that he would sooner fight for t'other king than for him." With regard to the rank and file of the Preston prisoners, who were not thought worth the expense of bringing to London, judges left the capital to dispose of them in a singular way. Every twentieth man taken by lot was to stand a trial, all the rest were transported. This was the sternest of jokes that the Whigs had ever had to laugh at, between the capture and the trial of the Jacobite prisoners of war in London.

MONSTRUM NULLA VIRTUTE REDEMPTUM.

HE following passage occurs in the journal of the Rev. J. Wesley, under the date of Thursday, 27th of December, 1744 :—"I called on the solicitor whom I had employed in the suit lately commenced against me in Chancery. And here I first saw that foul monster, a Chancery Bill! A scroll it was of forty-two pages in large folio, to tell a story which need not have taken up forty lines ; and stuffed with such stupid, sense_less, improbable lies—many of them, too, quite foreign to the question—as I believe would have cost the compiler his life in any heathen court, either of Greece or Rome. And this is equity in a Christian country ! This is the English method of redressing grievances !"

A CURIOUS HYBRID.

'CONNELL'S power of invective is well known. One of the best things he ever said in that way was against a remarkably combative attorney. The countenance of this individual was indicative of his disposition ; his face was bold and threatening, with the defiance of a pugilist. Upon either temple there stood erect a lock of hair, wiry like the bristles of Tom Twaddles. These tufts looked like horns, and added to the pugnacious expression of his face. He had a fiery deliverance, rather ejaculated than spoke, uttering his speeches in a series of short, hissing, spluttering sentences. Upon one occasion this individual gave repeated annoyance to O'Connell by interrupting him, speaking to the witnesses, and interfering in a manner altogether improper. In vain did the counsel engaged with O'Connell in the cause sternly rebuke him ; in vain did the judges admonish him to remain quiet : up he would jump, hissing and sputtering his remarks with vehemence. At last O'Connell lost all patience. He turned suddenly round, and, scowling at the disturber, shouted in a voice of thunder, " Sit down, you audacious, snarling, pugnacious ramcat." Roars of laughter rang through the court. The judge himself laughed outright at the humorous description of the combative attorney, who, pale with passion, gasped in inarticulate rage. The name of *ramcat* stuck to him through all his life.

THE LONGEST LAWSUIT.

HE famous " Berkeley Suit " is the longest suit on record in England, having lasted upwards of 190 years, for it commenced shortly after the death of Thomas, fourth Lord Berkeley, in 1416, and terminated in 1609. It arose out of the marriage of Elizabeth, only daughter and heiress of the above lord, with Richard Beauchamp, Earl of Warwick. Their descendants sought continually to obtain possession of the castle and lordship of Berkeley, in the county of Gloucester, which not only occasioned the famous lawsuit in question, but was often, at least during the first fifty or sixty years, attended with the most violent encounters. Thus, in 1469, Thomas Talbot, second Viscount Lisle, great-grandson of the above Elizabeth, residing at Wotton-under-Edge, was killed at Nibley Green in a furious fight between some 500 of his own retainers and about as many of those of William, Lord Berkeley, whom he had challenged to the field, and who led on his men. Besides the brave but ill-fated Lord Lisle, scarce of age at that time, about 150 of these followers were slain and 300 wounded, chiefly of the Wotton party, who fled at the fall of their leader. Lord Lisle's sisters were his heirs, and their husbands (one of whom succeeded to the title) followed up the suit, as their descendants did after them. It was not till 1609 that Henry, eleventh Lord Berkeley, obtained a decree in favour of his claims, and got full and quiet possession of the lands and manors so long in dispute.

TALKING AGAINST TIME.

REMARKABLE instances of this performance have been witnessed from Irish members in the parliamentary sessions of 1879, '80, and '81. But quite as copious flows of eloquence were poured out in the Emerald Island in the commencement of this century. In 1805 legal proceedings were taken in England against William Cobbett for having published in London letters under the signature of "Juverna," reflecting on the leading members of the Irish Government. The authorship of the letters, which were written in Ireland, was subsequently traced to Robert Johnson, then fourth justice of the Irish Court of Common Pleas. He was accordingly arrested in Dublin on the 18th of January, 1805, under a warrant issued by Lord Ellenborough, Chief Justice of England, as it was alleged in pursuance with an authority conferred by an Act of Parliament passed in 1804, shortly after the Union, "to render more easy the apprehending and bringing to trial offenders escaping from one part of the United Kingdom to the other, and also from one county to another." The summary arrest of an Irish judge by and under the warrant of an English judge, excited an intense sensation. The defendant applied for and obtained separate writs of *Habeas Corpus* out of the Courts of King's Bench and Exchequer, and his case was argued by the most eminent counsel at the Irish Bar, among others by the celebrated John Philpot Curran, whose argument will be found in his published speeches. These courts refused to liberate their learned brother.

Sir William Cusack Smith, baronet, then one of the barons of the Court of Exchequer, denounced from the bench the arrest as arbitrary and illegal. The prisoner not being satisfied with these decisions, determined to try the court of which he was himself a member. These litigated proceedings necessarily occupied a considerable time, and there were meanwhile rumours afloat that a change of ministry was possible, and even imminent. There was a barrister then at the Irish bar, John Barclay Scriven, who had previously been an officer in a black regiment in the West Indies, and who undertook, if employed, to speak on the case until the expected change of ministry should take place. This undertaking he actually accomplished, and after talking for over *ten* days, he replied, in answer to an inquiry from Lord Chief Justice Norbury, that he had eighteen questions to submit and argue, and that he hoped to finish the second point on to-morrow night! We may well imagine how the bench were startled by the announcement, but the change of ministry fortunately came before the finish of the speech. "All-the-talents-Administration" came into office ; the whigs, as those who were libelled, did not belong to their party, abandoned the prosecution, and Judge Johnson was allowed to retire on a pension. The lawyer who achieved so much for

his client, went ever after by the name of " Leather-Lungs
Scriven."

The Metropolis, written by the well-known Right Hon. John
Wilson Croker, then a young barrister in Dublin, contains the
two graphic sketches following, of Irish barristers endowed
with the peculiar talent for talk. One of these was Sir Jonah
Barrington, a queen's counsel, who afterwards aspired to be
an historian ; the other was " Leather-Lungs Scriven."

> " The world confesses Jonah's mighty powers,
> Who rants on nothing long, incessant hours ;
> Wide spreads the leaves of law, that weigh a grain
> With splish-splash morals of a schoolboy's brain.
> Warmth without cause, and reasons without strength,
> Wit without point, without connection length ;
> Topics that come and go, and nowhere tend,
> Jumbled without beginning, mean, or end.
> A hash of bombast, an unsavoury broth
> Of surplusage, tautology, and froth.
> As hounds ' do do ' run coupled words dingdong,
> Repeated burthens length'ning out the song.
> The jury yawns, the judges interpose ;
> Still drones his pipe, and still beats time his nose,
> Till drowsy languor deadens old and young,
> And mere fatigue constrains his struggling tongue.
>   *   *   *   *   *
> Who lifts his voice, this hostile hum to drown,
> And seems predestined never to sit down ?
> Scriven, with leather lungs and mill-clack tongue,
> Who on a nod can interruption hang,
> And make a whisper subject to harangue ;
> He trots 'gainst time, but time, once thought a trotter,
> Quakes every hour to find the contest hotter,
> Till on the brink of next vacation driven,
> He slacks his reins and yields the day to Scriven."

Scriven, although not a lawyer of the first class, was a very able
man and in constant employment. Not a day elapsed for many
years in which his harsh voice was not to be heard pleading in
the King's Bench, from the commencement to the close of
every term.

A REPORT IN OVID.

ERJEANT HILL once was pleading in a case concerning a hole being broken through a wall separating the houses of plaintiff and defendant. A question arose whether there was sufficient evidence to support an action of trespass. Lord Mansfield made a suggestion, " The hole was certainly there, and the defendant had used it ; but possibly it might have existed there long before." The learned serjeant was not wont to esteem the opinions of judges too highly, and he answered in rather an important manner, " I should like any *real lawyer* to tell me whether there be any authority in the books for such a presumption ? " Lord Mansfield replied, " I rather think, brother Hill, that you will find the point mooted in the case of Pyramus and Thisbe, and, in the report of the case, if I remember right, it is said—

> " Fissus erat tenui rimâ, quam duxerat olim,
> Cum fieret paries domui communis utrique.
> Id vitium nulli per sæccula longa notatum."
> OVID, *Metamor.*, iv. 65.

ADMINISTERING JUSTICE.

INGLE combat was formerly a very prevalent and favourite mode of *administering justice* : it was authorized by law, and frequently conducted before the high authorities and their ladies. " The last exhibition in Ireland of that nature which I have read of," says Sir Jonah Barrington in his *Personal Sketches*, " was between two Irish gentlemen, Connor MacCormac O'Connor and Teague MacKilpatrick O'Connor. They fought with broadswords and skeens, or large knives, in the castle of Dublin, in the presence of the archbishop and all the chief authorities and ladies of rank. They had hewed each other for a full hour, when Mr. MacKilpatrick O'Connor, happening to miss his footing, Mr. MacCormac O'Connor began to cut his head off with his knife, which, after a good deal of cutting, struggling, and hacking, he was at length so fortunate as to effect. And, having got the head clear off the shoulders, he handed it to the lords justices, who were present, and by whom it was most graciously received."

A LORD CHANCELLOR CHALLENGED BY AN EX-WAITER.

ONE of the most successful of the metropolitan club-houses, at the commencement of the last century, was White's, at the bottom of St. James's Street. This house having been destroyed by a fire, April 28, 1733, another house was opened at the top of the same street, where it still flourishes under the name of White's. The original founder, Mr. Arthur, died on June 6, 1761, and in the following October his only daughter married one " Bob " Mackreth, employed as a waiter at the club, who thus succeeded to the business. Two years after this Mackreth relinquished the business, and, as time passed on, in 1774 became M.P. for Castle Rising, in Norfolk, by the interest of Lord Orford, who in that manner paid him for a large sum of borrowed money. It was this Mackreth who, in 1793, sent a challenge to Sir John Scott (afterwards Lord Eldon) for having abused him in a speech delivered six years before. " The truth is," says Sir John, " these courts thought him so bad that they made him pay a young man, of whom they declared he had taken undue advantage, about £17,000 and all costs, and the fellow is fool enough to think he can retrieve his character by insulting me." Mackreth was convicted of a breach of the peace, and sentenced, by the Court of Kings' Bench, in May, 1793, to six weeks' imprisonment and a fine of £100. But, notwithstanding this reprehensible trans-action, he was two years afterwards knighted by George III. Sir " Bob " died in the month of February, 1819, in the ninety-fourth year of his age. This, I believe, is the only instance of an English lord chancellor being asked to fight a duel.

PERRY *VERSUS* MUM.

MR. PERRY, editor of the *Morning Chronicle*, being indicted by the attorney-general for an alleged political libel, conducted his own defence, made an able speech to the jury, and obtained a verdict of " Not guilty." Not long afterwards Cobbett was indicted for a seditious passage in his *Register*, and, prompted by the success of the *Chronicle's* editor, resolved to follow the same course. He did so, but failed, being convicted and sentenced to a heavy fine and imprisonment. The Hon. Henry Erskine's observation on this was that Cobbett tried to be Perry, when he should have been Mum.*

A GAY LOTHARIO.

DAVID RAE, subsequently Lord Eskgrove, was a most ludicrous personage. To be able to give an anecdote of Eskgrove, with a proper imitation of his absurd voice and manner, was a sort of fortune in Edinburgh society in the beginning of this century, when his lordship was in the zenith of his absurdity. In the trial of Glengarry for murder in a duel, a lady of great beauty was called as a witness. She came into the court veiled. But before administering the oath Eskgrove gave her this exposition of her duty : " Young woman ! you will now consider yourself as in the presence of Almighty God and of His High Court. Lift up your veil ; throw off all modesty and look me in the face."

---

* Mum also signifies a sort of beer much drunk in the last century. Malt, mum, cider, and perry were named together in an annually recurring act of parliament, relative to duties upon these articles.

RATHER LONG-WINDED.

ECHNICALLY the whole legislation of a session is called one act, and each statute or act is called a chapter of it. In the printed editions of the statutes each chapter is divided into sections. Such a section generally consists of but one sentence, and as it has often to give a long narration of things that must be done in particular cases, and others that may be done but are not imperative, and others again that must not be done, etc., the comprehension of the full meaning of this sentence requires a strong mental effort. Even the Duke of Wellington confessed that he had never been able to understand an act of Parliament in its "raw" state. Among the statutes there are individual sentences which, if printed in the type and form of a fashionable novel, would fill a hundred pages. Jeremy Bentham is said to have been at the trouble of counting the words in one Act of Parliament, and found that beginning with "Whereas," and ending with the word "Repealed," the act was precisely the length of an ordinary three-volume novel.

THE FLOWERS OF TYBURN TREE.

HE verses formerly repeated by the bellman of St. Sepulchre's, under the walls of Newgate, on the night preceding the execution of a criminal, are well known. Another curious custom anciently observed at the same church was the presentation of a nosegay to every criminal on his way to execution at Tyburn. No doubt the practice had its origin in some kindly feeling for the unfortunates who were so soon to bid farewell to all the beauties of the earth, or it may have been prompted by a feeling akin to that which caused the victims to be crowned with garlands of flowers. "Now I am a wretch indeed," says Polly, in the *Beggar's Opera*, alarmed on account of Captain Macheath ; "methinks I see him already in the cart, sweeter and more lovely than the nosegay in his hand." One of the last criminals who received a nosegay from the steps of St. Sepulchre's was John Rann, *alias* "Sixteen-string Jack," who was hanged in 1774, for robbing the Rev. Dr. Bell of his watch and eighteen-pence in money, in Gunnersbury Lane, on the road to Brentford. His execution was witnessed in his boyhood by John Thomas Smith, subsequently keeper of the print-room in the British Museum, who says that " the criminal was dressed in a pea-green coat, with an immense nosegay in the button-hole, which had been presented to him at St. Sepulchre's steps ; and his nankeen small-clothes, we were told, were tied at each knee with sixteen strings."

FORENSIC *TOURS-DE-FORCE.*

IT is reported to have been an amusement in the early life of John Scott (Lord Eldon) to turn pieces of poetry into the form of legal instruments. He is said actually to have converted the ballad of *Chevy Chase* into the shape and style of a bill in chancery. This marvellous production is unfortunately lost. But specimens of what may be described as an inverse process, viz., laws turned into rhyme as well as reason are not uncommon. The following, with attribution to various legal gentlemen, is almost too well known to bear repeating. I only place it here because it is so often quoted incorrectly.

Mr. Justice Powis, "a foolish old judge," as Lord Campbell calls him, habitually used in conversation the vulgarism, "Look ye, d'ye see?" Seeing one day Mr. Yorke (subsequently Lord Hardwicke), then a barrister, who was reputed to turn *Coke on Littleton* into verse, the judge asked him publicly how he was getting on with his undertaking. To which Mr. Yorke replied, "My Lord, I have only got as far as the first section, which I have arranged thus :—

> " He that holdeth his land in fee
> Need neither to quake nor to quiver,
> I humbly conceive ; for look, do you see,
> They are his and his heirs for ever."

Or according to another version :—

> " Tenant in fee
> Simple is he ;
> That hath lands of his own tight and clever ;
> For please you, my lord,
> And look 'e, d'ye see,
> They are his and his heirs for ever."

In 1742 a small book was published entitled the " Reports of Sir Edward Coke, Kt., in verse, wherein the title of each case and the principal points are contained in two lines, to which are added references in the margin to all the editions of the said Reports," etc. It was printed by Lintot, in the Savoy, for John Worrall, at the Dove, in Bell Yard, near Lincoln's Inn. This John Worrall was a writer on judicial questions, and pretended that it was " an ancient manuscript fallen accidentally into his hands." As this work may be unknown to some of my readers, a few specimens of the manner in which the subject is treated may be of interest, though they are by no means humorous or even amusing in any other way :—

> " PELHAM: 'T is forfeiture of a vouchee
> Tenant for life suffers recovery.

> DIGGS : A revoking power by deed, inroll'd
> By fine before inrolment is controul'd.

> WALCOT : 'Gainst wife and husband for wife's debt
> *Dum sola,* lay *debet* and *detinet.*

SNAG : If a person says he killed my wife,
No action lies, if she be yet alive."

A second edition of these " truths severe dressed in the fairy garb of verse," appeared in 1824, in 16mo.

A RACKET COURT.

MR. TOLER (subsequently Lord Norbury) was called to the Irish bar in 1770, up to which time he had been a sort of bully for the ascending party in the Irish House of Commons. He attained the bench through interest alone, and was tolerated in his post till 1829. His court, of the Common Pleas, in Dublin, was remarkable for repeated shouts of laughter re-echoed through the hall, as puns, quibbles, and quotations were bandied about from bench to bar, from bar to bench, and from both to the jury and the witnesses. A stranger traversing the halls of the Four Courts, might at any time distinguish that of the Common Pleas, by the bursts of merriment which issued from its portals. Of that place during the sittings of *Nisi Prius*, especially in summer, it is difficult even to shadow forth a description. As a matter of course his court was always crowded to the very ceiling, the atmosphere being almost tropical. In this above all things Norbury delighted. There he sat in all his glory, puffing his cheeks at the end of every sentence (whence he was nicknamed Puffendorf), punning and panting, till his Falstaffian countenance glowed like the setting sun. At last, grilled beyond all endurance by the atmosphere, off went the gown, and round went the wig, till its tails, reversed, dangled over his forehead. Mirth rose to uproar, and fun degenerated into downright insubordination. Of this his lordship himself has borne testimony. On pressing a reluctant witness one day to name his profession, and being at length told that he kept a racket court, "And a very good trade too," exclaimed the merry judge ; " so do I ; so do I," while he puffed and glanced for approbation at the " company."

HOUSEWIFELY.

HERE was a Sir Judkin Fitzgerald, who, being sheriff of Tipperary, had, it was said, during the rebellion of 1798, practised great cruelties. Among other things he was reported to have ordered the cat-o'-nine-tails to be dipped in *brine* before a flogging. One day he boasted in the presence of the witty Jeremiah Keller, a barrister on the Munster Circuit, that " by his firmness he had *preserved* the county." " No," said Jerry, " but you *pickled it.*"

DEGREES OF COMPARISON.

HE three degrees of comparison in a lawyer's progress are, getting on—getting onner (honour)—getting onnest (honest). Much sad truth in this jingle, which is a crumb from the bench table.

PROFESSIONAL JOKES.

HIEF JUSTICE TINDAL greatly enjoyed a joke. It is related that one of the learned serjeants coming too late for dinner at Serjeant's Inn Hall, found no place left for him. While waiting for a seat, " How now?" said the chief justice. "What's the matter, brother? You look like an outstanding term that's unsatisfied." Of another serjeant he was asked whether he thought him a *sound* lawyer? "Well, sir," said he, "you raise a doubtful point, whether *roaring* is unsoundness."

THE LAW ON DUELLING.

" REMEMBER well," says Charles Phillips in *Curran and his Contemporaries,* " at the Sligo Summer Assizes for 1812, being of counsel in the case of the King *v.* Fenton, for the murder of Major Hillas in a duel, when old

Judge Fletcher thus capped his summing up to the jury : 'Gentlemen, it's my business to lay down the law to you, and I will. The law says the killing of a man in a duel is murder ; therefore, in the discharge of my duty, I tell you so. But I tell you, at the same time, a *fairer duel* than this I never heard of in the whole *coorse* of my life ! ! ' It is scarcely necessary to add that there was an immediate acquittal."

ETYMON OF THE WORD BARRISTER.

HIS term is derived from the mediæval *barra*, whence *barraster*, one whose business is to be at the bar. This is confirmed by the old mode of spelling the word : *barrester* or *barraster*. Thus Spelman, under the word "Cancellarius," says, "Dicuntur etiam cancelli septem curiarum quæ barras vocant : atque inde juris candidati causas illic agentes Budæo cancellarii et nobiscum barrestarii."

TRUISM.

HE commencement of the preface to the third volume of *Modern Reports*, p. xiv., is curious : "Gentlemen—All human laws are natural or civil." "This puts us in mind," says a recent writer, "of a humorous introduction to death, which we have read somewhere—

" ' Death is common to all ;
It occurs but once.' "

"HATS OFF."

N the 7th of November, 1615, when Ann Turner, a physician's widow, was indicted at the bar of the Court of King's Bench, before Sir Edward Coke, as an accessory before the fact, for the murder of Sir Thomas Overbury, the learned judge observing she had a broad-brimmed hat on, told her "to put it off : that a woman might be covered in a church, but not when arraigned in a court of justice." Whereupon she said she thought it singular that she might be covered in the house of God and not in the judicature of man. Sir Edward told her " that from God no secrets were hid ; but that it was not so with man, whose intellects were weak. Therefore, in the investigation of truth, and especially when the life of a fellow-creature is put in jeopardy, on a charge of murder, the court should see all obstacles removed ; and because the countenance is often an index to the mind, all covering should be taken away from the face." Thereupon the chief justice ordered her hat to be taken off, and she covered her head with a handkerchief.

A BRILLIANT THOUGHT.

AT the Cork Assizes Curran had one day entered upon his case, and stated the facts to the jury. He then, with his usual impressiveness and pathos, appealed to their feelings, and was concluding the whole with this sentence : "Thus, gentlemen, I trust I have made the innocence of that persecuted man as clear to you as——" At that instant the sun, which had hitherto been overclouded, shot its rays into the courthouse. "As clear to you," continued he, "as yonder sunbeam, which now bursts in among us, and supplies me with this splendid illustration."

THE RETORT COURTEOUS.

A CERTAIN judge, who presided in the County Court of an American State, was fond of indulging occasionally in a joke at the expense of a counsellor, a practising attorney in the same court, with whom he was very intimate, and for whom he had a high regard. On one occasion, when pleading a cause at the bar, the counsellor observed that he would conclude his remarks on the following day, unless the court would consent to *set* late enough for him to finish them that evening. "*Sit*, sir, not *set;* hens set," corrected the judge, substituting one Americanism for another. "I stand corrected, sir," said the counsellor, bowing. Not long after, while giving an opinion, the judge remarked that under such and such circumstances an action would not *lay*. "Lie, may it please your honour," says the counsellor, "not *lay;* hens lay."

GRAY'S INN GARDENS.

HIS spot was a favourite resort of the Great Lord Chancellor Bacon during the period he resided in Gray's Inn. It appears by the books of the society that he planted a great number of the elm-trees, some of which, it is supposed, may still be in existence. In accordance with the custom of the times, he also erected a summer house on a small mound on the terrace, where it is not improbable that he often meditated and passed his time in literary composition. From the circumstance of Lord Bacon dating his *Essays* from his "Chambers in Graies Inn," it is not unlikely that the charming essay in which he dwells so enthusiastically on the pleasures of a garden was composed in, and inspired by, the floral beauty of this favourite haunt. "God Almighty," he says, "first planted a garden ; and, indeed, it is the purest of human pleasures. It is the greatest refreshment to the spirits of man, without which buildings and palaces are but gross handiworks." And he adds, "Because the breath of flowers is far sweeter in the air—where it comes and goes like the warbling of music— than in the hand, therefore nothing is more fit for that delight than to know what be the flowers and plants that do best perfume the air." As late as the year 1754 there was standing in the gardens of Gray's Inn an octagonal seat, covered with a roof, which had been erected by Lord Bacon to the memory of his friend, Jeremiah Bettenham.

A "VILLAGE HAMPDEN."

THE footway from Hampton Wick through Bushy Park had been for many years shut up from the public in the last century. An honest shoemaker, Timothy Bennett, of the former place, "unwilling" (was his favourite expression) "to leave the world worse than he had found it," consulted an attorney upon the practicability of recovering this road for the public good, and the probable expense of a legal process for that purpose. "I do not mean to *cobble* the job," said Timothy, "for I have £700, and I would be willing to give up the *awl* that great folks might not keep the *upper leather* wrongfully." The man of law informed him that no such sum would be necessary to try the right. "Then," said the worthy shoe- maker, "as sure as soles are soles I'll stick to them to the *last*," and Lord Halifax, then ranger of Bushy Park, was imme- diately served with the regular notice of action. Upon this his lordship sent for Timothy, and, on his being admitted to his presence, the earl said with some warmth, "And who are you that has the ensurance to meddle in this affair?" "My name, my lord, is Timothy Bennett, shoemaker, of Hampton Wick. I remember, an' it please your lordship, to have seen, when I was a young man sitting at work, the people cheerfully pass by my shop to Kingston market. But now, my lord, they are forced to go round about, through a hot, sandy road, ready to faint beneath their burdens. And I am unwilling to leave the world worse than I found it. This, my lord, I humbly repre- sent, is the reason why I have taken this work in hand." "Begone," replied his lordship; "you are an impertinent fellow." However, upon mature reflection, his lordship, convinced of the equity of the claim, began to compute the humiliation of a defeat by a shoemaker, desisted from his opposition not- withstanding the opinion of the Crown lawyers, and reopened the road, which is enjoyed by the public without molestation to this day. Honest Timothy died about two years after, in the 77th year of his age, and was followed to the grave by the great majority of the Hampton-Wickians.

BENEFITS OF LITIGATION.

THE spirit of litigation was perhaps never carried to a greater extent than in a cause between two eminent potters of Handley Green, Staffordshire, for a sum of £2 9s. 1d. After being in chancery eleven years, from 1749 to 1760, it was decided by John Morton and Rundle Wilbraham, esquires, to whom it was referred. These gentlemen determined that the complainant filed his bill without any cause, and that he was indebted to the defendant at the same time the sum for which he had brought this action. This they ordered him to pay, with a thousand guineas costs.

LAW VERSE.

ABOUT the fourteenth century it was a sort of fashion to put law matters into French verse. There exist metrical copies of the Statutes of Gloucester and Merton, and the compiler of a law-book in the reign of Edward I.* says, he preferred executing his task in " common romance " —that is, plain French prose—rather than to translate it into rhymes. It is not probable, however, that the lawyers, like the monks, attempted to rival the popular minstrels of those days, or that they designed *their* poetical compositions to be chanted to the harp. We may rather suppose that the object was to impress these matters more strongly on the memory, and even in this form they should be gotten by heart, not sung.

That traditionary law is frequently as permanent as written law is not a paradox. Letters being in common use amongst us, we hardly know how well the memory can be trusted. The

* *Lansdowne MSS. Catalogue*, part ii., p. 129.

verses of the Druids, as we collect from Cæsar, contained all
the laws of the Gauls, which means, in other words, that the
memory was assisted by an alliterative sentence or a jingling
line.   Amongst the Teutonic nations this application of the art
of poesy seems to have been universal, and even now we may
collect many an ancient verse, which taught the law in days
of old, and in which the rhyme assists the reason.   Such, for
instance, are the Kentish verses—*The father to the bough, The
son to the plough,* which, duly expounded, signify that land held
in gavelkind descends to the child, though the father be attainted.
A rhyme of remoter date declared the terms upon which the
Kentish freeholder was to regain the land he had forfeited :
*Nygonsith seld, And nygonsith geld, And five pund to the were,
Ere he be a healdere.*—Frailty worked the loss of the dower
of the Kentish widow : when " the child was born and heard
to cry," her tenancy in her husband's land expired.   The heir
entered and sent the wanton to her paramour, on whom she
henceforth was to depend for maintenance, according to the
monitory verse : *Se that hire wende, Se hire lende,* or as the
same has been waggishly paraphrased by Lambarde : *He that
doth turn or wend her, Let him also give unto her or lend her.*
The four indications of offence against the game laws in like
manner arrange themselves in rhyme : *Dog draw, stable stand,
Back berinde and bloody hand,* and this formed the precept of
the gamekeeper, and instructed him to seize the trespasser
whilst roaming in the greenwood shade.

Here also we see the origin of the old merry rhyming grants,
as King Athelstane's famous grant to the minster of Beverley :
As free mak I thee, As hert may think, Or eygh may see, which
perhaps was one of the ancient technical forms which constitute
a most important part of the law of the Northmen.   Another is
the grant of William the Conqueror to Powlen Royden : *My
hop and my hoplands, With all their bounds, Both up and down,
From heaven to earth, From earth to hell, For thee and thine,
Therein to dwell, From me and mine, To thee and thine, By a*

bow and a broad arrow, When I come to hunt upon Yarrow.
This language is poetical, though rugged ; but it yields in
picturesqueness to the charter which commemorates the gift
made by the Confessor : *To Ranulph Peperkyng and his
kindling, Of the Hundred of Chelmer and Daneing, With hart
and hind, doe and buck, Fox and cat, hare and brock, Wildfowl
with all his flock, partrich, fesant, hen, and cock; To keepen and
to geemen by all hire might, Both by day and eke by night, And
houndes for to hold, Good, swifte, and bolde, Four greyhounds
and six braches, For hare and fox, and wild cattes.* Earl
Sweyn of Essex, Bishop Wulstane, " book ylered," and Hovelyn,
the steward, are named as witnesses to the charter ; but the
lively enumeration of the franchises of the forest, rather be-
speaks the talent of the gleeman than the "book-learning" of
the bishop and the clerk.

While lands could pass by word of mouth, such rhyming
grants would strongly fix themselves upon the recollection of
the witnesses, and it was a kinder method than the ancient
custom still observed at beating of bounds, when the memory
is impressed through the feelings of the outward man. It is
hardly necessary to observe that neither Athelstane, nor the
Confessor, nor the Conqueror, could speak in the language
which is ascribed to them in the above rhymes. The modern-
ization, however, of the words of these monarchs does not
detract from the substantial antiquity of the rhythmical
memorials of their bounty. The royal grants became popular
saws, following the course of the language, as the Saxon
softened into English in the mouth of the burgesses of Beverley
and the tenants of the Hopton Manor. Their actual antiquity
is at all events considerable. The grant of Beverley is set out
in the petition presented to the House of Commons on behalf
of the Archbishop of York in 1466. Ranulph Peperkyng's
charter is at least as old as the reign of Edward II., it being
avouched in the record of a suit in one of the Courts at Westminster, 1324. It is also enrolled in the Forest Roll of Essex

The spelling is much altered in the latter copy, from which the above text is taken. Even though these whimsical instruments may be spurious, yet they may at least be received as good evidence of the antiquity of law-verse. If they were forged, similar precedents must have been extant, otherwise the forgers, who invented them, would have defeated their own ends. It is in the *Ancient Custumal of Kent* that we find the Kentish rhymes : two are preserved in the corrupt Saxon, used after the Conquest ; the third is English, but all have been equally derived from the Saxons. It is worth observation also that the Saxon laws are frequently couched in alliterative and assonant or rhyming sentences. Alfred strengthens the law which he set upon all ranks of men, by adding that the *Earl* and the *Churl* are equally to be subjected to its penalties. The *Thane* and the *Theow* always appear in conjunction. The clauses of the oath of fidelity, prescribed by the law of Athelstane, and which was probably much more ancient than the statute in which it is incorporated, are marked by alliteration and rhythm. In the Frisic laws, almost every sentence has as many "rhyme letters" as an Icelandic verse.

DAY-WORK.

ONCE when Judge Day went on the Munster Circuit, there were so many prisoners for trial in Limerick that he feared he could not open the Commission for Kerry at Tralee without sitting very late. When he continued long after the usual time, and showed no intention of leaving court, the members of the bar remonstrated, but without effect. At length, near midnight, as he still held on, a slip of paper was handed to him by the crier's wand. He read it, smiled, and announced "he would try no more cases that night." The paper contained these lines, written by a member of the bar—

> " Try men by night ! my lord, forbear ;
> Think what the wicked world will say !"

Methinks I hear the rogues declare
That justice is not done by Day."

This judge, a very tall man, was seen walking with Sir Arthur Clarke, a mere dwarf in comparison. "There goes," said a wit, "the longest Day, and the shortest (K)night." Of this pun-eliciting justice, Plunket said, "If a case were tried before Day, it would be tried in the dark."

CONSOLATORY.

NOT so very many years ago it was declared by Mr. (subsequently Justice) Williams, well-known to have had considerable practice in the Common Law Courts, that there were not more than *six* persons practising in them who could be considered as acquainted with the law of real property; and it was at one time asserted that there was *none* practising at the bar of the Court of Chancery who had this knowledge, with the exception of Sir Edward Burtenshaw Sugden, who became subsequently Lord St. Leonards.

JUDGE WITHOUT REASON.

THE story goes that a general officer of the army, on being appointed governor of a West Indian island, addressed Lord Mansfield in a voice of great concern : "What am I to do, my lord? The governor is commander-in-chief, and must he preside in the local Court of Chancery? I can command soldiers, but I know nothing of law." "Tut, man ; decide promptly, but never give any reasons for your decisions. Your decisions may be right, but your reasons are sure to be wrong." Acting on this rule, the military chancellor pushed on well enough ; but in an evil hour, forgetting the precept, he gave one day a good decision, which, however, was immediately appealed against. Recounting the above story to his grandson, Lord Mansfield said, " I was two or three years afterwards sitting at the Cockpit on Plantation Appeals, when there was one called from my friend and pupil the general, which the losing party had been induced to bring, on account of the ludicrously absurd reasons given for the judgment, which, indeed, were so singular, that he incurred some suspicion of corruption, and there was a clamour for his recall. Upon examining it, I found that the judgment itself was perfectly sound and correct. Regretting that my advice had been forgotten, I was told that the general, acquiring reputation by following it, began to suppose himself a great lawyer, and that this case brought before us was the first in which he had given his reasons, and was the first appealed against."

NEVER TOO LATE TO MEND.

JUSTICE KELLY almost always candidly admitted his legal mistakes. Mr. Johnson once pressed him fiercely for a decision in his favour, stating as an argument, in his usual peremptory manner, that there could be no doubt on the point, precedent was imperative in the matter, as his lordship decided the same point twice on the day before. "So, Mr. Johnson," said the judge, looking archly, shifting his seat and shrugging his shoulders, "because I decided wrong twice Mr. Johnson would have me to do so a third time. No, no, Mr. Johnson, you must excuse me; I'll decide the other way this bout." And so he did.

It is said that Lord Mansfield, after the determination of a cause, found reason to alter his opinion respecting the directions he had given to the jury, and when he next saw the counsel against whose client the verdict had been given, desired him to move for a new trial. Mentioning this circumstance a few days after at the judge's dinner, they expressed their surprise at the coolness with which he avowed his change of opinion. "Why," said he, "it is, after all, only showing the world that you are wiser to-day than you were yesterday."

Of Mr. Justice Lawrence, a most excellent man and able judge, it has been related that, at a trial at York, he summed up decidedly in favour of the defendant ; but having given the case further consideration, it appeared to him that he had altogether mistaken the law. A verdict having been recorded for the plaintiff, he had no redress ; but it is generally understood that the judge, feeling the hardship of his situation, left him in his will a sum of money sufficient to indemnify him for the loss he had sustained.

WHAT IS "SOME EVIDENCE"?

A LAWYER, in defending a case, having stated before a country jury that there was "some evidence" that his client had done so and so, Mr. Justice Maule thus ended his charge to the jury : " The learned counsel is perfectly right in his law ; there *is some* evidence on that point ; but he is a lawyer, and you're not, and you don't know what he means by *some* evidence, so I'll tell you. Suppose there was an action on a bill of exchange, and six people swore that they saw the defendant accept it, and six others swore they heard him say he should have to pay it, and six others knew him intimately and swore to his handwriting. And suppose, on the other side, they called a poor old man who had been at school with the defendant forty years before, and had not seen him since, and he said he rather thought the acceptance was not his writing, why there'd be *some* evidence, that it was not ; and that's what Mr. —— means in this case."

POISONING IN SCOTLAND.

A STATUTE of the reign of James II. of Scotland emphatically provided that any person importing poison " through the which any Christian man or woman may take bodily harm, shall tyne and forfeit to the king life, lands, and goods." This law induced Sir John Mackenzie seriously to consider whether poison destined for a Jew, pagan, or infidel, or for an excommunicated person came within the act.

It is an indication of the mysterious importance attached to everything connected with the operation of poison, while so slight a scientific control could be exercised over its influence, that in 1601 an important trial before the High Court of Justiciary, in which James I. took a personal interest, related to no more formidable crime than the slaughter of a couple of fowls. Thomas Bellie, burgess of Brechin, and his son, were accused of " having and keeping of poison, mixing the same with daich (dough), and casting down thereof in Janet Clerk's yard in Brechin, for the destruction of fowls, by the which poison they destroyed to the said Janet two hens." For this crime the two accused were banished from the kingdom for life.

WIGS.

IGS are comparatively a modern fashion on the bench and bar. As late as the reign of Queen Anne a lord keeper wore his own hair instead of the wig. In 1705, Lady Sarah Cowper records of her father, when the queen had made him Lord Keeper of the Great Seal, in his forty-first year: " He looked very young, and wearing his own hair made him appear still more so, which the queen, observing, obliged him to cut it off, telling him the world would say she had given the seal to a boy." At the close of the seventeenth century, however, English barristers almost universally wore wigs ; though Scotch advocates powdered their hair so late as the middle of the eighteenth century.

Occasionally, however, wigs have been discarded. When Lord Campbell argued the great privilege case, he obtained permission to appear without a wig ; but this concession to a counsel was accompanied with an intimation that " it was not to be

drawn into precedent.' Still, the same formidable innovation
has been repeated from time to time by bench and bar.

At the Summer Assizes at Lancaster, in 1819, Mr. Scarlett,
having hurried into court without his wig and gown, apologized
to the judge, and expressed a hope that the time would shortly
come when these mummeries would be entirely discarded. In
accordance with this wish all the counsel appeared the next
day in court without the usual professional badges of wisdom.
This change of fashion lasted but for a day.

Again, we read in the *Times*, July 24, 1868, at the end of the
law reports of July 23rd :—

"During the last two days the learned judge and the bar
have been sitting without their wigs, and in opening a case Sir
William Collier called attention to the innovation, and apologized
for not appearing in full forensic costume. His lordship said
he had set the example of leaving off the wig in consequence of
the unprecedented heat of the weather, as he thought there were
limits to human endurance. Sir William Collier expressed a
wish that this precedent might be generally followed, and hoped
that the obsolete institution of the wig was coming to an end—
a hope in which many members of the bar heartily concurred."

This took place in the Court of Probate and Divorce, Sir
J. P. Wilde being on the bench.

On July 22, 1874, when Dr. Kenealy rose to open the case
for the defendant in the famous Tichborne suit, he obtained
leave to remove his wig on account of the excessive heat. Yet
he forthwith plunged into an harangue in many respects so extraordinary as to show that the precaution to keep his head cool
had neither been superfluous nor altogether effective.

No wigs appear to have been discarded during the days of
tropical heat in July, 1881, and it seems the wig-makers are
destined to have still as important a share as ever in making
foolish faces look wise, and wise faces look foolish.

A WILD BULL.

URING one of the scenes of tumult, too common in the court of Lord Norbury, in Dublin, Judge Mayne, who was sitting at his lordship's left hand, seeing a man in court with his hat on, exclaimed solemnly, and speaking from the bench : " I see you standing there like a wild beast with your hat on."

OBSCURUM PER OBSCURIUS.

HE bar and the public would be rather astonished, at the present day, to hear one of the learned judges of the Court of Queen's Bench, in giving judgment in some important case, pursue a line of observation similar to that which we find in the decision of that court in the once cele-brated case of Stowe *v.* Lord Zouch (Plowden, *Comment. or Reports*, p. 353).   Mr. Justice Catline, speaking of a fine levied in pursuance of the 4 Hen. VII., compared it to " Janus, who," he said, "was Noah, but the Romans *occasionally* called him Janus, and used to paint him with two faces—one looking backward, in respect that he had seen the former world, which was lost by the flood ; and the other looking for-wards,—for which reason they called him Janus Bifrons. And also he carried a key in his hand, his power to renew the new world by his generation. *So* here the act creates, as it were, a flood, by which all former rights before the fine shall be drowned by non-claim, for non-claim is the flood, and the fine begets a new generation, which is the new right, for the fine makes a new right, and is the beginning of a new world, which proceeds from the time of the fine downwards."

A CATHOLIC DISCLAIMER.

HE following anecdote was related by Sir Robert Peel to Charles Phillips, the commissioner of the Court for the Relief of Insolvent Debtors :—Charles Kendal Bushe, the solicitor-general (subsequently chief justice), although attached to what was called the Tory party, was more than suspected of entertaining liberal opinions, particularly on the Roman Catholic question. During the viceroyalty of the Duke of Richmond in Ireland, politics ran high, his grace being a Whig. The duke, however, as a convivial spirit, much culti-vated the society of his witty and accomplished solicitor-general. Dining one day with a right-trusty Orangeman and " something more," the charter toast, as a matter of course, was given. Bushe seemed to hang fire. The duke vociferated, " Come, come, Mr. Solicitor, do justice for once to the 'im-mortal memory.'" Hours passed on, and the master of the revels did this toast such ample and repeated justice that at last he tumbled from his chair. The duke immediately raised and reinstalled him. "Well, my lord duke," said Bushe, "this is indeed retribution. Attached to the Catholics you may declare me to be ; but one thing is certain, at all events, *I* never assisted in the *elevation of the Host.*"

LOCKE-D UP.

R. ERSKINE, in defending a client, under prosecution for a libel upon the government, quoting a sentence or two from a printed book, was hastily interrupted by Justice Buller, who said " it was no defence of one libel to quote another, and a worse libel in support of it." Erskine immediately turned to the jury and said, "You hear, gentlemen, the observation of his lordship, and from that observation I maintain that you must acquit my client. His lordship says that the work under pro-

secution is not so libellous as the quotation I have just read.
Now, gentlemen, that quotation is from a work universally
allowed to be classical authority on the character of British
government. It is from the pen of the immortal Locke. Shall
we condemn a writer who is declared not to go the length of
that great and good man?"

HARD LABOUR.

ONE day Jekyll observed a squirrel in Colman's Chambers
in the Temple, performing, in the usual revolving cage,
the same operation as a man on the treadmill. After
looking at it for a minute in silence, he exclaimed feelingly,
"Ah! poor devil, he is going the Home Circuit."

LONGS AND SHORTS.

THERE were two barristers at the Irish bar who formed
a singular contrast in their stature—Ninian Mahaffy,
Esq., was as much above the middle size as Mr. Collis
was below it. When Lord Redesdale was Lord Chancellor of
Ireland, these two gentlemen chanced to be retained in the
same cause, a short time after his lordship's elevation and before
he was personally acquainted with the Irish bar. Mr. Collis
was opening the motion when the lord chancellor observed,
"Mr. Collis, when a barrister addresses the court he must
stand." "I am standing, my lord," said Collis. "I beg a
thousand pardons," said his lordship, somewhat confused. "Sit
down, Mr. Mahaffy." "I am sitting, my lord," was the reply
to the confounded chancellor.

A barrister, who was present on this occasion, penned down
the following impromptu :—

> " Mahaffy and Collis, ill-paired in a case,
>   Representatives true of the rattling-size ace ;
>   To the heights of the law, though I hope you will rise,
>   You will never be judges, I'm sure, of a(s)size."

LOGICAL.

THE *Albany Law Journal* makes mention of a statute of New York, which allowed deductions of a certain number of days to be made, on account of good behaviour, from the term of imprisonment of convicts, with a wise proviso that the statute should not apply to any person *sentenced for the term of his natural life.*

DE MINIMIS CURAT LEX.

THE following anecdote is related on the indisputable authority of the late Judge Burton, to whom it was narrated by Mr. Sankey, one of the actors in the scene. Walter Hussey Burgh, a man of high eminence at the Irish bar at the close of the last century, had one foible—he imagined that he could do everything better than anybody else. He was one day travelling to Galway with a brother barrister, Mr. Sankey, both having been retained in a special cause at the approaching assizes at that town. They stopped at a country village, and, while enjoying their bottle of port after dinner, their attention was attracted by some urchins playing at marbles beneath the window. "I was once a famous marble-player," said Sankey. "I was the most celebrated of my day," replied Burgh; "what think you of a game to see which of us is the better player?" The challenge was accepted, marbles were procured, a ring was made, and the grave lawyers, with their right forefingers chalked, *secundum artem*, set to with all the zest and rivalry of boyhood. "I won," said Sankey: "Burgh was much excited and much chagrined. He uttered not a word during the remainder of the evening, and from that day forward never spoke to me!"

IN RE BARDELL *V.* PICKWICK.

JOHN ADOLPHUS, the eminent barrister and historian, often longed to tell Charles Dickens how he overlooked a point in the trial of *Bardell* v. *Pickwick*. In the celebrated speech of Serjeant Buzfuz he reads Pickwick's letter : "'Garraway's, 12 o'clock. Dear Mrs. B——, chops and tomato sauce.—Yours, PICKWICK.' Gentlemen," says the learned serjeant, "what does this mean?" etc., etc. Now, here Dickens misses his triumphant point, which was this : "Gentlemen, I need not tell you that the popular name for the tomato is the love apple ! Is it not clear what this base deceiver meant? The outpouring of love and tender feelings implied by tomato sauce cannot be misunderstood."

JUDICIAL MALVERSATION.

THE latest proceedings against a judge for malversation in his office were in the case of the Earl of Macclesfield, lord chancellor, who was impeached in the year 1725 of high crimes and misdemeanours, found guilty, and sentenced to a fine of £30,000. The standard of public principle must be miserably low when those who are appointed to distribute justice are the first to pollute the pure fountains from which it ought to issue ; and yet in our history we find innumerable instances of this practice. The concluding words of chapter twenty-nine of Magna Charta are : "Nulli vendemus, nulli negabimus aut differemus rectum vel justitiam,"—a clause calculated to prevent abuses in the Crown. Yet for centuries after it was usual to pay fines for delaying law proceedings, even to the extent of the defendant's life. Sometimes they were exacted to expedite process and to obtain right ; in other cases the parties litigant offered part of what they were to recover to the Crown. Madox, in his invaluable history of the Exchequer,

collects many instances of fines for the *king's favour*, and
notably of the Dean of London's paying twenty marks to the
king that he might assist him against the bishop in a lawsuit.
William Stutevill presented to King John three thousand marks
in order to obtain judgment with relation to the Barony of
Mowbray, which Stutevill claimed against William de Mowbray. To the honour of the very pure administration of justice
in this country, since the Revolution such a practice has been
impossible. But it flourished up to that period. Charles II.,
in appeals to the House of Lords, used to go about whilst the
cause was hearing, and solicit particular lords for appellant or
respondent. Whitelock, when a barrister, applied to the judges
with regard to a prosecution for a libel on his father, who
had been on the bench, and was then dead. The libeller was
indicted after this previous conversation, and convicted. Oliver
Cromwell also interfered in the decision of the Scottish judges
whilst he was protector, whence the bitter lines—

> " In sessions and sizes we bear the stroke and sway,
>   In patents and commission of quorum always chief,
>   So that to whether soever we did weigh,
>   Were it by right or wrong, it passed without reprief,
>   The true man let hang, sometimes to save a thief,
>   Of gold and of silver our hands were never empty,
>   Offices, farms, and fees fell to us in great plenty."

From this practice being so universal, Hobbes contends
" that he whose private interest is to be decided in an assembly
may make as many friends as he can ; and though he procures
them with money, yet it is not injustice."

During the reign of the Stuarts this evil appears to have
mounted to a higher pitch than at any other period of our
history : and so blunt was the moral feeling of the public upon
the subject, that the crime was scarcely regarded in an odious
light. Clarendon somewhere mentions a message which he
received from the queen to favour a particular suitor, and simply
records the fact without that reprobation which the act merited.

The corruption of Lord Bacon has been sometimes ex-
tenuated, on the ground that in the acceptance of gratuities he
was merely following the example of his predecessors, and that
his offence partook strongly of the spirit of the age.   It cannot,
however, be supposed that Bacon was not aware of the magnitude of his crime.   In his address to Serjeant Hutton on his
becoming a judge, he solemnly cautioned him to beware of
corruption.   " That your hands, and the hands of your hands
(I mean those about you) be clean and uncorrupt from gifts,
from meddling in titles, and from serving of turns, be they great
ones or small ones."   With regard to himself he endeavoured
to frame an excuse out of the prevalence of the evil.   " And for
the briberies and gifts, wherewith I am charged," he writes, in
a letter to the king, " when the book of hearts shall be opened,
I hope I shall not be found to have the troubled fountain of a
corrupt heart, in a depraved habit of taking rewards to pervert
justice ; howsoever I may be frail *and partake of the abuses of
the times*."   It is singular to observe the different shapes in
which the bribes were administered in Lord Bacon's case.   In
several causes he received large sums in money.   In one cause
" a dozen of buttons after the cause ended, to the value of £50 ;"
in another, " £200 in money, and a diamond ring worth £500
or £600."   " Of the apothecaries, besides a rich present of amber
grease, £150."   In the cause of Kenday and Valore, "a cabinet
worth £800."

The conduct of Sir Thomas More is in beautiful contrast
with this corruption.   When he was chancellor he received two
presents from certain suitors of his court.   A glove filled with
gold pieces, and a golden goblet.   Sir Thomas returned the
money but retained the glove, because it came from a lady
suitor ; and after drinking the gentleman's good health out of
the golden goblet, he restored it to the donor.

A NOVEL DOMESTIC PET.

OME years since a country gentleman in West Corkshire complained of being very *blasé.* He could find no excitement either in drinking, gaming, or foxhunting. He grew tired of keeping an open house, and a pack of hounds. In order to procure excitement a friend of his recommended him to *keep an attorney !*

NATURAL HISTORY QUESTION.

N the trial of a cause respecting the right of a copyholder to dispose of some "boulderstones" on the land, Mr. Serjeant Wilde, subsequently chancellor, contended that he would have the same right to do so as he would have to pick up any meteoric stones which fell on his land. "I think he would burn his fingers if he tried it, brother Wilde," observed Baron Alderson with a smile.

CRIMINAL RESPONSIBILITY AGE.

N criminal matters a person of the age of fourteen may be capitally punished for any capital offence, but under the age of seven he cannot. The period between seven and fourteen is subject to much uncertainty, the rule applicable to it depends upon the infant's capacity to discern good from evil. We take that age from the East, where puberty comes early, and it is not the sole trace of an origin from Constantinople in many of our statutes. The *Code Napoléon* is wiser. It determines that if an accused person be under the age of— not fourteen, but—sixteen, it shall be inquired of by the jury whether he acted with, or without discernment. In the latter case he is acquitted, but is liable to be under due control. If, on the contrary, he is found to have acted with discernment, his punishment, it is decreed, shall be regulated in proportion to the full punishment of the offence, but never equal to it. On the strength of the maxim, *Malitia supplet ætatem,* our old laws took little thought at all of any such distinction. In 1629, a child between the ages of eight and nine was hanged at the Abingdon Assizes. As late as the year 1780 a boy of fourteen was hanged for participation in a riot about Catholic emancipation. It might be argued, however, that a London street arab is mature at ten. Account was given in the beginning of this century to a parliamentary committee of one of these unhappy creatures, who, during a career of five years, had robbed to the amount of £3000. Besides numerous minor punishments, he had been sentenced to death, but from compassion he was sent to the Philanthropic Asylum instead of the gallows. Thence he escaped, and was for another offence transported for life—all before the age of thirteen.

WHO'S WALKER?

"RECOLLECT," says Mr. Cyrus Jay, "the late Lord Ellenborough sitting in the old Court of Queen's Bench at the end of the hall ; the counsel who argued before him first-class men. Lord Brougham was then one of the juniors behind the bar : and he seemed always to have a dislike to him. I remember on one occasion Brougham pronounced a word improperly. Lord Ellenborough alluded to it, and Brougham said, "That is the way Walker pronounces it." "Who's Walker?" inquired Lord Ellenborough superciliously.

ENGLISH AND IRISH KITES.

IN a bill case Mr. Plunket (afterwards Lord Chancellor of Ireland) applied to accommodation bills of exchange the common expression "flying kites." Lord Chancellor Redesdale, who was slow at taking a joke, observed,

"The learned counsellor talks of 'flying kites :' what does it mean? I recollect flying kites when I was a boy in England." "Oh, my lord," replied Plunket, "the difference between kites in England and in Ireland is very great. In England the wind raises the kite, but in Ireland the kite raises the wind."

PAR NOBILE FRATRUM.

IT is said that James I., soon after his accession to the English throne, was present in a court of justice to observe the pleadings in a cause of some importance. The counsel for the plaintiff having finished, the king was so perfectly satisfied, that he exclaimed, "This is a plain case," and was about to leave the court. Being persuaded, however, to stay and hear the other side of the question, the pleaders for the defendant made the case no less plain on their side. On this the monarch rose, and departed in a great passion, exclaiming, "They are all rogues alike."

RAISON D'ÊTRE OF SPECIAL DEMURRERS.

LORD HOBART remarked that special demurrers "exist that law may be an art."

LIVE AND LET LIVE.

ONE of the most extraordinary reasons which any lawyer has alleged against effecting law reforms, is that assigned by the Chancellor d'Agnesseau. He was once asked by the Duke de Grammont whether he had ever thought of any regulations by which the length of suits and the chicanery practised in the courts could be terminated. "I had gone so far," said the chancellor, "as to commit a plan for such a regulation to writing ; but after I had made some progress I reflected on the great number of advocates, attorneys, and officers of justice whom it would ruin; compassion for these made the pen fall from my hands. The length and number of special lawsuits confer on gentlemen of the long robe their wealth and authority, one must continue *therefore* to permit their infant growth, and everlasting endurance."

PRIVILEGE OF PEERAGE.

T the commencement of the reign of Edward **VI.** an act was passed, from which no very favourable inference can be drawn as to the morals, habits, or accomplishments of the English nobility in the middle of the sixteenth century. Housebreaking, by day or by night, highway robbery, horse-stealing, and stealing from a church having been made capital offences, it was provided "that any lord or lords of the parliament, including the bishops and archbishops, and any peer or peers of the realm having place and voice in parliament, being convicted of any of the said offences for the first time upon his or their request, or prayer, though he cannot read, be allowed benefit of clergy and be discharged without burning in the hand, loss of inheritance, or corruption of blood." "It seems strange to us," says Lord Campbell (*Lives of the Chancellors*), "that this privilege of peerage should have been desirable, or should have been conceded; but it continued in force till taken away by an act passed, after the trial of Lord Cardigan, in the reign of Queen Victoria."

"COULD AULD ACQUAINTANCE BE FORGOT."

ENTLEMEN at the bar, owing to their profession, make a wide and very varied circle of acquaintances, there can be no doubt. One evening, as Mr. John Adolphus was walking through St. Giles's by way of a short cut home, an Irish woman came up to him, "Why, Misther Adolphus! and who'd a' thought of seeing you in the Holy Ground?"

"And how came you to know who I am?" said the barrister. "Lord bless and safe ye, sir! not know ye? Why, I'd know ye if ye was boiled up in a soup!"

Lord Kaimes used to relate a story of a man who claimed the honour of his acquaintance on rather singular grounds. His lordship, when one of the justiciary judges, returning from the north circuit of Perth, happened one night to sleep at Dunkeld. The next morning he was walking towards the ferry, but, apprehending he had missed his way, he asked a man whom he met to conduct him. The other answered with much cordiality, "That I'll do wi' all my heart, my lord, for I ken ye fine. Does not your lordship recollect me? My name is Jimmy Skeate; I have had the honour to be before your lordship for stealing sheep." "Oh, Jemmy, I remember you well; and how is your wife? She had the honour to be before me too for receiving them, knowing them to be stolen." "At your lordship's service. We were o'er lucky: we got off for the lack o' evidence, and I'm still going on in the flesher's trade." "Then," replied his lordship, "we may have the honour of meeting again."

VERY POINTED.

SIR JOHN HAMILTON, who had severely suffered from dealings with the law, used to say that an attorney was "like a hedgehog; it was impossible to touch him anywhere without pricking one's fingers."

SUPREMACY OF THE JURY.

PRACTICAL effect was once given to the idea of supremacy of juries by a Colonel Martin, who was tried at Reading, and who caused the jury to put on their hats, telling them that it was their right, inasmuch as they were the chief judges in the court (*State Trials*, iv. p. 1381). Another colonel, Lilburne by name, at his trial in 1649, thus addressed the judges, "You that call yourselves judges of the law, are no more but Norman intruders; and in deed and in truth, if the jury please, are no more but cyphers to pronounce their verdict." A doctrine which provoked Mr. Justice Jermin to exclaim, "Was there ever such a damnable blasphemous heresy as this is, to call the judges of the law cyphers!"

TOP AND BOTTOM.

THE following playful exchange of epigrams took place at a dinner-table between Sir George Rose and James Smith (author of *Rejected Addresses*) in allusion to Craven Street, Strand, where the former resided :—

J. Smith—

> "At the top of the street ten attorneys find place,
> At the bottom ten coal barges are moored ;
> Fly, honesty, fly, to some safer retreat,
> For there's *craft* in the river and *craft* in the street."

Sir George replied—

> "Why should honesty fly to some safer retreat,
> From attorneys and barges, od rot 'em?
> For the attorneys are *just* at the top of the street,
> And the barges are *just* at the bottom."

CONSOLATORY.

LORD ESKGROVE, a Scotch judge of the end of the last century, as great a "character" as ever graced the bench, rarely failed to signalize himself in pronouncing sentences of death. It was almost a matter of style with him to console the prisoner by assuring him that "Whatever your religious persuasion may be, or even if, as I suppose, you be of no persuasion at all, there are plenty of reverend gentlemen who will be most happy for to show you the way to y-eternal life."

SWEARING ON THE BENCH.

ONE instance may be found in the Yearbook, 2 Hen. V. 5, cited in 11 Rep. 53*b*, of a judge venturing to use an oath upon the bench : " A dyer was bound that he should not use the dyer's craft for two years, and there Hull held that the bond was against the common law, and *by God*, if the plaintiff was here, he should go to prison till he paid a fine to the king."

ORIGIN OF SOLICITORS.

THIS branch of legal practice seems to have arisen, in great part, out of the suits of the Star Chamber. In its origin the calling appears to have been of doubtful legality, and their reputation not over good. Time has, however, established their right to practise, whatever may have been its effect upon their character. Peter Hudson, a barrister of Gray's Inn, thus speaks about them in *The Divine Right of Government*, 1647 : " To our age there are stepped up a new sort of people called solicitors, unknown to the records of the law, who, like the grasshoppers in Egypt, devour the whole land ; and these, I dare say (being authorized by the opinion of the most reverend and learned lord chancellor that ever was before him), were express maintainers, and could not justify their maintenance upon any action brought ; I mean not where a lord or gentleman employed his servant to solicit his cause, for he may justify his doings thereof; but I mean those which are common solicitors of causes, and set up a new profession, not being allowed in any court, or, at least, not in this court, where they follow causes ; and these are the retainers of causes and devourers of men's estates, by contention and prolonging suits to make them without end."

WILLS AGAINST MOUSTACHES.

MR. TEGG, in his curious and interesting volume, *Wills of Their Own*, quotes two testators whose aversion to moustaches continued to exhibit itself even after death. The will of Mr. Henry Budd, which came into force in 1862, declared against the wearing of moustaches by his sons in the following terms : " In case my son Edward shall wear moustaches, then the devise herein before contained in favour of him, his appointees, heirs, and assigns, of my said estate called Pepper Park, shall be void ; and I devise the same estate to my son William, his appointees, heirs, and assigns. And in case my said son William shall wear moustaches, then the devise hereinbefore contained in favour of him, his appointees, heirs, and assigns of my said estate, called Twickenham Park, shall be void ; and I devise the said estate to my said son Edward, his appointees, heirs, and assigns."

Another instance is the will of Mr. Fleming, an upholsterer of Pimlico, proved in 1869, who left £10 each to those of the men in his employ who did not wear moustaches. Those who persisted in wearing them to have only £5 each.

CUIQUE SUA VOLUPTAS.

PETER PEEBLES, in *Redgauntlet*, " whose voluminous course of litigation served as a sort of essay-piece to most young men who were called to the bar" in Edinburgh, is no creature of the great magician's brain. He is a type of a class not uncommon in Scotland, simple men of difficult and captious tempers, cursed with an over-strong sense of right or of wrong, under which they prefer by many degrees utter ruin to making the slightest concession. Peebles used to tell his friends sometimes that he had at present thirteen causes in hand, but was *only* going to move in seven this session.

When anxious for a consultation, he would walk in the night from Linlithgow, where he lived, to Edinburgh, and on reaching that town at four in the morning, would go about ringing the bells of the principal lawyers in the vain hope of getting one to rise and listen to him, to the infinite annoyance of many a poor servant-girl, and no less of the town guard, in whose hands he generally fell.

Another specimen of the class was Campbell of Laguine, who has perhaps been longer at law than any man in modern times. He was a store-farmer in Caithness, and had immense tracts of land under lease. When he sold his wool, he put the price in his pocket—no petty sum—and came up to Edinburgh to waste it in the Court of Sessions. His custom was to pay double for every meal he made at the inns on the road, that he might have a gratis meal on his return from the courts of justice, knowing that he would not bring a " bawbee " away in his pocket. He once told a learned counsel that his laird and he were nearly agreed now—there was only about ten miles of country contested betwixt them. When finally this little matter was adjusted, his agent said, " Well, Laguine, what will ye do now ? "—rashly judging that one who had lived upon law for years, would be at a loss how to occupy his mind now. " No difficulty there," replied Laguine ; " I'll dispute your account, and go to law with you."

Other insane fishers in the troubled waters of the law were Macduff of Ballenloan and Andrew Nicol. The former had two cases before the court at once. His success in the one depended upon his showing that he had capacity to manage his own affairs ; and in the other, upon his proving himself incapable of doing so. He used to complain, with some apparent reason, that he lost them both. Andrew Nicol was at law for thirty years about a *midden-stead* (*Anglice*, " the situation of a dunghill "). He used to frequent the Register House as well as the courts of law, and was encouraged in his foolish pursuits by the roguish clerks of that establishment, by whom he was denominated *Muck* Andrew, in allusion to the object of his litigation. This wretched being, after losing property and credit, and his own senses, in following a valueless phantom, died in 1817 in Cupar jail, where he was placed by one of his legal creditors.

CHALLENGING THE JURY.

AT the trial of Captain Gillespie for having killed William Barrington in a duel, the brother of the deceased, Henry French Barrington, declared that the jury had been " packed," and was told by Sir Jonah Barrington (subsequently judge of the High Court of Admiralty in Ireland), another brother of the victim, that they would have to " challenge the array." " That was my own opinion, Jonah," said he, " and I will do it now." An hour after French returned, apparently quite cool and tranquil. " I have done it," cried he exultingly, and with that he produced from his coat-pocket a long queue and a handful of powdered hair and curls. " See here," continued he, " the cowardly rascal! I went directly to the grand jury-room to ' challenge the array,' and there I challenged the head of the array—that cowardly Lyons. He peremptorily refused to fight me, so I knocked him down before the grand jury and cut off his curls and tail, and my brother Jack is gone to flog the sub-sheriff."

The too literal gentleman had taken the words of the law term in their common acceptation. He had seen the high sheriff coming in with a great *array*, and, repairing to the grand jury dining-room, had challenged Mr. Lyons, the high sheriff, to mortal combat. Mr. Lyons, conceiving the young man to be intoxicated, refused the invitation in a most peremptory manner. French then collared him, tripped up his heels, and, putting his foot on his breast, cut off his side curls and queue with a carving knife from the dinner-table handed him by an old waiter who had been butler in the Barrington family.

The same evening French Barrington tied the curls and queue to a lamp which hung in the centre of a room where a grand ball was given, and made loud proclamation of the whole transaction. Next day he paraded the streets with the curls and queue, newly powdered, suspended from the bridle of his hunter. After having exhibited the spoils for a considerable time, he rode home, "and," says Sir Jonah Barrington in his *Personal Sketches of His Own Time*, "he was never called to account or molested on the subject in any way whatsoever." This extraordinary fact is confirmed by Mr. Townsend Young, LL.D., editor of the third edition of the above work.

OUR OLD DRACONIAN LAWS.

UP to the commencement of the present century a sanguinary and barbarous penal code prescribed one indiscriminate penalty, capital punishment, for nearly three hundred offences, embracing all degrees and varieties of guilt. Keeping company with gipsies, the picking of pockets to the value of twelvepence, shoplifting to the value of five shillings, robbery from a dwelling-house to the value of forty shillings, soldiers or mariners to wander and beg without a pass from their commanding officers or the magistrate, and many other offences of an almost equally trivial nature were placed on a level with the most atrocious murder. The law's remedy in each case was that the culprit should be hanged by the neck until he was dead. That the extreme penalty was seldom enforced in later times against many of the criminals who were threatened by it, it is needless to remark. It would have been too shocking to humanity had it been otherwise.

The maxim that too severe laws are never executed was illustrated in various ways. The victims of petty theft would not prosecute when they knew that their evidence might send a man to the gallows ; and juries, in violation of their oaths but

K

in obedience to the dictates of humanity, returned verdicts
which were ridiculously at variance with the evidence laid before
them. A number of cases of this kind were cited by Sir
Samuel Romilly in his *Observations on the Criminal Law*, published in 1810. He mentions the instance of a woman who
pleaded guilty to the charge of stealing two guineas, two half-
guineas, and forty-four shillings in money from a private
dwelling-house. The jury persisted in finding a verdict that
she had stolen only thirty-nine shillings, in order to save her
from the capital penalty. In another case a man stole goods
from a shop which he was proved to have afterwards sold for
£1 5s. The jury mercifully determined that the value of the
articles was only 4s. 10d. These are but illustrations of what
was continually occurring. In order to protect criminals from
undue severity, juries deliberately disregarded their judicial
oaths, and the law became the abettor of its own violation.

LEGAL PITFALLS.

THE framing of acts of parliament, apart from considerations of how they are to be passed, is a matter
of no small difficulty. Mr. Austin (*On Jurisprudence*,
vol. ii., p. 371), who had himself tried his hand at the craft,
says, " I will venture to affirm that what is commonly called
the *technical* part of legislation is incomparably more difficult
than what may be styled the *ethical*. In other words, it is far
easier to conceive justly what would be useful law than so to
construct that same law that it may accomplish the design of
the lawgiver." Even legal members of parliament sometimes
are caught tripping ; witness the following amendment proposed by an eminent queen's counsel :—

"*Dogs trespassing on enclosed land.*

" Every dog found trespassing on enclosed land unaccompanied by the registered owner of such dog, or other person who shall, on being asked, give his true name and address, may be then and there destroyed by such occupier or his order."— *Monday, May* 22, 1865.

The following definition, the result of the combined efforts of a parliamentary committee, parliamentary counsel, and parliamentary agent, is a legislative illustration of the homely saying, that "too many cooks spoil the broth " :—

"*Darlington Improvement Act,* 1872.

" The term 'new building' means any building pulled or burnt down to or within ten feet from the surface of the adjoining ground."—See Report of Board of Trade under " Tramways Act, 1870," etc., *6th February,* 1873.

FREE TRANSLATIONS.

A LATE venerable practitioner in a humble department of the law, says Mr. Burton in *The Bookhunter,* who wanted to write a book, and was recommended to try his hand at a translation of Latin law-maxims, as a thing much wanted, was considerably puzzled with the maxim, "Catella realis non potest legari ; " nor was he quite relieved when he turned up his Ainsworth and found that catella means "a little puppy." There was nothing for it, however, but obedience ; so that he had to give currency to the remarkable principle of law that " A genuine little whelp cannot be left in legacy." He also translated " Messis sequitur sementem," with a fine simplicity into " The harvest follows the seed time " : and " Actor sequitur forum rei," he made " The agent must be in court when the case is going on." Copies of the book containing these gems are exceedingly rare, some malicious person having put the author up to their absurdity.

ROYAL PERQUISITES.

O purloin one more anecdote from the above delightful work : I am not sure, says Mr. Burton, but in the very mighty heart of all legal formality and technicality— the statutes at large—some funny things might be found.   The best that now occurs to the memory is not to be brought to book, and must be given as a tradition of the time when George III. was king.   Its tenor is, that a bill which proposed, as the punishment of an offence, to levy a certain pecuniary penalty, one half thereof to go to his majesty, and the other half to the informer, was altered in committee, in so far that, when it appeared in the form of an act, the punishment was changed to whipping and imprisonment, the destination being left unaltered.

JEJUNE VERDICTS.

HE first mention of the jury being prohibited from having meat or drink, occurs, I believe, in *Fleta* (*Commentarius Juris Anglicani*, iv. 9), written in the reign of Edward I., where it is said that the sheriff is to cause the jurors in an assize to be kept without food or drink until they are agreed.   Nor did England stand alone in the exercise of such a regulation.   It was a law of the Lombards, *ut judices jejuni causas audiant et decernant.*   And by one of the Welsh laws of Hoel-dda (*Leg. Wall.* v. § 48), no court could sit after noon (*nulla causa post meridiem orari debet*).   The origin of such rules is obvious.   They arose no doubt from the general propensity in ancient times to indulge in excess at meals, and were dictated by a fear lest jurors should, if they had access, when empannelled, to food and drink, become incapacitated from a due discharge of their duty.   And so strictly was this rule enforced that Blackstone quotes instances from the year.

books, where judgment was stayed and a new *venire* awarded, because the jury had eaten and drunk without consent of the judge.

THEMIS AND TERPSICHORE.

THE art of dancing has seldom come judicially before our courts of law. The only case on the books, so far as I know, connected with this subject is reported in Littleton's *Rep*. 268. It is thus cited by Chief Baron Gilbert in his *Treatise on Tenures*, 288 : "There is the case of Caslon and Uthert, where a widow had copyhold lands, and divers persons came for rent, whom she put off with delays ; at last comes a young gentleman and demands it ; she answered that she did not know him, *but if he would dance before her, if she liked his dancing*, she would pay him. This denial was adjudged no forfeiture not being wilful."

Out of court, however, it is well known that dancing was one of the favourite amusements, and, indeed, stated exercises of our old lawyers. Upon certain solemn occasions the ceremony of dancing round the coal fire was performed by the greatest dignitaries of the law. But that lapse of time which encrusted the shield of Scriblerus with its invaluable rust, has deprived us of many of our most ancient and excellent customs. The last time this ceremony took place was in 1733, when Mr. Talbot took leave of the Inner Temple, on having the Great Seal delivered to him. An account of these judicial gambols is to be found in Wynne's *Eunomus*.

After describing the dinner, and the play which was afterwards acted in the Inner Temple, the narrative thus proceeds : "After the play, the lord chancellor, master of the Temple, judges and benchers, retired into their parliament chamber, and in about half an hour afterwards came into the hall again, and a large ring was formed round the fireplace (but no fire or embers were in it). Then the master of the revels, who went first, took the lord chancellor by the right hand, and he, with his left, took Mr. Justice Page, who, joined to the other judges, serjeants, and benchers present, danced, or rather walked, round about the coalfire, according to the old ceremony, three times, during which time they were aided in the figure of the dance by Mr. George Cooke, the prothonotary, then of sixty. And all the time of the dance the ancient song, accompanied by music, was sung by one Toby Aston, dressed in a bargown, whose father had formerly been master of the Plea Office in the King's Bench."

How amicable and how engaging must this spectacle have been ! No doubt the custom was founded in the wisest purposes· Thus to mingle the festive amenities of life with the stern prac- tice of the bar, was well calculated to soften that ruggedness of character and harshness of feeling which the pursuits of a lawyer are but too apt to superinduce. However, if report speaks true, these results were not perceived in the case of Mr. Justice Page.

COUNTRY QUARTER SESSIONS IN THE LAST CENTURY.

IN the *Universal Magazine*, 1736, a country quarter session is satirically described in the following lines :—

> " Three or four parsons, three or four 'squires,
> Three or four lawyers, three or four liars ;
> Three or four parishes bringing appeals,
> Three or four hands, and three or four seals ;
> Three or four bastards, three or four w——,
> Tag-rag and bob-tail, three or four scores ;
> Three or four bulls, and three or four cows,
> Three or four orders, three or four bows ;
> Three or four statutes not understood,
> Three or four paupers praying for food ;
> Three or four roads that never were mended,
> Three or four scolds—and the session is ended."

THE SCALES OF JUSTICE.

O N Monday, December 4, 1871, at the Warrington Borough Court, before the Mayor, Joseph Davies, Esq., H. Bleckly, Esq., and C. Broadbent, Esq., Patrick Flanagan was charged with having had an unjust half-pound weight in his possession. The mayor requested the clerk, Mr. H. Brown White, to see how many quill pens would be required to balance the scales when the just and unjust weights had been placed at either end. They would fine the defendant one shilling for each quill. Mr. White: "Nine quills make the scale balance." The Mayor: "Then we will fine the defendant nine shillings, one for each quill."

LORD ELDON'S FIRST YEAR'S EMOLUMENTS.

" W HEN I was called to the bar," says Lord Eldon, "Bessy [his wife] and I thought all our troubles were over; business was to pour in, and we were to be almost rich immediately. So I made a bargain with her, that during the following year all the money I should receive in the first eleven months should be mine, and whatever I got in the twelfth month should be hers. What a stingy dog I must have been to make such a bargain! I would not have done so afterwards. But, however, so it was; *that* was our agreement; and how do you think it turned out? In the twelfth month I received half-a-guinea; eighteen-pence went for fees, and Bessy got nine shillings. In the other eleven months I got not one shilling."

A "WRINKLE" TO O'CONNELL.

M ANY of O'Connell's legal triumphs in defending prisoners were owing to his skill in detecting flaws in the indictments. Thus, a man was charged with stealing a cow; the prosecutor swore that the prisoner was caught in the field where he left the cows to graze, but that the carcase was found in the next field. O'Connell submitted that the indictment was bad, for when the cow was killed it was no longer a cow ; and if the prisoner was to be tried for stealing a dead animal, it should be so stated. He relied on the dictum of Judge Holroyd, that an indictment for stealing a dead animal should state it was dead ; for upon a general statement that a party stole the animal, it is to be intended that he stole it alive (Edwards's Case : Russell and Ryan, 497. *Vide* Roscoe's *Dig. of Crim. Evid.* p. 77). And here the only evidence was that the animal was dead.

The court held the indictment bad, and directed the jury to acquit the prisoner. It was said the cow in question was the fattest of a number of cows, and the night on which it was killed was pitch dark. The grateful cattle-stealer came in the evening to O'Connell's lodgings to thank him for having saved his life—for in those days cattle-stealing was punished by hanging. " How did you contrive to select the fattest cow when the night was quite dark ? " inquired O'Connell, wishing to increase the stock of his useful knowledge. "Well, your honour, you saved my life," replied the culprit, "so I'll put you up to the dodge. When you go to steal a cow, and wish, av coorse, to take the best—for ' in for a penny in for a pound '—be sure to take her that's on the outside. The wakest craturs always make for the ditch for shelter, but the fat bastes are outside."

YO EL REY OUTLAWED.

" THE King of Spain," says Selden, in his *Table Talk*, "was outlawed in Westminster Hall, I being a counsel against him. A merchant had recovered costs against him in a suit, which, because he could not get, we advised him to have his majesty outlawed for not appearing, and so he was. As soon as Gondemar, the Spanish ambassador, heard this, he presently sent the money ; by reason if his master had been outlawed, he could not have had the benefit of the law, which would have been very prejudicial, there being then many suits between the King of Spain and our merchants."

WORSE THAN CANNIBALS.

VERY stick is said to be good enough when you want to beat a dog, and almost every word in the dictionary, every circumstance in life, every object in the universe, seems to furnish a fit text for invective against the much abused legal profession. In Clement's Inn pretty garden there is a bronze figure of a kneeling negro supporting a sun-dial, which was brought from Italy early in the eighteenth century by Lord Clare, by whom it was presented to the Inn. On this object the following biting epigram was made :—

> " In vain poor sable son of woe
> Thou seek'st the tender tear ;
> For thee in vain with pangs they flow ;
> For mercy dwells not here.
>
> From cannibals thou fled'st in vain,
> Lawyers less quarter give ;
> The first won't eat you till you're slain,
> The last will do't alive."

BRIEF BUT SWEET.

HEN a lawyer is called out of his own circuit to plead for plaintiff or defendant in another, he is described as " specially engaged," and receives a large fee or hono-rarium accordingly, generally from one to five hundred pounds sterling. Perhaps the largest fee ever received in England was by Lord Truro (then Sir Thomas Wilde), who had nine thousand guineas for going out of his circuit to plead in some great property case. His brief—so called like *lucus a non lucendo*, because of the prolixity of such documents—extended to over two thousand pages.

LORD CLONMEL'S MAXIMS.

WO maxims of Lord Chief Justice Clonmel are worthy of being remembered. One was, "Whatever may be done in the course of the week always do on Monday morning." The other, which he gave as applicable to married life, was, "Never do anything for *peace sake*, if you do you buy all future tranquillity only by concession." Being asked if this last was his own rule of practice, he confessed that it was not, as a philosopher had an easier life of it than a soldier.

HABEAS CORPUS.

N Pepys' time playgoers could not engage seats before-hand, but used to send their servant-man, or even a street boy, to take a seat and occupy it till they came. Something similar appears to have been done in the courts in the days of Queen Bess—witness the following anecdote, pre-served by John Manningham, of the Middle Temple, in his *Diary.* "Mr. Prideaux, a great practiser in the Exchequer, and one that usurps upon a place certain at the bar, left his man one day to keep his place for him, but Lancaster of Grays Inn coming in the mean time, would needs have the place, though the man would have kept it. 'For,' said Lancaster, 'knowest thou not that I believe nothing but the real presence (meaning that he was a papist); and besides, I could not think it to be *corpus meum* except Mr. Prideaux himself were there.'"

LAWYERS' POINTS.

"T is very odd," said Serjeant Channell to Thesiger, "that Tindall should have decided against me on that point of law, which seemed to me as plain as *a, b, c.*" "Yes," replied Thesiger, "but of what use is it that it should have been as plain as *a, b, c* to you, if the judge was determined to be *d, e, f* (deaf) to it?"

A PRETTY PAIR.

THERE were two attorneys, father and son, of the name of Priddle. In point of character they stood very low. Lord Mansfield used to say to the father, "Don't read your affidavit, Mr. Priddle; we give the same credit to what you say as to what you swear." They had a cause, father against son. The father called to leave a retainer with Lord Eldon against the son, representing him as the most worthless of human beings. Lord Eldon declined to interfere in this family business. Soon afterwards the son called to retain him against the father, representing in his turn the old gentleman as the most worthless of human beings. This retainer his lordship also declined to accept. The elder of these persons had got possession of a house belonging to the crown. The Attorney-General Macdonald had great difficulty in dispossessing him by proceedings at law, but at last succeeded; and when Mr. Chamberlayne, the Treasury solicitor, went with due authority to demand possession, Priddle said, "If you will take the house, you shall take all that's in it. Poor Mrs. Priddle died a day or two ago; she lies a corpse upstairs in bed, and there I shall leave her. If you must have the house, you shall have her also." The Treasury solicitor took possession of the house and of her, and Priddle rejoiced in saving the expense of burying his departed spouse.

FILII TERRAE.

WHILE "pleasant Ned Lysaght" was living in college there were two sprigs of newly manufactured nobility there, who made themselves ridiculous. These were

the two sons of the notorious Lord Norbury, the chief justice
of the Court of Common Pleas. Lord Norbury, when plain
John Toler, had married the heiress of the Norwood estates,
and while he was serving the office of attorney-general, he had
influence enough to get his wife made Viscountess Norwood,
in her own right, with remainder to her second son. In the
course of time John Toler was himself raised to the peerage
as Lord Norbury, his eldest son, of course, succeeding him in
the title. Many were the mistakes about the two Hon. Messrs.
Toler, the future Norwood being often confounded with the
future Norbury, and *vice versâ.* Lysaght one day, meeting the
two young conceited Tolers in the square of the college, went
up to them, and said, " Pray tell me which is which. Which
of you is *Bog*berry and which of you is *Bog*wood ? " The semi-
plebeian *filii nobiles* by no means relished the allusion to bogs.

MORE PUNNING.

A PERSON who had long been a familiar friend of Sir
Thomas More, came to visit him when he was in the
height of his prosperity. The lord chancellor enter-
tained him hospitably, and among other pastimes, showed him
his gallery of paintings, at the same time desiring him to say
which picture he liked best. The friend could not decide,
whereupon Sir Thomas showed him the picture of a skull
with the motto *Memento Morieris,* which he commended as an
excellent device and conceit. The gentleman being desirous to
know what his host could see so extraordinary in such a trite
device, More replied, " Sir, you must remember sometimes
you borrowed money of me, but I cannot remember that you
have ever remembered to repay it. It is not much, truly, but
though I be chancellor I have use for that little, and now
methinks that picture speaks unto you : *Memento Mori Æris.*"

BEGGING A LIFE.

" IT is the custom, not the law," says John Manningham, an Elizabethan lawyer, in his *Diary,* " in France and Italy that if any notorious professed woman of ill-fame will beg for a husband a man who is going to execution, he shall be reprieved, and she may obtain a pardon, and marry him, that both their ill lives may be bettered by so holy an action. Hence originated a jest when a scoffing gentlewoman told a gentleman that she heard that he had been in some danger to have been hanged for certain villainy. ' Truly, madam,' he answered, ' I was afeard of nothing so much as that you would have begged me.' Montaigne tells of a Picard who was going to execution, and when he saw a limping woman come to beg him, he exclaimed : ' Oh, she limps ! she limps ! dispatch me quickly,' preferring death to life with a lame wife. In England it has been used that if a woman will beg a condemned person for her husband, she must come in her smock only, and a white rod in her hand, as Sterrill says he has seen."

Daines Barrington, in his *Observations on the more Ancient Statutes,* is inclined to consider this a vulgar legal error. " To these," he says, " may *perhaps* be added the notion that a woman marrying a man under the gallows, will save him from execution. This probably arose from a wife having brought an appeal against the murderer of her husband, who afterwards repenting the prosecution of her lover, not only forgave the offence but was willing to marry the appellee." Unless we assume that this romantic but ill-told incident had happened in several countries, with the same *dénouement,* Daines Barrington's explanation may be dismissed. The detail about the " smock " given by Manningham may have been taken from another ancient vulgar legal error, which asserted that when a man designs to marry a woman who is in debt, if he take her from the hand of the priest *clothed only in her shift,* it is supposed that he will not be liable to her engagements.

LORD ELLENBOROUGH'S PLAYFULNESS.

LORD ELLENBOROUGH had no mean power of ridicule, as playful as a mind more strong than refined could make it ; while of sarcasm he was an eminent professor, but of the kind which hacks and tears and flays its victims, rather than destroys by cutting keenly. His interrogative exclamation in Lord Melville's case, when the party's ignorance of having taken accommodation out of the public fund was alleged—indeed, was proved,—may be remembered as very picturesque, though, perhaps, more pungent than dignified. "Not know money ! Did he see it when it glittered ? Did he hear it when it chinked ?" On the bench he had the very well-known though not very eloquent Henry Hunt before him, who, in mitigation of some expected sentence, spoke of some who "complained of his dangerous eloquence." "They do you great injustice, sir," said the considerate and merciful chief justice, kindly wanting to relieve him from all anxiety on *this* charge. On another occasion, after he had been listening for a whole day to two conveyancers of a long and most technical argument in silence, and with a wholesome fear of lengthening it by any interruption whatever, one of them, in reply to a remark from another judge, said, " If it is the pleasure of your lordship that I go into that matter." " We, sir," said the chief justice, " have no pleasure in it any way."

A MEMORIAL OF SHAKESPEARE.

THE Middle Temple Hall, one of the finest ancient structures in the metropolis, is the only edifice now in existence in which a play of Shakespeare's was acted in the poet's lifetime. Here the play of "Twelfth Night" was recited before Queen Elizabeth, on February 2, 1601, witness the following entry in the *Diary* of John Manningham, of the Middle Temple Barrister-at-Law—

"Febr. 2, 1601. At our feast wee had a play called 'Twelve Night, or What you Will,' much like the 'Commedy of Errors,' or 'Menechmi' in Plautus," etc.

FAULTY JUSTICE.

A STORY is told of Lord Hailes (Sir David Dalrymple, appointed a Scotch judge in 1762), once making a series of objections to a law-paper, and in consequence to the whole suit to which it belonged, on account of the word *justice* being spelt without an *e* at the end. Hence the line in the doggerel ballad, *Court of Session Garland*, supposed to have been a joint composition of James Boswell and John Maclaurin, advocates—

"'This cause,' cries Hailes, 'to judge I can't pretend,
For *justice*, I perceive, wants an *e* at the end.'"

Perhaps no author ever affected so much critical accuracy as Lord Hailes, and yet there never was a book published with so large an array of "corrigenda et addenda" as his first edition of the *Annals of Scotland.*

HIMSELF A HOST.

MR. THOMAS BAIRD was once, in a dull technical way, stating a dry case to Lord Meadowbank, who was sitting single. This did not please the judge, who thought that his dignity required a grander tone. So he dismayed poor Baird, than whom no man could have less turn for shining in the Forum, by throwing himself back in his chair, and saying, "Declaim, sir! why don't you declaim? Speak to me as if I were a popular assembly."

AGGRAVATION OF CRIME.

THE French juries have a great talent for discovering "attenuating circumstances," yet I am not aware that their ingenuity ever went so far as to take into consideration the sacredness of the dinner hour, and the propriety of a criminal in not having chosen that hour for the commission of his crime. In the opinion of Lord Eskgrove, a Scottish judge, the invasion of a house in that sacred hour of the day was an aggravation of crime. His lordship had to condemn three persons to death for having broken into a house at Luss, assaulted Sir James Colquhoun and others, and robbed them of a large sum of money. He first, as was his almost constant practice, explained the nature of the various crimes, assault, robbery, and *hame sucken*, of which last he gave them the etymology. Then he reminded them that they attacked the house and the persons within it, and robbed them, concluding with this climax : " All this you did ; and God preserve us ! *ioost when they were sittin' doon to their denner.*"

SUMMA LEX, SUMMA INJUSTITIA.

THE following curious case appears in the *Daily Telegraph*, October 20, 1881 :—

"CHELMSFORD.—Joseph Hale, Wm. Preest, and Ruth Preest were charged at the Essex Quarter Sessions here, to-day, with stealing 56lb. of grapes. For the prosecution it was stated that the law did not permit an indictment for stealing growing grapes, and in this case they were cut from the vine. The prisoners, however, were also charged with taking the scissors with which they cut them. The charge was established, and Hale was sentenced to two months' and the two Preests to one month's imprisonment each."

Verily it is not without cause that our law is said to be "the perfection of human reason" and "the mother of justice." *

EXPLICITNESS.

OF a certainty there could be no doubt left on the mind of the executioner of the law, concerning the spot where the blow of the sword had to be administered on the body of the delinquent, sentenced to death for highway robbery on October 13, 1568, by the Court of Arnhem, in Gelderland, Holland. The curious sentence, verbally, naively, and superabundantly ran as follows: "That Jacob van der Bosch, alias Boschman, be executed by the headsman with the sword, and divided in two parts between the shoulders and the head, of which two parts the head is to be the smaller one : and further, that his dead body be placed on a wheel on the spot where he has committed the said act of felony of which he stands convicted."

A HANGWOMAN.

IN the first quarter of this century the executioner in the county of Connaught was a woman, nicknamed Lady Betty. She is described in the *Dublin University Magazine*, 1850, as a person of a violent temper, though in manner rather above the common, and possessing some education. It was said that she was a native of County Kerry, and that the occasion of her having adopted her horrible profession was the following :—By hard usage she had driven her only son from her at an early age. The son enlisted, and after many years returned with some money in his pocket, acquired in his campaigns. In order to be able to judge of his mother's character, he asked for a night's lodging, without making himself

---

* "No man out of his private reason ought to be wiser than the law, which is the perfection of reason" (*Co. Litt.* 97*b*) ; "so as in truth justice is the daughter of the law, for the law bringeth her forth" (*Ibid.* 142*a*).

known. The woman did not recognize her visitor, but granted his request. Having discovered that he possessed some money, the wretched mother murdered and robbed her own son in his sleep. For this crime she was sentenced to be hanged with a batch of other prisoners. No executioner being at hand, and "the sheriff and his deputy being men of refinement, education, humanity, and sensibility, who could not be expected to fulfil the office which they had undertaken—and for which one of them, at least, was paid"—the wretched woman was permitted to save her life by becoming the executioner of the other prisoners, sheep-stealers, white-boys, shop-lifters, and cattle-houghers, who, to the amount of seven or eight, were destined to be turned off on the same occasion. She officiated unmasked and undisguised, and after this first attempt continued to practise as executioner for a great number of years for the Connaught circuit, and Roscommon in particular. She used also to flog publicly in and through the streets as a part of her profession, and was always considered extremely severe, particularly on her own sex. The above authority describes her as "a middle-aged, stout-made, dark-eyed, swarthy complexioned, but by no means forbidding-looking woman." Numerous were the tales related of her exploits, and few children were born or reared in Connaught at that period, who were not occasionally frightened into being good, by the cry "Here's Lady Betty." One extraordinary trait of her character was that she used to draw with a burnt stick, upon the walls of her room, portraits of all the persons she executed.

FALSE TRUTHS.

IN his judgment in *Moens* v. *Heyworth*, Baron Alderson observed : "I consider that if a person makes a representation, or takes an oath of that which is true, if he intend that the party to whom the representation is made should *not* believe it to be true, that is a false representation ;

and so he who takes an oath in one sense, knowing it to be administered to him in another, takes it falsely. This may be illustrated by an anecdote of a very eminent ambassador, Sir Henry Wotton, who, when he was asked what advice he would give to a young diplomatist going to a foreign court, said, ' I have found it best always to tell the truth, as they will never believe anything an ambassador says ; so you are sure to take them in.' Now Sir Henry Wotton meant that he should tell a lie. This, no doubt, was only said as a witticism, but it illustrates my meaning."

THE FIRST QUARTER OF THE MOON.

BROUGHAM, speaking of the salary attached to a rumoured appointment to a new judgeship, said it was all moonshine. Lyndhurst, in his dry and waggish way remarked : " May be so, my lord Harry, but I have a strong notion that moonshine though it be, you would like to see the first quarter of it."

A BITER BIT.

CURRAN was always ready for the ring, and eager to throw down the gauntlet in the list of raillery and re-joinder. What could be cleverer than his repartee in a horse cause, when he asked the jockey's servant his master's age, and the man retorted with ready gibe : " I never put my hand into his mouth to try." The laugh was against the counsellor till he made the bitter reply : " You did perfectly right, friend ; for your master is said to be a great bite."

BAR AND BENCH.

THE altercations of the late Dr. Kenealy with Lord Chief Justice Cockburn stand out in strong relief as one of the few instances in modern courts of justice of a public and extreme collision between the advocate and judge.

Formerly it was not so with our volatile countrymen across St.
George's Channel, who delighted in a scene, and excused the impropriety for the sake of the point, wit, and fun. Thus we read of
a sharp sparring match between Judge Robinson and Mr. Hoare,
where the judge charged the barrister with a design to bring
the king's commission into contempt. "No, my lord," said
Hoare, "I have read in a book, that when a peasant, during
Charles the First's reign, found the king's crown in a bush, he
showed it all marks of reverence ; but I will go further—I will
respect it on a bramble."

COLOURABLE TRESPASS.

WHEN Justice Buller, at the age of forty-two, was frequently called upon to preside not only over the chief
Court of Common Law, but over the Court of Chancery
also, his assumption over his seniors was noticed by the bar,
and one of them having remarked to Cowper, the king's counsel,
how Buller trespassed on the province of Ashurst, "Pooh!"
said Cowper, "that's nothing ; don't you see," pointing to the
senior's rubicund face, "how he himself gives *colour to the trespass.*" My readers who are not professional must be willing to
believe that the jest was a good one, for I dare not hazard in
their behalf that most forlorn of all Quixotic undertakings, the
attempting to explain a joke.

LORD MONBODDO'S HORSE.

LORD MONBODDO, who had a Gulliver-like admiration
of the horse, once embroiled himself in an action
respecting a horse which belonged to him. His lordship had committed the animal, when sick, to the charge of a
farrier, with directions for the administration of a certain medicine. The farrier gave the medicine, but went beyond his commission, in as far as he mixed in it a liberal *menstruum* of

treacle, in order to make it palatable. The horse dying next morning, Lord Monboddo raised a prosecution for its value, and actually pleaded his own cause at the bar. He lost the case, however, and is said to have been in consequence so enraged at his brethren, that he never afterwards sat with them upon the bench, but underneath among the clerks. The report of this action is highly amusing on account of the appalling quantity of Roman law quoted by the judges, and the strange circumstances under which the case appeared before them.

DUTIES OF A MASTER OF THE ROLLS.

AN old book of precedents, now in the possession of Mr. Colville, of the Registrar's Office, and which belonged, in the latter part of the last century, to Mr. Green, another celebrated registrar, has a paper attached to it containing this passage in print :—" The following description of the duties of a master of the Rolls is given by a lord chancellor not a hundred years ago : ' I look upon my court and that of the Rolls to be somewhat like a stage-coach, which, besides the skill of the coachman, requires the assistance of an able postillion to lead the horses and pick out the best parts of the road. Now if I have got an ignorant furze-bush-headed postillion he may overset the coach and tumble us both into the ditch.'"

TWO SIDES OF THE LAW.

HROAT. And how think'st thou of law?
　　Dash.　Most reverently :
　　Law is the world's great light ; a second sun
To this terrestrial globe, by which all things
Have life and being, and without the which
Confusion and disorder soon would seize
The general state of men : war's outrages,
The ulcerous deeds of peace, it curbs and cures.

It is the kingdom's eye, by which she sees
The acts and thoughts of men.
   Throat. The kingdom's eye!
I tell thee, fool, it is the kingdom's nose;
Nor is't of flesh, but merely of wax;
And 'tis within the powers of us lawyers
To wrest this nose of wax which way we please.
Or, it may be, as thou say'st, an eye, indeed;
But if it be, 'tis sure a woman's eye,
That's ever rolling.
                LODEWICK BARRY, " Ram Alley,"
                Old Plays, vol. v., p. 381.

A BARBER-OUS FIGURE.

LORD KENYON was not only given to fanciful quotations from the classics, but so partial to rhetorical ornaments and metaphorical language, that some of his discourses show faults as glaring as the compositions of a fashionable auctioneer. When sitting in the Rolls Court, indignant at the conduct of one of the parties who had tried every artifice to gain time, the Master astonished his staid and prosaical audience by exclaiming, " This is the last hair in the tail of procrastination!" Whether he plucked it out or not the reporter has omitted to inform us.

A GOLDEN EGG.

WHEN the author of *The Lay of the Last Minstrel* obtained the appointment of Clerk to the Sessions, Erskine complimented him upon it in a punning manner. The scheme to bestow this office on Sir Walter Scott had been begun by the Tories, but was completed by the Whigs, and after the fall of the latter cabinet, Erskine met the new clerk and congratulated him on his appointment, which he liked all the better, he said, as it was *the lay of the last ministry.*

A SPECIAL CASE.

N 1780, Jerry Keller dined at the house of one Garrett Moore, grocer and whisky vendor, in Aungier Street, Dublin. When the mirth grew "fast and furious" an intimation was made that the lady of the house had just been confined. "Let us adjourn," said the host. "Certainly,' replied Jerry, "*pro re nata.*" The young stranger whose somewhat unexpected arrival disturbed the feast, was Thomas Moore, the poet.

MISTAKING SIDES.

"HAD," says Lord Eldon in his *Anecdote Book,* "very early after I was called to the bar, a brief in business in the King's Bench, as junior to Mr. Dunning. He began the argument, and appeared to me to be reasoning very powerfully against our client. Waiting till I was quite convinced that he was mistaken for what party he had been retained, I then touched his arm, and, upon his turning his head towards me, I whispered to him that he must have misunderstood for whom he was employed, as he was reasoning against our client. He gave me a very rough and rude reprimand for not having sooner set him right, and then proceeded to state, that what he had addressed to the court was all that could be stated against his client, and that he had put the case as unfavourably as possible against him, in order that the court might see how very satisfactorily the case against him could be answered ; and accordingly very powerfully answered what he had before stated."

This was one way of getting out of the difficulty. Another mode is related by Mr. Smirke, who, writing in *Notes and Queries,* states that an eminent counsel, who afterwards presided in the Divorce Court, was on one occasion his leader on an argument before Lord Denman, in a case relating to the principle on which railway companies should be rated. "To my surprise he very soon showed the court that he had mistaken his real client, and was prepared to argue in support of the wrong party. I interfered as soon as I could, by privately explaining to him the error under which he was labouring, when he declined to retrace his steps, and left his duty at once in the hands of his junior counsel, without saying more."

A third instance of this unfortunate mistake occurred in the Rolls Court on the 11th of June, 1788. An eminent counsellor, whose initial only is given, Mr. A——, received a brief in court a short time before the cause was called on, for the purpose of opposing the prayer of a petition. Mr. A——, conceiving himself to be the petitioner, spoke very ably in support of the petition, and was followed by a counsel on the same side. The master of the rolls then inquired who opposed the petition? Mr. A——, having by this time discovered his mistake, rose in confusion, and said that he really felt much ashamed for a blunder into which he had fallen, but that instead of supporting the petition it was his business to have opposed it. The master of the rolls, with great good humour, desired him to proceed now on the other side, observing that he knew no counsel who could answer his arguments so well as himself."

There is still another instance on record which occurred in the Vice-Chancellor's Court, in 1829. A case. was set down on the paper to be spoken to, and Messrs. Horne and Pemberton were heard on one side. Mr. Sugden, subsequently Lord St. Leonards, followed, concurring in the argument of his learned friends : "The law here was quite clear," etc. "Then Mr. Sugden is with you, Mr. Horne," said the vice-chancellor. Mr. Horne replied that "the argument of his learned friend was to his great surprise on his side, but his friend happened to be on the other side." This excited great laughter in court. Mr. Sugden, who after consulting with his junior, Mr. Jacob, seemed not a little disconcerted, said he "had mistaken his side. What he had said, however, was said in all sincerity, and he never would for any client, be he whom he might, argue against what he thought a settled point of law. As his learned friends had differed on the present point, he hoped his honour would decide it without reference to what had fallen from him." This the vice-chancellor promised to do.

FREE BENCH.

SOME allusions are made in a former page * to certain consequences anciently following on the frailties of widow tenants in Kent. An analogous custom, called Free Bench, existed in other parts of England, and is thus described in the *Law Dictionary* of Giles Jacob, the learned lawyer, whom Pope immortalized as a "blunderbuss of law." In the manors of East and West Enbourne in the County of Berks, in the manor of Torre in Devonshire, and in other parts in the West of England, there is a custom, that when a copy-hold tenant dies his widow shall have "free bench" in all his customary lands, *dum sola et casta fuerit;* but if she commits incontinency she forfeits her estate. Yet, nevertheless, on her coming into the court of the manor, riding backwards on a black ram with his tail in her hand, and saying the words following, the steward is bound by the custom to re-admit her to her free bench. The words are these:—

> " Here I am
> Riding on a black ram
> Like a w—— as I am ;
> And for my crincum crancum
> I've lost my bincum bancum ;
> And for my tail's game
> Have done this worldly shame.
> Therefore, pray, Mr. Steward, let me have my lands again."

This is a kind of penance among jocular tenures to purge the offence.

* " Law Verse," p. 104.

A HOUSE OF CORRECTION.

ORD CHANCELLOR BATHURST possessed a lively
wit.   In one session of parliament there was an unusual number of bills sent up from the Commons, in
a state so imperfect that they had to be amended by the
Lords.   One was brought in by Mr. Gilbert, famous for his
activity in establishing and improving houses of correction.
The chancellor said to him, when he brought his bill up to the
Lords, "You have been a long time, Mr. Gilbert, wishing for
a good house of correction, and I now congratulate you on
having found one ; for this House has been nothing but a house
of correction for the errors and mistakes of your House the
whole session."

JOHN-A-NOAKES AND JOHN-A-STYLES.

HE law formerly used to compel jurymen, if they acquitted
any man accused of murder, not merely to acquit him,
but to name the guilty person.   Whenever they could
not do this to the satisfaction of their consciences, the juries declared that the real murderer was John-a-Noakes.   That person
of whom we speak so often as Jack Noakes, in friendly terms,
has been declared guilty by jury after jury of horrible atrocities.

The history of John-a-Noakes and his brother John-a-Styles
is still to be written.   "To whom" they were "related and of
whom begot," is a mystery.   They are only known as legal fictions,
like that other pair of legal turtle-doves John Roe and Richard
Doe, and as subjects of humorous distinction in some old
writers :—

" Prythee, stay a while ;
Looke you, comes John-a-Noke and John-a-Style."

MARSTON, *Scourage of Villainy,* ii. 7, 1599.

And again :—

" John-a-Nokes was driving his cart towards Croydon, and

by the way fell asleep therein. Meanwhile a good fellow came up, and stole away his two horses, and went fair away with them. In the end he awakening and missing them, said, 'Either I am John-a-Noakes, or I am not John-a-Nokes. If I am John-a-Noakes, then have I lost two horses, and if I be not John-a-Noakes, then have I found a cart." (Copley *Wit, Fits, and Fanceys,* 1614.)

A writer in the *Spectator,* August 6, 1714, penned a " Humble Petition of John-a-Nokes and John-a-Stiles," showing " That your petitioners have had causes depending in Westminster Hall above five hundred years, and that we despair of ever seeing them brought to an issue ; that your petitioners have not been involved in these lawsuits out of any litigious temper of their own, but by the instigation of contentious persons ; that the young lawyers in our Inns of Court are continually setting us together by the ears, and think they do us no hurt, because they plead for us without a fee ; that many of the gentlemen of the robe have no other clients besides us two ; that when they have nothing else to do, they make us plaintiffs and defendants, though they were never retained by either of us ; that they traduce, condemn, or acquit us, without any manner of regard to our reputations and good names in the world," etc.

END OF MR. GAMMON.

AT the bar mess at York, shortly after the late Mr. Serjeant Murphy took the coif, the following conversation took place.

Mr. S. Murphy. Well, Warren, I have been reading your *Ten Thousand a Year.*

Warren. Have you? I hope you liked it.

Mr. S. Murphy. Pretty well. But what became of Mr. Gammon, who appears in the first and second volumes, and then suddenly disappears?

Warren. Well, I'll tell you, serjeant; the fact is, Gammon took the coif, and never was heard of after.

This was a severe and well-deserved hit to Murphy, whose business had declined ever since he took the coif.

LEGAL CHARGES.

AT the close of the last century, when all ranks of Britons shouldered the musket in order to be ready for any attempts Republican France might think proper to make against their liberties and constitution, the Inns of Court formed two corps of volunteers—the Temple corps, christened by Sheridan the "Devil's Own," and the Lincoln's Inn volunteers, nicknamed the "Devil's Invincibles." The Temple corps numbered all the legal grandees in its ranks, including judges, and admitted no lawyer or student who was not a member of an Inn of Court. The Lincoln's Inn volunteers were less fastidious, and admitted even attorneys in their ranks. As may be expected, many jokes were made on this corps. One of these was that when Colonel Cox, the master in Chancery, who commanded the corps, gave the word "Charge," two-thirds of his rank and file took out their note-books and wrote down 6s. 8d.

SUBTRACTING EVIDENCE.

FEW cases are more laughable than that which describes the arithmetical process by which Baron Perot arrived at the value of certain conflicting evidence. "Gentlemen of the jury," this judge is reported to have said, in summing up the evidence in a trial where the witnesses had sworn with noble tenacity of purpose, "there are fifteen witnesses who swear that the watercourse used to flow in a ditch on the north side of the hedge. On the other hand, gentlemen, there are nine witnesses who swear that the watercourse used to flow on the south side of the hedge. Now, gentlemen, if you subtract nine from fifteen, there remain six witnesses wholly uncontradicted ; and I recommend you to give your verdict for the party who called those witnesses."

RUDIS INDIGESTAQUE MOLES.

AID Lord Bacon, "So great is the accumulation of statutes, so often do those statutes cross each other, and so intricate are they, that the certainty of the law is entirely lost in the heap." Lord Bacon said this when the number of our public statutes was two thousand one hundred and seventy-one. Thus the profoundest brain that ever wig covered pronounced itself to be lost in the maze of a law constructed of two thousand one hundred and seventy-one disjointed statutes. From his day to our own the maze has been incessantly in progress of enlargement. New laws are hung on to the outskirts of the rest faster than new streets on the outskirts of this metropolis : new legal neighbourhoods spring up, new streets of law are pushed through the heart of old-established legislation, and all this legal building and improvement still goes on with little or no carting away of the old building materials and other rubbish. If, therefore, two thousand odd hundred statutes perplexed Bacon, what sort of a legal genius must he be who can feel easy with some twenty-five thousand on his mind ? It is manifest that in these law-making days it would need twelve Bacons, at the very least, to make one judge.

Simple additions to the statutes have been made since the happy accession of her Majesty, of a number actually double the whole sum known in Bacon's time. The following chronological table comprises all acts passed in this reign, classed by the Queen's printers as " Public " or " Public General " :—

1 & 2 Vict., 1837-38,	120	4 & 5 Vict., 1841	61
2 & 3 „ 1839	97	5 „ 1841	11
3 & 4 „ 1840	113	5 & 6 „ 1842	123

6 & 7 Vict.,	1843	99	25 & 26 Vict.,	1862	114
7 & 8 „	1844	113	26 & 27 „	1863	125
8 & 9 „	1845	130	27 & 28 „	1864	121
9 & 10 „	1846	117	28 & 29 „	1865	126
10 & 11 „	1847	115	29 & 30 „	1866	122
11 & 12 „	1847–48,	133	30 & 31 „	1867	146
12 & 13 „	1849	111	31 & 32 „	1867–68,	130
13 & 14 „	1850	116	32 & 33 „	1868–69,	117
14 & 15 „	1851	106	33 & 34 „	1870	112
15 & 16 „	1852	88	34 & 35 „	1871	117
16 & 17 „	1852–53,	137	35 & 36 „	1872	98
17 & 18 „	1854	125	36 & 37 „	1873	91
18 & 19 „	1854–55,	134	37 & 38 „	1874	94
19 & 20 „	1856	120	38 & 39 „	1875	96
20 „	1857	85	39 & 40 „	1876	81
21 & 22 „	1857–58,	110	40 & 41 „	1877	69
22 „	1859	35	41 & 42 „	1878	79
22 & 23 „	1859	66	42 & 43 „	1879	78
23 & 24 „	1860	154	43 „	1880	19
24 & 25 „	1861	134	43 & 44 „	1880	48

DUBIOUS HONOUR.

ONE of the most infamous conspiracies known to English advocates has been the attempt—and upon one occasion sadly successful—to take life by regular criminal procedure. One plan has been to incite others to commit robbery, and then, for the sake of the reward, to procure such evidence as would be sufficient to convict them. Another plan was to discover a robbery and charge an entirely innocent person. Serjeant Davy once was counsel for some miscreants of this character. They had connived with the prosecutor that he should be robbed by two strangers, innocent, not of the robbery, but of the conspiracy. The serjeant delivered an elaborate argument on the subject, and his clients, although subsequently convicted of conspiracy, were discharged as to the felony. The serjeant's opening for the conspirators was sufficiently humorous : "I have the honour of attending your lordships as counsel for the prisoners ; and I must own that I could not have been prevailed upon to have been counsel for such a set of rogues had I not been appointed by your lordships."

FROG-MORGAN.

THE way Mr. Morgan obtained his nickname of Frog-Morgan was as follows. The law reports of Mr. Justice Croke are usually quoted according to the reigns to which they refer—Elizabeth, James, Charles, etc. Morgan, one day in arguing a case in the King's Bench, quoted so frequently from Croke Charles, Croke James, and Croke Elizabeth, that the whole bar became convulsed with laughter, and he, in consequence, obtained the sobriquet of "Frog-Morgan."

COMPARATIVE ENTOMOLOGY.

WHEN Sir William Jones, in his younger days, lived in the Middle Temple, he one day took a book from a shelf, which caused a large spider to fall to the floor. "Kill that spider, Day," cried Jones to his friend Thomas Day, who happened to be present. "No," said Day, deliberately, "I will not kill that spider ; I do not know that I have a right to kill it. Suppose, when you were going in your coach to Westminster Hall, a superior being, who perhaps may have as much power over you as you over that spider, should say to his companion, 'Kill that lawyer,' how should you like that, Jones ? And I am sure, to most people, a lawyer is a more noxious animal than a spider."

THE RIGHT NAME.

N innkeeper not many years ago appeared at the Borough Police Court on a summons which charged him with having his house open before one o'clock on the 19th of August, that being "the Lord's day." It was objected by the counsel who appeared for the defendant that the term "the Lord's day" was a misnomer according to the act of parliament, which specified "Sunday;" and the objection being sustained by the magistrates, the case was dismissed.

DOCKING AN ENTAIL.

PHYSICIAN once reproached a learned counsel with what Bentham would have called the "uncognoscibility" of the technical terms of the law. "Now, for example," said he, "I never could comprehend what you meant by *docking an entail*." "My dear doctor," replied the barrister, "I don't wonder at that, but I will soon explain the meaning of the phrase. It is doing what your profession never consents to—*suffering a recovery*."

THE BULWARKS OF THE CONSTITUTION.

"ROTHER of Winchester," said Cranmer to Lord Chancellor Gardyner, "you like not anything new unless you be yourself the author thereof." "Your grace wrongeth me," replied the inveterate Conservative. "I have never been author yet of any one new thing : for which I thank God." "Such a Conservatism," says Sumner (*Works*, vol. ii. p. 127), "is the bigotry of science, of literature, of jurisprudence, of religion, of politics. An example will exhibit its character. When Sir Samuel Romilly proposed to abolish the punishment of death for stealing a pocket-handkerchief, the Commons of England consulted certain officials of the law, who assured the House that such an innovation would endanger the whole criminal law of the realm. And when afterwards, this illustrious reformer and model lawyer (for of all men in the history of English law, Romilly was most truly the model lawyer) proposed to abolish the obscene punishment for high treason, requiring the offender to be drawn and quartered, and his bowels to be thrown into his face, while his body yet palpitates with life, the attorney-general of the day, in opposing this humane amendment, asked, "Are the safeguards, the ancient landmarks, the bulwarks of the constitution, to be thus hastily removed?" Which gave occasion for the appropriate exclamation in reply, "What! to throw the bowels of an offender into his face one of the safeguards of the British constitution! I ought to confess that until this night I was wholly ignorant of this bulwark."

A HARD NUT TO CRACK.

OLD Judge Henn, a very excellent man, was dreadfully puzzled on circuit in 1789 by two pertinacious young barristers, who flatly contradicted one another as to the "law of the case." At last they requested his lordship to decide the point. "How, gentlemen," said the judge, "*can* I settle it between you? You, sir, positively say the law is *one way*, and you" (turning to the opposite party) "as unequivocally affirm that it is the other way. I wish to goodness, Billy Harris" (to his registrar), "I knew what the law *really* was!" "My lord," replied the registrar most sententiously, "if I possessed that knowledge I would tell your lordship with a great deal of pleasure." "Then we'll *save the point*, Billy Harris!" exclaimed the judge.

FASHIONABLE BENCHERS.

N 1557 the subject of the dress of Middle Temple benchers was discussed, and an order was made "that none should wear any great breeches in their hose, made either after the Dutch, Spanish, or Almain, *i.e.* German, fashion, or lawn upon their caps, or cut doublets upon paine of 3*s.* 2*d.* for the first default, and expulsion for the second." More enactments "concerning reformation in apparel" are registered in the reign of the dress-loving Elizabeth, according to which the members of the society were to wear no great ruffs, nor white doublets, or hose ; nor velvet facings to their gowns (except benchers). None were to walk the streets in cloaks, but in their gowns, and those of a sad colour. No hats or long-curled hair were tolerated.

Again, in 1575, an order was made " that every man of the Society of Gray's Inn should frame and reform himself for the manner of his appearel, according to the proclamation then last set forth, and within the time therein limited : else not to be accounted of this house." And that no one should wear any gown, doublet, hose, or outward garment of any light colour, upon penalty of expulsion ; and within ten days following it was also ordered that no one should wear any white doublet in the house after Michaelmas term ensuing.

Hats were forbidden to be worn in the hall at meal-time, in 1586, under a penalty of 3*s.* 4*d.* for each offence. In 1600 the gentlemen of the society were instructed not to come into the hall with their hats, boots, or spurs, but with their caps decently and orderly, "according to the ancient orders." When they walked in the city or suburbs, or in the fields, they had to go in their gowns, or they were liable to be fined, and at the third offence to be expelled and lose their chamber.

Laws, however, cannot oppose fashion ; and though the benchers might talk grandly in their council chamber of its being frivolity, and issue instructions about wearing this and not wearing that, it is to be feared they were not always attended to. "Even in the time of Elizabeth," says one writer, "when authority was most anxious that either barristers should, in matter of costume, maintain that reputation for 'sadness' which is the proverbial characteristic of apprentices of the law, counsellors of various degrees were conspicuous through the town for 'brave' attire. At Gray's Inn, Francis Bacon was not singular in loving rich clothes, and running into debt for satin and velvet, jewels and brocade, lace and feathers. Even of that contemner of frivolous men and vain pursuits, Edward Coke, biography assures us that "the jewel of his mind was put into a fair case—a beautiful body with a comely countenance : a case which he did wipe and keep clean, delighting in good clothes well worn, being wont to say that the outward neatness of our bodies might be a monitor to the purities of our souls."

In the reign of Queen Elizabeth sumptuary laws were also made to regulate the dress of the members of Lincoln's Inn, who were forbidden to wear long hair or great ruffs, cloaks, boots, or spurs. Beards were prohibited at the great table under Henry VIII., under pain of paying double commons. His daughter Elizabeth, in the first year of her reign, confined them to a fortnight's growth—not a beautiful object to look at—under penalty of 3*s*. 4*d*. Attempts to regulate trifles of this sort, however, have always been found more difficult than any others, the impertinence of the interference being in proportion. Think of the officers watching the illegal growth of the beard ; the vexation of the "swells" who wanted their beards out of doors ; and the resentment of the unservile party of the elders ! He that parted with his beard, rather than his 3*s*. 4*d*., would be looked upon as an alien. No laws can stop fashions. The prohibition was repealed, and no manner of size limited to that venerable hirsute excrescence on the chin.

LEZE MAJESTY OF A BELLY-BAND.

LORD ESKGROVE, as was usual with stronger heads than his in the beginning of this century, considered republicanism the prime mover and aggravating circumstance of every crime. One day, in condemning a tailor to death for murdering a soldier by stabbing him, his lordship thus aggravated the offence: "And not only did you murder him, whereby he was berea-ved of his life, but you did thrust, or push, or pierce, or project, or propel the le-thall weapon through the belly-band of his regimen-tal breeches, which were his majesty's!"

He rarely failed to signalize himself in pronouncing sentences of death. It was almost a matter of style with him.

THE WAY WITH THE JURY.

IT is related that when Sir Robert Peel was Chief Secretary for Ireland, he met an Irish country squire, remarkable for his vulgarity. Charles Kendal Bushe, the eminent advocate, was a neighbour, and the squire was loud in his praises, so Peel inquired "what was Mr. Bushe's *forte?*" This was quite a puzzle for the squire, and Mr. Peel had to put the inquiry in more intelligible shape: "What was Mr. Bushe most remarkable for?" "Ah, I understand—the jury." "And how does he manage the jury?" said Peel. "Troth, this way," was the reply: "he blarneys them: he first *butthers* them up, and then he *slithers* them down."

WAGER OF BATTEL.

WHEN Achan took the "goodly Babylonish garment and the two hundred shekels of silver," the men of Ai smote and chased the Israelites, and a miracle was wrought by the Almighty in order to discover the transgressor. Hence, in times long after, trials by "presumptuous appeals to Providence," to use the words of Blackstone, were frequent among the Saxons and Normans. Ordeals of various kinds were resorted to instead of trials, and one of these was the "wager of battel." For a considerable period the challenge and fight were simple. The charge was made, and the conflict forthwith ensued. The man who fell was judged guilty either of the offence or of the falsehood of making the charge. But when trial by jury was fully established, and an acquittal took place in a case of murder, it became a question how far the near relatives of the deceased, if dissatisfied with the verdict, were to be appeased? For this ordeal, therefore, twelve men bade fair to supersede the old mode of proceeding by battle. Therefore an appeal was allowed against the finding, and a second jury might be called upon to review the facts. If the second verdict were favourable to the prisoner, he was free for ever from the charge ; but if pronounced guilty upon the fresh inquiry, not having "waged the battel," he was inevitably executed, the prerogative · of mercy being upon this occasion withheld. Still the trial by battle remained ; although much disused, it was not abolished. Certainly, if the appellant were a woman, a priest, an infant, or of the age of sixty, or lame, or blind, or a citizen of London, he or she might refuse to fight ; otherwise the ancient usage was within reach of the person appealed against. And there was one special ground for rejecting the application on the part of the prisoner to resort to arms. This was where great and violent presumptions of guilt existed, admitting of no denial, "as if," to use the language of Blackstone, "the accused was taken in the room with a bloody knife." In such cases the second jury must have been empannelled.

Those who desire to know all the formalities observed in a "wager of battel," will find them related at length in Blackstone's *Commentaries*, and in Dugdale's *Origines*. The battle took place in the presence of the court, and, if people of the lower rank were concerned, in the following form. At sunrise the parties assembled, the lists were set by the court, the accuser and the accused were to be bare-headed, bare-armed, bare-legged, each armed with a wooden truncheon of an ell long, and a square wooden target. They then took each other's hands, and each swore—the accuser that the accused did kill the deceased, and the accused swore that he did not. After this both took oaths that they had about them "ne bone, ne stone, ne charm of any sort, whereby the law of the devil may be exalted, or the law of God depressed." Then they commenced fighting. If the accused could make good his defence till the stars appeared in the evening, he was acquitted; but if either cried *craven*, *i.e.* surrender, or was defeated, he was hanged. Even if he was slain in the field, his body was hanged on the gallows.

The last time but one that the trial of battle was awarded in this country was in the case of Lord Rea and Mr. Ramsey, in 1632. The king, by his commission, appointed a Constable of England to preside at the trial, who proclaimed a day for the duel, on which occasion the combatants were to appear with a spear, a long sword, a short sword, and a dagger. But the combat was prorogued to a further day, and in the mean time the king revoked the commission (Woolrych, *Lives of Eminent Serjeants*).

It is not a little curious that, after having been disused for nearly two centuries, this antiquated form of defence should have been resorted to so recently as the year 1817. This was in the trial of Abraham Thornton, at the Warwick Assizes, August 8, 1817, for the murdering of Mary Ashford. Mr. Justice Holroyd presided, and the trial lasted the whole day. The evidence against the prisoner, though strong, was entirely circumstantial. His defence was well got up, and the jury, to the infinite dissatisfaction of the people of the locality, acquitted him. This dissatisfaction was so loudly expressed, that the brother of the unfortunate girl was induced to obtain a writ of appeal. Thornton consequently was again taken into custody, and on November 17th placed at the bar of the Court of King's Bench in Westminster Hall, two of the presiding judges being Lord Ellenborough and Mr. Justice Bailey. Mr. Reader, as counsel for the prisoner, commenced the proceedings by moving that " he do now plead." By order of the court the record was then read to the prisoner ; it, of course, charged him with the murder of Mary Ashford, by casting her into a pit of water; and he was asked what he had to plead to the charge. He at once rose up ; his counsel placed in his hands a pair of large horseman's gloves, one of which he immediately put on, and handed him a paper, from which Thornton read : " My lords, I am not guilty, and I am ready to defend myself with my body." He then waved the other glove, and flung it into the middle of the court, where it lay until the close of the day's proceedings, when it was handed up to the care of the officer for the crown.* The " gage " having been flung, William Ashford, the appellant, was formally called. He appeared—a mere stripling of short stature, apparently weak, and about the age of twenty-two. Mr. Clark, his counsel, then expressed surprise that the charge against the prisoner should be put to issue in this way. He submitted that the court had a right to restrain the defendant from his plea, and adduced the appellant's weakness of body as a circumstance cogent enough to warrant the interference of the court. This, however, was declined, and time, until November 21st, given to the appellant to counter-plead. The counter-plea merely recapitulated the facts of the case, and concluded thus : " Wherefore the said William Ashford prays the judgment of the court, that the said Abraham Thornton may not be permitted to wage battel, on his the said Abraham's plea." Time was now granted to the defendant to reply, and on January 24, 1818, he delivered in a long replication, in which he quoted the evidence used at his former trial, asserted his innocence, and repeated his prayer to be

* It is to be observed that in this case the appellant did not take up the glove, because he denied the " right of battel " upon legal grounds.

allowed to "wage battel" with William Ashford.   The sufficiency
of this replication was denied on January 29th, when Mr. Reader,
for the prisoner, joined issue on the demurrer.   The argument
took place on, and occupied the whole of the 6th and 7th of
February, when the case was further adjourned to April 16th.
Then the court decided that the law gave the defendant a right
to his "wager of battel."   The appellant, Ashford, craved until
April 20th, to consider the course he should adopt ; and on that
day his counsel gave up the appeal.   "The appellant," says
Mr. Gurney, "does not feel himself justified in accepting the
challenge."   The defendant was thereupon discharged from
custody.

Early in the session of 1819, the attorney-general took charge
of a bill for abolishing the custom.   Sir Francis Burdett rose to
move an amendment, denouncing it as calculated to increase
the power of the crown, "inasmuch as it would deprive the
subject of an appeal against what might be an illegal and unjust
extension of the power of the crown in pardoning criminals in
cases of murder."   But a majority of eighty-six to four decided
the success of the bill.   Then Sir Robert Wilson made another
effort, but the numbers were sixty-four to two ; and so it passed.

LEGAL TERMINOLOGY.

THERE are one or two legal terms of which the meaning
is not perhaps generally known.   No one need be
reminded that the term lunacy is derived from an idea
that madness is connected with the moon.   But many may not
be aware that felony is derived from an idea that felons are
prompted by excess of gall, "*fel.*"   Felonies were crimes committed *felleo animo*, with a mind affected by gall; and Sir
Matthew Hale was of opinion that the reason why a lunatic
cannot be guilty of a crime is a want of gall.   Then, again,
maiming is not any kind of wounding in general, but such
wounding as lessens a man's power of battling in his own de-

fence. Therefore it was ruled that to knock out a man's front tooth is to maim him ; but that he is not maimed by the knocking out of a grinder ; because with a front tooth he can bite and tear an enemy, but with a grinder he can only masticate his food.

A BURNING QUESTION.

A VAST number of puns, each paragraphed as " Lord Norbury's Last," appeared in the Irish newspapers in the lifetime of that merry judge. Every editor who made a joke sent it upon the world as one of the Norbury family. His own jests were better than most of the imitations. A man of rank was tried before him for arson, and acquitted. Norbury met him soon after at a castle *levée*. " Glad to meet you *here*," said the judge. " This is my last bachelor visit, my lord ; I am going to turn Benedict." Norbury looked him full in the face while he responded, "Ay, St. Paul says better marry than *burn*."

Lord Norbury had his joke to the very last. His neighbour, Lord Erne, was far advanced in years and bedridden. When Norbury's own health failed, he heard of his friend's increased illness. " James," he said to his servant, " go next door, and tell Lord Erne, with my compliments, that it will be a *dead heat* between us."

SEMPRE IL MAL NON VIEN PER NUOCERE.

I T is a curious coincidence that the two greatest Chancery lawyers of their day, Romilly and Lord Tenterden, should have been forced into the profession by incidental circumstances. Romilly said that what principally influenced his decision was the being thus enabled to leave his small fortune in his father's hand, instead of buying a sworn clerk's seat with it. " At a later period of my life, after a success at the bar which my wildest and most sanguine dreams had never painted to me--when I was gaining an income of £8000 or £9000 a-year,—I have often reflected how all that prosperity had arisen out of the pecuniary difficulties and confined circumstances of my father."

Lord Tenterden's early destination was changed by a disappointment. When he and Mr. Justice Richards were going the home circuit, they visited Canterbury Cathedral together. Richards commended the voice of a singer in the choir. "Ah," said Lord Tenterden, "that is the only man I ever envied! When at school in this town, we were candidates for a chorister's place together, and he obtained it."

JUSTICE AND COUNSEL.

IN the famous trial of the patriotic Dean of St. Asaph, at Shrewsbury, for publishing Sir W. Jones's famous "Dialogue," Erskine, who defended, put a question to the jury relative to the meaning of their verdict. Mr. Justice Bullen objected to its propriety. The counsel reiterated his question, and demanded an answer. The judge again interposed his authority in these emphatic words : "Sit down, Mr. Erskine. Know your duty, or I shall be obliged to make you know it." Mr. Erskine, with equal warmth, replied, "I know *my* duty as well as your lordship knows *your* duty. I stand here as the advocate of a fellow-citizen, and I will *not* sit down." The judge was silent, and the advocate persisted in his question.

IN THE CONDEMNED CELL.

CHARLES DICKENS used to relate an anecdote of the last moments of Fauntleroy, the great banker, hanged for forgery in 1824. His elegant dinners had always been followed by some remarkable and matchless curaçao, the origin of which he kept a deep secret. Three of his boon companions had an interview with him in the condemned cell the day before his execution. They were about to retire when the most impressive of the three stepped back and said, "Fauntleroy, you stand on the verge of the grave. Remember the text, my dear man, that 'we brought nothing into this world, and it is certain we can take nothing out.' Have you any objection, therefore, to tell me now, as a friend, where you got that curacao?"

A NICE COMPLIMENT.

M R. BETHEL, an Irish barrister, when the question of the Union was in debate, like all the junior barristers, published pamphlets upon the subject. The witty Ned Lysaght met this pamphleteer in the hall of the Four Courts, and in a friendly way said, "Zounds! Bethel, you never told me you had published a pamphlet on the Union. I only saw it this morning, and I must say it contained some of the best things I have yet seen in any pamphlet upon the subject." "I am very proud you think so," said the other, rubbing his hands with satisfaction; "and pray, what are the things that pleased you so much?" "Why," replied Lysaght, "as I passed by a pastry-cook's shop this morning, I saw a girl come out with three hot mince-pies wrapped up in one of your works."

LAMB-ENTABLE SHEEPISHNESS.

I N the course of conversation Lord Erskine observed how much confidence in speaking was acquired from habit and frequent practice. "I protest I do not find it so," said Counsellor Lamb; "for though I have been a good many years at the bar, and have had a good share of business, I don't find my confidence increase, indeed rather the contrary." This remark having been repeated to Lord Erskine, the relentless joker observed, "No wonder; every one knows the older a lamb grows the more sheepish he becomes."

WITHOUT BEGINNING OR END.

THE principal charge brought against that consummate lawyer, Lord Eldon, who presided in the Court of Chancery for nearly twenty-five years, was dilatoriness. Sir Thomas Plumer, the first vice-chancellor appointed under the act of 1813, although displaying much learning in his judgments, was prolix and tedious to an insufferable degree. In reference to this state of affairs the following epigram was made :—

> " To cause delay in Lincoln's Inn
> Two different methods tend :
> His lordship's judgments ne'er begin,
> His honour's never end."

A HOME-THRUST.

AT the sittings of Guildhall, an action of debt was tried before Lord Mansfield, in which the defendant, a merchant of London, complained with great warmth of the plaintiff's conduct, in having caused him to be arrested upon the Exchange, where all the merchants of London were assembled. Lord Mansfield stopped him with the greatest composure, saying, " Friend, you forget yourself ; *you* were the defaulter in refusing to pay a just debt ; and let me give you this piece of advice : for the future do not put it in any man's power to arrest you, either in public or in private."

HUMBLE CONFESSION.

SERJEANT SAYER once went the circuit for some judge who was indisposed. He was afterwards imprudent enough to move *as counsel* to have a new trial of a cause heard before himself, " for a misdirection by the judge." Lord Mansfield said, " Brother Sayer, there is an act of parlia-

ment which, in such a matter as that before you, gave you direction to act as you thought right." "No, my lord," said the
serjeant, "I had no discretion." "You may be right, brother,"
said Lord Mansfield: "for I am afraid even an act of parliament could not give you discretion."

AMBIGUOUS COMPLIMENT.

MR. JOHN CLERK, afterwards Lord Eldon, when at the
bar was remarkable for the *sang froid* with which he
treated the judges. On one occasion a junior counsel,
on hearing their lordships give judgment against his client, exclaimed that he was "surprised at such a decision." This was
construed into a contempt of court, and he was ordered to
attend at the bar next morning. Fearful of the consequences
he consulted his friend John Clerk, who told him to be perfectly
at ease, for he would apologize for him in a way that would
avert any unpleasant result. Accordingly when the name of the
delinquent was called, John Clerk arose, and coolly addressed
the bench: "I am very sorry, my lord, that my young friend
should have so far forgotten himself as to treat your honourable bench with disrespect. He is extremely penitent,
and you will kindly ascribe his unintentional insult to his
ignorance. You must perceive at once that it originated in that.
He said that he was surprised at the decision of your lordships.
Now, if he had not been very ignorant of what takes place in
this court every day, had he known you but half so long as I
have done, he would not be surprised at *anything* you did."

COKE'S BLUSTERING.

COKE appears in all the State prosecutions of his time in
no favourable light; the bitterness of spirit which he
always appears to have felt towards those against whom
he was retained, prompted him to indulge in the most unfeeling

taunts. To the court he was disrespectful, to the culprit insulting, unrelenting. "In your pleadings," Lord Bacon once wrote to him, "you were wont to insult over misery, and to inveigh bitterly at the persons, which bred you many enemies." The judicial proceedings of their time furnished our elder dramatists with many hints. Ben Jonson appears to have borrowed largely in his *Epicœne* from the proceedings in the case of the Earl of Southampton and the Countess of Essex. There is a passage in Shakespeare's *Twelfth Night* where Sir Toby Belch says to Sir Andrew Aguecheek, "If thou *thou'st* him some thrice, it shall not be amiss." These words are supposed to allude to Coke's conduct to the gallant and unfortunate Sir Walter Raleigh on his trial, to whom he addressed the most opprobrious epithets : "Thou art a monster," he said, "thou hast an English face and a Spanish heart. Thou viper! for I *thou* thee, thou viper."

PROFESSIONAL COURTESY.

KILKENNY cats are famous for pugnacity, and to them the rhymes of Isaac Watts may be applied with as much justice as to "little dogs ;" but what would the poet have said of the following squabbles of bench and bar, who, according to his theory, ought certainly to have "agreed." At the conclusion of the Kilkenny sessions in 1857, the assistant-barrister, Mr. Nicholas Purcell O'Gorman, made some strong observations upon the indecorous conduct of the attorneys of his court, "I'll bear it no longer," exclaimed the enraged judge, "and this very night I shall write off and insist upon being transferred to another county." "Does your worship think," said Mr. Michael Hyland, solicitor, addressing himself to the irate law-dispenser, "that a memorial signed by all the attorneys of this court backing your application would be of any assistance in obtaining your object ?" A look of peculiar ferocity was the only response to the generous offer.

A MOMENTOUS MONOSYLLABLE.

HE case of Captain Donellan is well known. He had been a man of pleasure, and, becoming involved in difficulties, poisoned his brother-in-law, Sir Theodosius Boughton, on whose demise he had a considerable reversion expectant. Walsh, well known at the Beef-steak Club, accompanied Donellan to his trial. Getting close to the dock, Walsh kindly explained to him all the solemnities before his eyes. "There, Donellan," he said, "there's the jury; there's the judge. If you are found guilty, he will put on his black cap and sentence you to be hanged. But it all depends upon the jury; for they have only to say one single monosyllable more or less, guilty or not guilty, and you will be hanged or set at liberty."

CONSIDERATE.

"LEATHER-LUNGED SCRIVEN," the Irish barrister, was a very ugly man; his complexion was "like wash-leather which had never been washed." Being of high Tory politics, his practice in the Irish law courts frequently brought him into collision with Daniel O'Connell. Once O'Connel was retained in a Kerry case, in which the *venue*, or place of trial (it being in law a transitory action), was laid in Dublin. O'Connell was instructed to try and change the *venue*, so that the case might be tried in Tralee. This motion was resisted by Scriven, the counsel opposed to O'Connell. He stated that he had no knowledge of Kerry, and had never been in that part of Ireland. "Oh," replied O'Connell, "we'll be glad to welcome my learned friend, and show him the lovely lakes of Killarney." "Yes," growled Scriven, "I suppose the bottom of them." "Indeed no," retorted Dan, "and for this simple reason: your face would frighten the fish."

COMPULSORY KNIGHTHOOD.

EMPORA mutantur, etc. Charles I., being in constant want of money, at the instigation of Robert Heath, attorney-general, compelled all who had a landed estate of £40 a year, to *submit* to knighthood on payment of a heavy fee, or on refusal to pay a heavy fine. This caused a tremendous outcry, and was at first resisted. But the question being brought before the Court of Exchequer, Heath delivered an argument in support of the claim, in which he traced knighthood from the ancient Germans down to the reign of the Stuarts, showing that the prince had always the right of conferring knighthood upon all who held of him *in capite*—receiving a reasonable compliment in return. In this instance Mr. Attorney not only had the decision of the court, but the law on his side. Blackstone says, " The prerogative of compelling the king's vassals to be knighted, or to pay a fine, was expressly recognized in parliament by the statute *de Militibus* I Ed. II., but yet was the occasion of heavy murmurs when exerted by Charles I., among whose many misfortunes it was that neither himself nor his people seemed able to distinguish between the arbitrary stretch and the legal exertion of prerogative." Compulsory knighthood was abolished by the Long Parliament (16 Car. I., c. 20).

LAW *v.* JUSTICE.

HE best case which I have seen of law *v.* justice and common sense, is one which Montaigne relates (lib. iv. ch. 17) as having happened in his own days. Some men were condemned to death for murder ; the judges were subsequently informed by the officers of an inferior court that certain persons had confessed themselves guilty of the murder in question, and had told so circumstantial a tale that the fact was placed beyond all doubt. Nevertheless, it was deemed so bad a precedent to revoke a sentence and show that the law could err, that the innocent men were delivered over to execution and duly hanged.

JUDICIAL PROMOTIONS.

N 1818, there were great changes in the law courts. Of these judicial promotions Jekyll said that they came by titles very different, viz., Chief Justice Abbott *by descent*, Justice Best by *intrusion*, and Richardson by the *operation of the law*. The wit of the two first is pungent; the last a deserved compliment. It was expected, said Jekyll, that Vaughan would come in by *prescription*. This was not so good. Sir Henry Halford, the king's physician, was his brother.

A JURYMAN'S IDEA.

IR ALBERT PELL, serjeant-at-law, on one occasion had been more than ordinarily tautologous, and a hint to that effect was given him by some friend. He instantly pleaded guilty to the charge. " I certainly was confoundedly long," said he, "but did you observe the foreman, a heavy-looking fellow in a yellow waistcoat? No more than one idea could stay in his thick head at one time, and I was resolved *that that idea should be mine*, so that I hammered on till I saw by his eye that he had got it."

A KNOTTY POINT.

T was a serious question among the lawyers of the Restoration " Whether the act of severing the head of Charles I. from his body could be alleged to have been committed in his own life-time," and " whether it should be laid as against the peace of the late or the present king." Judge

N

Mallet made the confusion more confounded, by maintaining that " by the law of England a day is indivisible ; and that as Charles II. certainly was our lawful king during a part of that day, no part of it had been in the reign of Charles I."

DAUNTLESS ADVOCATE.

MR. (subsequently Lord) Erskine, in his defence of Horne Tooke, made the following remarkable declaration :— " Gentlemen, Mr. Tooke had an additional motive for appearing to be a supporter of Mr. Paine. The constitution was wounded through his side. I blush, as a Briton, to recollect that a conspiracy was formed among the higher orders to deprive this man of a British trial. This is the clue to Mr. Tooke's conduct ; and to which, if there should be no other witness, I will step forward to be examined. I assert that there was a conspiracy to shut out Mr. Paine from the privilege of being defended ; he was to be deprived of counsel ; and I, who now speak to you, was threatened with the loss of office if I appeared to be his advocate. I was told, in plain terms, that I must not defend Mr. Paine. *I did defend him, and I did lose my office.*" Mr. Erskine had been deprived, in consequence of his noble obstinacy, of the attorney-generalship of the Duchy of Cornwall.

Lord Erskine, when at the bar, was always remarkable for the fearlessness with which he contended against the bench. In one of these contests he explained the rule of his conduct in the following noble terms :—" It was," said he, " the first command and counsel of my youth always to do what my conscience told me to be my duty, and to leave the consequence to God. I shall carry with me the memory, and, I trust, the practice of this paternal lesson to the grave. I have hitherto followed it, and have no reason to complain that my obedience to it has been even a temporal sacrifice. I have found it, on the contrary, the road to prosperity and wealth, and I shall point it out as such to my children."

A STRIKING QUALIFICATION.

AT the Norwich Assizes, in 1824, a case occurred which exhibited the wretched state of the laws at that time. A gang of burglars was brought up for trial, against whom there was a complete case if the evidence of an aecomplice were receivable, but none without. Now, that accomplice had been convicted of felony, and sentenced by a Court of Quarter Sessions to imprisonment *alone*, without the addition of a fine or a whipping; and the statute restoring competence requires imprisonment, *and* a fine or a whipping. Chief Baron Gazelee * refused to attend to this objection, and all were convicted; but Serjeant Robinson, who defended the burglars, called on Edgell, the clerk of assize, and told him that unless the men were discharged he would memorialize the Secretary of State, and in consequence the men were in a few days discharged. Sir Robert Peel, at the opening of the session of parliament, brought in a short act amending the law.

UNPARDONABLE.

SERJEANT HILL once began an argument in the King's Bench thus : " My Lord Mansfield and judges, I beg your pardon." " Why, brother Hill, do you ask our pardon?" " My lords," said he, " I have seventy-eight cases to cite." " Seventy-eight cases," said Lord Mansfield, " to cite ! You can never have our pardon if you cite seventy-eight cases !"

---

* Sir Stephen Gazelee : before he retired from the bench, his faculties became considerably impaired ; and Dickens, in *Pickwick*, ridicules him under the name of Judge Stareleigh.

THE PROGENY OF THE EVIL ONE.

DEAN SWIFT, having preached an assize sermon in Ireland, was invited to dine with the judges, and, having in his sermon considered the use and abuse of the law, he then pressed a little hard upon those counsellors who plead causes which they know in their consciences to be wrong. When dinner was over, and the wine began to circulate, a young barrister retorted upon the dean, and, after some fencing, the counsellor asked him whether, if the devil were to die, a parson might not be found who, for money, would preach his funeral sermon. "Yes, sir," said Swift; "I would gladly be the man, and I would then give the devil his due, as I have this day done his children."

GOLD FOR BRASS.

SERJEANT DAVY is known to have stood up for his professional gains—a great merit when there are so many attorneys from whom the just honorarium cannot, sometimes, be without difficulty acquired. He once had a very large brief, with a fee of two guineas only at the back of it. His client asked him if he had read his brief. He pointed with his finger to the fee, and said, "As far as that I have read, and for the life of me I can read no further."

When he was called to account for taking silver from a client, and so disgracing the profession, he replied, "I took silver because I could not get gold, but I took every farthing the fellow had in the world; and I hope you don't call *that* disgracing the profession."

A somewhat similar story is told of a namesake of Serjeant Davy, but who flourished centuries back in a darker age, when fees were not what they are now. He was accused once upon a time, by his brethren of the court, of having degraded their order by taking from a client a fee in copper; and on being solemnly arraigned for this offence at their Common Hall, he defended himself by the following plea of confession and avoidance :—"I fully admit that I took a fee from him in copper, and not one but several, and not only fees in copper but fees in silver : but I pledge my honour, as a serjeant, that I never took a single fee from him in silver until I had got all his gold, and that I never took a fee from him in copper until I had got all his silver,—and you don't call *that* a degradation of our order."

A SOOTABLE JOKE.

LORD NORBURY, giving judgment in a case in the Court of Common Pleas in Dublin, observed that it was not for the defendant in a writ of right to say he "claimed by descent." "That," continued his lordship, "would be a very shrewd answer for a sweep, who had got into your house by coming down the chimney. 'Pray, sir, how did you get into my house?' 'I got in by descent—*facilis descensus Averni.*' And this would be an easy and sweeping way of getting in."

LAWS FOR THE DOGS.

I CAN find no reference to this useful animal in the statutes at large before the reign of our Most Gracious Majesty Queen Victoria. Up to that period the humble friend of man appears to have been totally disregarded by the law—an oversight so much the more astonishing as there was an unmistakable family connection between the canine race and the language in which our ancient jurisconsults delivered their oracles. Since the accession of her Majesty, however, this disregard has been handsomely made up for by a not inconsiderate amount of legislation. Parliament commenced in 2 & 3 Vict. by increasing the "resources of civilization" against the lawless doings of Irish curs. In 12 & 13 Vict. dog-fighting, bull- and bear-baiting were abolished, which statute cannot fail to have been received with considerable satisfaction in the canine world.   Between 17 & 18 Vict. and 43 & 44 Vict. not less than eight statutes were passed regarding the condition and social status of the dog in England, one of which placed him in the honourable and enviable position of a taxpayer.   All these acts were of course applicable to the dogs of the United Kingdom ; but in addition to these, one little Act had to be framed to curb the sheep-worrying propensities of the sportive Scotch "tyke." Certainly if the dog still deserves his reputation for gratitude, he ought to wag his tail when he passes the Houses of Parliament.   How different was his position in the bad old times ! In Filow's case (*Year-b.* 12 Hen. VIII. 3, pl. 3), Justice Eliot goes so far in his depreciation of the "friend of man" as to lay down that dogs were vermin, and for that reason the Church would not degrade itself by taking tithes of them.   Nor did the law condescend to take notice of such base animals.   A dog was not the subject of larceny at common law, because, as it was said, "a man shall not hang for a dog" (*Law Reporter,* i. c. c., p. 59 : see Regina *v.* Robinson, Bel. c. c., 34).

BARRED BY STATUTE.

ISAAC BURKE BETHEL, an old member of the Irish bar, was ever ready to accept any meals he could get, or take any fee that was offered.   On one occasion, when engaged in a prosecution, he said very pompously, "I appear for the crown, my lord."   "Oftener for the *half-crown,*" whispered a wit, who knew Burke Bethel's line of practice. When Thomas Goold, Master in Chancery, had taken the house in Merrion Square, Bethel called and expressed his wish to see it.   The master had no desire to encourage his visits, but could not refuse to show him the house.   As he did not offer him luncheon, which was what Bethel sought, the disappointed barrister, on going down a back stair where the light was dim, grumbled, "A man might easier break his neck, than break his fast in this house." Even this broad hint was not taken; so, when parting, Bethel said, "I declare, master, it is more than six years since you gave me a dinner." "Six years, is it?" said the master, as he bowed his importunate visitor out; "then you are barred by the statute of limitations, sir."

LAWYER'S BAGS.

HAT lawyers towards the end of the seventeenth century carried green bags, instead of the crimson or blue bag in use at the present day, is evident from various passages in the dramatists of that period. Thus, in Wycherley's *Plain Dealer*, one of the principal characters is Widow Black-acre, "a petulant litigious woman, always in law, and mother of Jerry Blackacre, a true raw squire, under age and his mother's government, bred to the law." In act i., sc. i., we find the following stage directions: "Enter Widow Blackacre, with a mantle and a green bag, and several papers in the other hand. Jerry Blackacre, her son, in a gown, laden with green bags, following her." In Act iii., sc. i., of the same play, the widow is called impertinent and ignorant by a lawyer, of whom she demands back her fee on his returning her brief and declining to plead for her. This draws from her the following reply: "Impertinent again, and ignorant to me! Gadsbodikins! you puny upstart in the law to use *me* so! You green-bag carrier, you murderer of unfortunate causes!" And further on in the same scene, Freeman, "a gentleman well educated, but of broken fortune," thus admonishes his young Jerry: "Come, squire, let your mother and your trees fall as she pleases, rather than wear this gown, and carry green bags all your life, and be pointed at for a tony."

The green bags still held sway in the reign of Queen Anne, for in Dr. Arbuthnot's *History of John Bull*, part i. c. 25, we read: "I am told, cousin Diego, you are one of those that have

undertaken to manage me, and that you have said you will
carry a green bag yourself, rather than we shall make an end of
the lawsuit."

It is not known when the crimson bag was substituted for
the more modest green one, which at present is chiefly seen
in the hands of shoemakers, upholsterers, and other artificers.

Henry Crabb Robinson writes, in his *Diary and Reminiscences*, in the year 1818 : "In the Spring Term of this year,
Gurney, the king's counsel's clerk, brought me a bag, for which
I presented him with a guinea. This custom is now obsolete,
and therefore I mention it. It was formerly the etiquette of the
bar that none but serjeants and king's counsel could carry a
bag in Westminster Hall. Till some king's counsel presented
him with one, however large the junior (that is stuff-gowned)
barrister's business might be, he was forced to carry his papers
in his hand. It was considered that he who carried a bag was
a rising man."

The actual existing use "*in re bags*," is minutely regulated
by that unwritten law of etiquette which no lawyer can trans-
gress with impunity. Barristers' bags are either red or dark
blue. Red bags are strictly speaking reserved for queen's
counsel and serjeants ; but a stuff gownsman may carry one
if presented therewith by a "silk." It is an imperative rule
that only red bags may be taken into court ; blue bags are not
to be carried further than the robing room. Such at least is
the practice of the Common Law bar. With regard to solicitors,
it seems they may please themselves, and carry a blue, red, or
purple bag, just as their fancy dictates.

SHARING FATIGUE.

WAS waiting for some case in which I was a counsel,"
says Mr. O'Flanagan in *The Irish Bar*, "when the
crier called, 'Pluck and Diggers,' and in came James
Scott, Q.C., very red and heated, and throwing his bag on the

table within the bar, he said, ' My lords, I beg to assure your lordships I feel so exhausted, I am quite unable to argue this case. I have been speaking for three hours in the Court of Exchequer, and I am quite tired. Pray excuse me, my lords; I must get some refreshment.' The chief justice bowed, and said, ' Certainly, Mr. Scott ; ' so that gentleman left the court. ' Mr. Holmes, you are in this case,' said the chief justice ; ' we'll be happy to hear you.' ' Really, my lord, I'm very tired too,' said Mr. Holmes. ' Surely,' said the chief justice, ' you have not been speaking for three hours in the Court of Exchequer ? What has tired you ? ' ' Listening to Mr. Scott, my lord,' was Holmes' sarcastic reply."

AN UNGENTLE PAGE.

N November 20, 1727, the poet Savage, illegitimate son of Ann, Countess of Macclesfield, committed a manslaughter in a drunken brawl at an ill-famed coffeehouse near Charing Cross. For this crime he stood his trial at the Old Bailey, in the following December, before Sir Francis Page. Mr. Justice summed up the evidence in a clear and logical manner, but what he is further reported to have said is not quite so creditable to him. The conclusion of his address was in these words: " Gentlemen of the jury, you are to consider that Mr. Savage is a great man, a very great man, a much greater man than you or I, gentlemen of the jury; that he wears very fine clothes, much finer clothes than you or I, gentlemen of the jury ; that he has abundance of money in his pocket, much more money than you or I, gentlemen of the jury : but, gentlemen of the jury, is it not a very hard case, gentlemen of the jury, that Mr. Savage should therefore kill you or me, gentlemen of the jury ? "

JUSTICE WITH OPEN EYES.

COKE says that when the king is party, one shall not challenge the array for favour; for which he assigns the startling reason, "because in respect of his allegiance the sheriff ought to *favour the king more.*"

SWALLOWING THE *CORPUS DELICTI.*

PETER BURROWS, the friend of Grattan and of Plunkett, though an eminent lawyer, was of a very childlike nature and the most absent-minded of men. It is recorded of him, that, on a circuit, a brother barrister found him at breakfast time standing by the fire, with an egg in his hand, gravely boiling his watch in the saucepan. His grandest exploit, however, came off in one of the assize towns on his circuit. A murder which caused much excitement had been committed, and he had to state the case for the prosecution. In one hand—having a heavy cold—he held a box of lozenges, and in the other the pistol-bullet, by which the man met his death. Ever and anon, during the pauses in his address, he kept lubricating himself with a lozenge, until at last, in the very middle of a sentence, his bosom heaved, and his eyes starting, a perfect picture of horror, Peter bellowed out, "Oh—h—h—gentlemen! by the heavens above me—*I've swallowed the bull—llet.*" It is attempted by the orthography to give an idea of the pronunciation; as to the manner, neither pen, nor pencil can convey it.

INSURANCE AND ASSURANCE.

"INSURANCE of contingencies," says Malcolm, in his *Anecdotes of Manners and Customs of London,* " was known before 1682, as in that year a widow attempted to file a bill in chancery, which implicated nearly five hundred individuals, whom she would have called upon to answer what sums were due from them to her deceased husband, 'a kind of usurer,' as he is termed by my authority, the *London Mercury*. This curious bill consisted of sixty-six skins of parchment and three thousand sheets of paper. The lord chancellor amazed at the effrontery of the woman, and considering the enormous expense each defendant would incur by procuring a copy of it, dismissed it, and directed Mr. Newman, the counsellor who had signed it, to refund the charges already incurred, and to take his labours for his pains."

SERJEANT GLYNN'S GRATITUDE.

HERE is a story told of Glynn, Cromwell's chief justice, vouched to be authentic, which reflects much credit on him. When Glynn, in his youth, was a scholar of Westminster school, he one day unluckily tore the curtain which at that time was drawn across the school, dividing the upper from the lower forms. This crime was sure to be visited with fearful punishment by the redoubtable Dr. Busby, in those days head-master of the school. A generous schoolfellow, taking compassion at the terror of the offender, took the blame on himself, and bore the flogging. Time rolled on, the boys became men, and the civil wars ensued. Each took different sides. Glynn, the culprit who tore the curtain, was on the commission to try the prisoners taken in Penruddock's rebellion in 1654. Some were condemned to die, and among these Glynn saw a face which struck him as not unfamiliar. He found upon inquiry that the man was no other than his school-fellow William Wake, who had taken the flogging to save him. Glynn said nothing at the moment, but took horse and rode straight to the Protector, from whom he obtained his friend's life as a personal favour.

CIRCUMSTANTIAL EVIDENCE.

HE following curious case occurs in Lord Eldon's *Anecdote Book*: " I remember, in one case where I was a counsel, for a long time the evidence did not appear to touch the prisoner at all, and he looked about him with the most perfect unconcern, seeming to think himself quite safe. At last the surgeon was called, who stated deceased had been killed by a shot, a gunshot in the head ; and he produced the matted hair, and the stuff cut from and taken out of the wound. It was all hardened with blood. A basin of warm water was brought into court, and as the blood was gradually softened, a piece of printed paper appeared, the wadding of the gun, which proved to be the half of a ballad. The other half had been found in the pocket of the accused when he was taken. He was convicted and hanged."

PLURALITY OF COUNSEL.

N the time of the Stuarts it was customary, especially in the Court of Chancery, to retain on either side in every cause, whether involving points of great difficulty or not, a great number of counsel. Ten advocates on one side have been heard to speak to a motion of course. This practice of retaining many counsel is now generally discountenanced by the courts as tending to increase the expense and protract the settlement of the suit. Consequences still more injurious have resulted from the practice. In the case of Mr. Shelley, which was argued in the Court of Chancery not half a century ago, *all* the king's counsel were retained for Mr. Shelley. A cause was tried at Carlisle about a century ago, the parties to which were the then Earl of Lonsdale and the three orphan children of his deceased steward. The peer managed to retain every counsel in the place, and succeeded in obtaining a verdict by which the poor children, of which the poet Words-worth was one, were deprived of an estate lawfully their own. Upon the decease of the oppressor, his son returned the property, so unjustly acquired, to the orphans with interest, as well as the costs of the suit.

"OUR ABSENT FRIENDS."

THE general bar-mess in Galway, in the earlier years of this century rejoiced in a barmaid named Honor Slaven, whose quick repartee, to the not always very delicate jokes addressed to her by the gentlemen of the bar, had spread beyond the provinces. John Philpot Curran, having been called specially on the Connaught Circuit, heard of this ready-witted Hebe, and was determined to test her smartness. Curran, however, was far superior to those whom she had defeated in these often unseemly combâts, and was expected to come off with flying colours from the contest. Among the customary toasts of that time was a succession of three alliterate ones, of which the last was a flagrant indecency, and this Curran resolved should fall to Honor's turn to propose in due rotation. Making her take a seat at the table, with one gentle-man interposed between himself and the " neat-handed Phillis," he began with the first toast : " Honor "—bowing to *her*—" and Honesty." " Love and Loyalty " followed, by his next neighbour. " Come, Honor," said Curran, filling a bumper, " you know the next : be not squeamish, and let us have it." " No, sir," she replied with an arch smile, " I cannot do that, but I will pledge you in your own toast : ' Honor and Honesty, or *your absent friends.*' " These last words were uttered with marked emphasis, and in their provoked application, well sustained the barmaid's reported character, which indeed was promptly acknowledged by Curran himself.

That witty Irishman figures in another anecdote in con-nection with the above toast. Lord Avonmore was a very absent man. One day, at a dinner-party, Curran, who sat next to the chief baron, observing him quite oblivious of what was passing around him, when the toast "Our Absent Friends" was drunk, nudged him, "My lord," he said, "our host has just proposed your health, which has been received in very cordial terms; surely you will respond?" "Thank you, Curran; really I was not aware of it," replied the chief baron, and up he got, and to the surprise of many and the amusement of more, made an eloquent speech in reply to a toast which was not given.

A CASE IN POINT.

ONCE Robert Holmes, a distinguished member of the Irish bar, having in vain pressed a point upon the Barons of the Exchequer, who, one and all, were quite against him, he said he would be content if they allowed him to refer to a very recent judgment of the Court of Appeal in England, which he thought in point. "No use at all, Mr. Holmes," said the Chief Baron O'Grady, who perhaps suspected what was coming. "Only two lines, my lord," persisted Holmes. "Well, Mr. Holmes, as you say it is in point, let us hear it," remarked Baron Pennefather. Holmes thereupon opened a recent number of the House of Lords cases, and read from the judgment of an appeal case, reversing the decision of the barons: "The Court of Common Pleas in Ireland is seldom right—the Exchequer Court never."

Bench and bar were quite taken aback by this instance of Holmes' sarcasm; while Chief Baron O'Grady drawled out, "Now, brother Pennefather, see what you have got for your politeness."

LAWYERS' CLERKS *TEMP.* CHARLES I.

MR. LOWTON, of Gray's Inn, in *Pickwick*, is a capital picture of the lawyer's clerk in the year of grace, 1827. The type has since been modified, toned and sobered down to the spruce youth of the present day, who rides on a bicycle in a semi-military costume, is member of some volunteer corps, rows his "enribbon'd fair" on the Thames on Saturday afternoons and the blessed St. Lubbock's days, smokes pipes in the streets, patronizes the Alhambra and the pit of theatres, and is adorned with a great variety of other accomplishments. What the lawyer's clerk was like when Charles I. reigned and Cromwell brooded, may be gathered from "*Picturæ Loquentes, or Pictures Drawne Forth in Character*, by Wye Saltonstall, sold by Tho. Slater, at his shop in the Black Fryars, 1631 :"—

"His father thought him too chargeable to keep him at school till he could read Harry Stotle [Aristotle], and therefore preferred him to a man of law. His master is his genius, and dictates to him before he sets pen to paper. If he be to make a bond or bill, for fear of writing false Latin, he abbreviates the ending and termination of his word with a dash, and so leaves it doubtful. He sits near the door to give access to strangers, and at their going forth gives them a leg in expectation [of a tip]. His master is a cunning juggler of lands, and knows how to convey them underhand, he only copies them over again, and looks for a fee for expedition. His utmost knowledge is the names of the courts and their several offices, and he begins after a while, like a magpie that has had its tongue slit, to chatter out some terms of law, with more audacity than knowledge. At a new play he'll be sure to be seen in the threepenny room,*

---

* *i.e.* the upper gallery. Nearly a century later Defoe, in his *Comical Pilgrim*, describes the audience in this part as "composed of lawyers' clerks, valets-de-chambre, exchange girls [shop-girls], chamber-maids, and skip-kennels." The latter term is synonymous to the French *saute ruisseau*, the youngest of all clerks in a lawyer's office.

and buys his pippins before he goes in, because he can have more for money [than if he bought them in the house]. When he hears some stale jest (which he best understands), he fills the house with an ignorant laughter. He wears cut fingered dog-skin gloves for his ease, or the desire of bribes makes his hands grow itchy. In the vacation his master goes into the country to keep courts [on circuit], and then he is tied to a cloak-bag and rides after him. He calls himself the hand of the law, and commends the wisdom thereof in having so many words go to a bargain, for that both lengthens them and makes his fee the larger. He would fain read *Littleton*, if he might have a comment on him, otherwise he's too obscure, and dotes much on West's *Symboliography** for teaching him the form of an acquittance. In his freshmanship he hunts after cheap food, and is in debt to the cook for eel-pies on fasting days and feeding nights. The corruption of him is a weak attorney, then he trafficks with countrymen's businesses, and brings them down a bill of charges worse than a tailor's for a suit in the last fashion ; and here we leave him, for now he is at the highest [point he can reach]."

DANGER OF UPRIGHTNESS.

WHILE Sir Thomas Richardson, appointed Chief Justice of the Common Pleas in 1626, was attending the assizes at Salisbury, a prisoner whom he had sentenced to death, for some felony, threw a brickbat at his head ; but as the justice happened to stoop at the time, it only knocked off his hat.† When his friends congratulated him on his narrow

* William West, of the Inner Temple, attorney at the Common Law : "Symboliography, which may be termed the art description or image of instruments, covenants, contracts, etc., or the notary or scrivener collected and disposed in four severall books." The first edition appeared in 1590. In the next half century this work ran through fourteen editions.

† A proof that judges in those days did not wear wigs, but sat with their hats on.

escape, he said, "You see, now, if I had been an upright judge, I had been slain." The additional punishment upon this offender is recorded by Chief Justice Trevy, in the margin of Dyer's *Reports*, p. 188, in the following rich specimen of law French :—"Richardson, C.J. de C.B. at Assizes at Salisbury, in Summer 1631, fuit assault per Prisoner condemne pur Felony : que puis son condemnation ject un Brickbat a ledit Justice, que narrowly mist. Et pur cet immediately en fuit Indictment drawn pur Noy envers le Prisoner, et son dexter manus ampute et fixe al Gibbet sur que luy mesme immediatement hange in presence de Court."

ACCOMPLISHMENTS.

LORD ELDON at all times remained fond of studying the law, but in his younger days his thirst for legal knowledge was so great that he abandoned the pursuit of almost every other species of information, and never sacrificed one moment from his legal studies beyond what was absolutely necessary for his health. Law was "his food, his sleep, his study, and his pastime." His brother William (afterwards Lord Stowell, was fond of society, and used to join the literary parties at the Mitre, in Fleet Street, where Dr. Johnson, Goldsmith, and others of the highest ornaments of literature, used to assemble. Occasionally he would endeavour to induce his brother John to accompany him thither, saying, "Where do you sup to-night?" To this question John invariably answered, "Brother, I sup with Coke to-night." William would then demur with, "Nay, but come to 'the Mitre with me ; you'll meet Dr. Johnson ;" whereupon John argued concerning the doctor, "What's the use of him ? He can't draw a bill."

DISSECTING CRIMINALS.

THE bodies of executed criminals formerly were "begged" from the sheriff, for the use of the anatomical lessons; but in 1752 parliament passed an act "for the better preventing the horrid crime of murther," by which, to add further terror to the punishment of death, it was directed that the body of the criminal should be delivered at Surgeons' Hall to be dissected and anatomized. This expedient, it is said, carried some terror with it at first, but the impression soon wore off, for, on comparing the annual average of convictions for twenty-three years previous and subsequent to the statute, it was found that the number of murders had not decreased.

The Surgeons' Hall stood in the Old Bailey, on the site of the New Sessions House, till 1809. Pennant, in his *London*, remarks that the erection of the Hall in this neighbourhood was an exceedingly convenient circumstance. "By a sort of second sight," he says, "the Surgeons' Theatre was built near this court of conviction (the old Court of Justice) and Newgate, the concluding stage of the lives forfeited to the justice of their country, several years before the fatal tree was removed from Tyburn to its present site. It is a handsome building, orna-mented with Ionic pilasters, and with a double flight of steps to the first floor. Beneath is a door for the admission of the bodies of murderers and other felons, who, noxious in their lives, make a sort of reparation to their fellow-creatures by becoming useful after death." The act thus disposing of the bodies of executed criminals was only repealed in the reign of William IV.

A LUCKY BREACH OF PROMISE CASE.

T. JOHN LONG, a native of Doneraile, after having been by turns a basket-maker, a sign-painter, an engraver, a colour-grinder to Sir Thomas Lawrence, and, lastly, a portrait painter—failing in all these callings, set up as a quack. Though the impostor was of forbidding countenance, yet he succeeded in obtaining a large practice among the upper classes, earning so much as his £10,000 a year. Having been jilted by a young lady in Exeter, he ordered a Mr. Paxton, a solicitor of Gray's Inn Road, to send a writ for breach of promise. The writ was served by the clerk of an attorney practising in Exeter, but, by a mistake, upon the sister of the unfaithful beauty. The lady concerned in the writ, in order to avoid the lawsuit, fled to Italy. At Naples she became acquainted with the Prince of Capua, who married her. After this alliance she introduced her sister to the Earl of Dinorben, (?) an extremely wealthy nobleman, to whom she was soon united. Through these marriages the ladies' brother was introduced to Lord Tenterden, and married his lordship's daughter; and thus were these three marriages effected through the mistake in the service of a writ.

LEGAL TAUTOLOGY.

" HOPE," says the lawyer in Steele's comedy, "to see the day when the indenture shall be the exact measure of the land that passes by it. For it is a discouragement to the gown that every ignorant rogue of an heir should, by a word or two, understand his father's meaning, and hold ten acres of land by half an acre of parchment. Let others think of logic, rhetoric, and I know not what impertinence, but mind thou tautology. What's the first excellence in a lawyer? Tautology. What's the second? Tautology. What's the third? Tautology; as an old pleader said of action."

" When I think," says Cobbett, who for some years was clerk in the chambers of a gentleman in Gray's Inn, "of the saids and so forths, and the counts of tautology that I scribbled over— when I think of those sheets of seventy-two words, of those lines two inches apart—my brain turns. Gracious Heaven ! If I am doomed to be wretched, bury me beneath Iceland snows, and let me feed on blubber ; stretch me under the burning line, and deny me the propitious dews ; nay, if it be thy will, suffocate me with the pestilential airs of a democrat's club-room ; but save me, whatever you do, save me from the desk of an attorney ! "

AN HONEST LAWYER.

HE man of law is "damned to fame" on the signboard under the style and title of the " Honest Lawyer." The picture represents him with his head in his hand, that being considered the only condition in which a lawyer by any possibility could be honest ; though in the case of a bad man of law, the proverb *Morta la bestia, morto il veleno* does by no means apply.

Old jest-books tell us that Ben Jonson, passing once through a church in Surrey, and seeing a number of poor people weeping round an open grave, asked one of the women whose loss they deplored. " Oh ! " said she, " we have lost our precious lawyer, Justice Randall ; he kept us all in peace, and always was so good as to keep us from going to law : the best man ever lived." "Well, then," said Ben Jonson, "in that case I will write you an epitaph to inscribe on his tomb," which was—

> " God works wonders now and then ;
> Here lies a lawyer, an honest man."

When Sir John Strange, Master of the Rolls, died, a wit proposed for him the epitaph—

> " Here lies an honest lawyer, that is Strange."

Sir John's remains rest within the walls of the chapel of Clifford's Inn, but without the quibbling line.

The character of an honest lawyer has been sketched by an essayist of the seventeenth century, from which I extract the concluding sentence, for the benefit of the learned saints of the present day :—" While he lives, he is the delight of the courts, the ornament of the bar, the glory of the profession, the patron of innocency, the upholder of right, the scourge of oppression, the terror of deceit, and the oracle of his country. And when death calls him to the bar of heaven by a *habeas corpus cum causis*, he finds his judge his advocate, nonsuits the devil, obtains a *liberate* from all infirmities, and continues still one of the long robe in glory."

CHESHIRE CHEESE JOKE.

LORD LYNDHURST did not succeed in attracting public attention until the year 1817, when Serjeant Copley was counsel, in conjunction with Sir Charles Wetherell, for James Watson the elder, who was indicted for high treason. Lord Campbell, in his Life of Lord Ellenborough, says that Lord Castlereagh was sitting on the Bench during the trial, and he adds the statement, which Lord Lyndhurst resented, viz., that Lord Castlereagh, expressing great admiration of Mr. Serjeant Copley's republican eloquence, is said to have added, " I will set my rat trap for him, baited with *Cheshire cheese.*" This anecdote was probably a joke of circuit invention; but it had just this base of actual fact in it, that Mr. Serjeant Copley in the year following was made by Government Chief Justice of Chester.

SUICIDED BY THE EXECUTIONER.

THERE are some extraordinary instances recorded in the criminal annals of persons committing a crime solely in order to perish by the law, and thus prevent themselves, as they imagined, incurring the guilt of suicide. One Samuel Burr was tried for forgery at the Old Bailey in 1787. When called upon by the Recorder in the usual manner, he ended his address to the bench with the words, "I have forfeited my life, and I wish to resign it into the hands of Him who gave it. To give my reasons for this would only satisfy an idle curiosity. No one can feel a more sensible heartfelt satisfaction in the hopes of shortly passing into eternity, wherein I trust I shall meet with great felicity. I have no desire to live; and as the jury and court in my trial thought proper to recommend me to mercy, if his Majesty should, in consequence thereof, grant me a respite, I here vow, in the face of Heaven, that I will put an end to my own existence as soon as I can. It is death that I wish for." His end was frustrated, however, for he was respited. A much more horrible instance happened at Philadelphia, in 1760, when a Captain Bruluman tired of life, murdered a gentleman in a billiard saloon. After having shot two bullets through the man's body, he went up to him and said, "I have no malice or ill-will against you; I never saw you before: but I was determined to kill somebody that I might be hanged, and you happened to be the man, and I am very sorry for your misfortune." Bruluman died on the gallows, exulting in the success of a scheme by which he deemed himself not guilty of his own death.

INNS OF COURT IN OLDEN TIMES.

IN the reign of Henry VI. the students in each of the Inns of Courts were computed at two hundred. The reason given by the celebrated judge, Sir John Fortescue, for the smallness of their number at that time is rather curious, and is but one of a thousand facts which might be adduced to prove the vast increase of wealth in this country. His words are these :

" In these greater inns there can no student be maintained
for less expenses by the year than twenty marks ; and if he
have a servant to wait upon him, as most of them have, then so
much the greater will this charge be. Now, by reason of these
charges, the children only of noblemen do study the laws in
those inns, for the poor and common sort of people are not able
to bear so great charges for the exhibition of their children.
And merchant men can seldom find in their hearts to hinder
their merchandise with so great yearly expenses. And thus it
falleth out that there is scant any man found within the realm
skilful and cunning in the laws, except he be a gentleman born,
and come of a noble stock. Wherefore they, more than any
other kind of men, have a special regard to their nobility and to
the preservation of their honour and fame. And to speak up-
rightly, there is in these greater inns, yea, and in the lesser too,
beside the study of the laws, as it were, an university, or school,
of all commendable qualities requisite for noblemen. There
they learn to sing, and to exercise themselves in all kinds of
harmony. There also they practise dancing, and other noblemen's pastimes, as they use to do, who are brought up in the
king's house. In the working days most of them apply themselves to the study of the law ; and on the holy days to the
study of holy scripture ; and out of the time of divine service
to the reading of chronicles. For there, indeed, are virtues
studied, and vices exiled. So that for the endowment of virtue
and abandoning of vice, knights and barons, with other states
and noblemen of the realm, place their children in those inns,
though they desire not to have them learned in the laws, nor to
live by the practice thereof, but only upon their fathers' allowance."

"Whereunto I shall add," says Dugdale, in his *Origines
Juridiciales*, alluding to the above passage, " what Mr. John
Ferne, sometime a student of the Inner Temple, in his learned
book entitled *The Glory of Generosity*, expresses : Nobleness of
blood, joined with virtue, makes the person most meet to the

exercising of any public service. And for that cause it was, not for nought, that our ancient governors in this land did, with a special foresight and wisdom, provide that none should be admitted into the houses (Inns of Court, being seminaries, sending forth men apt to the government of justice) except he were a gentleman of blood. And that this may seem a truth, I myself have seen a calendar of all those which were together in the society of one of the same houses, about the last year of King Henry V., with the arms of their house and family marshalled by their names. And I assure you, the self-same monument doth both approve them all to be gentlemen of perfect descents, and also the number of them much less than now it is, being at that time in one house scarcely three score."

So late as the beginning of the reign of James I. it was intimated at a " pension," or meeting, that none but gentlemen of descent should be admitted to the society of Gray's Inn. The names of all candidates were therefore ordered to be delivered to the bench, that inquiries might be made as to their " quality." The exemplary conduct and refined manners praised by Fortescue appear to have considerably deteriorated in course of time however ; for ere the sixteenth century had elapsed the Inns of Court gentleman acquired a very different reputation, and edicts, rules, and enactments had constantly to be made and renewed in order to keep his buoyant spirits within bounds. Fuller, who writes in the reign of Charles I., says in his character of the Degenerous Gentleman, " at the Inns of Court, under pretence to learn law, he learns to be lawless : not knowing by his study so much as what an execution means till he learns it by his own dear experience. Here he grows acquainted with the Roaring Boys ; I am afraid so called by a fearful prolepsis *here* for *hereafter*. What formerly was counted the chief credit of an orator these esteem the honour of a swearer, pronunciation, to mouth an oath with a graceful grace. These, as David says, ' clothe themselves with curses as with garments,' and therefore desire to be of the latest fashion, both in clothes and in curses."

SCOTCH LAW JARGON.

IT has been a usual complaint that the difficulty of understanding law is greatly aggravated by the barbarous
phraseology used by its professors. Technical terms
must always seem uncouth to the uninitiated, and be unintel-
ligible to those to whom the sense in which they are used is
unknown, and perhaps lawyers will say that, abstractly speaking,
law phrases are not one whit more barbarous and uncognoscible
than those of any other science. Be that as it may, it is certain
that the phrases used in Scotch law are even more difficult and
obscure than those in use on this side of Tweed. This arises
from the circumstance that the Scotch lawyers employ words in
ordinary use in a certain technical sense. Thus, to *see* is to
appoint the petition against the judgment pronounced to be
answered. When a judge wishes to be peremptory in an order,
he ordains parties to *condescend;* when he intends to be mild,
he recommends them to *lose* their pleas. When anybody thinks
proper to devise his estates for the benefit of the poor, he is
considered by the law of Scotland to *mortify* them. Witnesses
are brought into court upon a *diligence,* and, before they can be
examined, they must be *purged.* If a man loses his deceased
elder brother's estate, it is called a *conquest.* The elegant phrases
of "blasting you at the horn," "poinding your estate," "consign-
ing you to the fisc," exceed any barbarism for which Westminster
Hall need to blush. The consequence of these uncouth terms
is that when Scotch lawsuits find their way across the border
they lead sometimes to curious misunderstandings. There are
two old methods of paying rent in Scotland: *kane* and *carriages*
—the one being rent in kind from the farmyard, the other an
obligation to furnish the landlord with a certain amount of
carriage, or rather cartage, the *corvée* of the old *régime* in France.
In one of the vexed cases of domicile which had been brought
before the House of Lords, a Scotch lawyer argued that a

landed gentleman had shown his determination to abandon his residence in Scotland by having given up his *kane* and *carriages*. It is said that the argument went further than he expected— the English lawyers admitting that it was indeed very strong evidence of an intended change of domicile, when the laird not only ceased to keep a carriage, but actually divested himself of his walking-cane.

AN OLD MARRIAGE LAW.

BY a statute of August, 1653, the betrothed couple were allowed to choose whether they would be "asked" in church or chapel on three several Sundays, or cried in the open market on three consecutive market days, in the parish nearest their ordinary place of worship. This was the assertion with a vengeance of the civil nature of the marriage contract. If the loving pair chose to be cried, their proposed union was in most cases proclaimed by the bellman, though the kind assistance of that official was not legally required for making the announcement. "In the absence of conclusive evidence on the matter," says Mr. Jeaffreson, the historian of *Brides and Bridals*, "I have no doubt that the street bans of our forefathers in Cromwell's England, were rarely proclaimed by clergymen. On the other hand, it is certain that the bellman was, in many places, regularly employed to cry aloud for impediments to the wedding of precise lovers." One of the registers of the church of St. Andrew's, Holborn, containing entries from 1653 to 1658, is wholly occupied with proclamations during the interregnum, published in the market place. They run generally in this style : "An agreement and intent of marriage between John Law and Ffrances Riley, both servants to the Lady Brooke, of this parish, was published three several markett days, that is to say," etc.

IN A FIX.

LORD BACON relates, in his *Apothegms*, that in Chancery one time when the counsel of the parties set forth the boundaries of the land in question by the plot, and the counsel of one part said, " We lie on this side, my lord," and the counsel on the other part said, " We lie on this side," the Lord Chancellor Hatton stood up and said, " If you lie on both sides, whom will you have me to believe ? "

TEMPORA MUTANTUR.

THE irony of history was once more exemplified—and in a manner not generally realized—when Sir George Jessel, the first person of Jewish birth, who ever sat on the English bench, took his seat in the Rolls' Court as master. Once on a time the rolls, or public records, were kept in a chapel which had been originally founded for the benefit of converted Jews. But so few of them got converted, that, in Edward the First's reign, our choleric ancestors thought to make quicker work by turning them out of the country in a body. As for the chapel, it was annexed " for ever " to the office of the Mastership of the Rolls. At length the whirligig of time has raised an unconverted Jew to that lucrative eminence—if £6000 a year is to be considered a good thing in these expensive days.

LINCOLN'S INN AND THE REPORTERS.

IT is well known that a considerable number of reporters for the public press are bar students, and that many of the most eminent men in the legal profession owed their subsistence during their studentship to the same source. Serjeant Spankie was a reporter on the *Morning Chronicle*, so also was Sir John Campbell ; the late Master Stephens was also employed in a similar capacity, and Lord Plunkett was a reporter for, and afterwards editor of, the *Dublin Patriot.* Talfourd for many years earned money as a reporter, and many other names just as good will occur to the reader.

In the early part of this century the benchers of Lincoln's Inn passed a by-law, excluding gentlemen who wrote for the newspapers from their society. This illegal proceeding was brought under the consideration of the House of Commons, by one of the gentlemen against whom it operated, and there it met with such unmingled condemnation, that the benchers were shortly afterwards induced to rescind the obnoxious resolution. In the discussion to which the subject gave rise, Sheridan observed that there were among those who reported parliamentary debates no less than twenty-three graduates of the Universities of Oxford, Cambridge, Dublin, and Edinburgh. He quoted the examples of Dr. Johnson and of Burke, for whom this employment had long been the chief means of existence. Mr. Stephen followed Sheridan in a very manly speech, declaring that he had been a member of Lincoln's Inn for thirty-five years, but that he had not the most remote connection with the framing of this offensive by-law, which he thought a scandal rather to its authors than to its objects. Sir John Anstruther was also a member of Lincoln's Inn, but reprobated the by-law referred to. Obnoxious as it was, it is a curious fact that it originated with an individual who had been particularly loud in his professions of regard for the liberty of the press: Mr. Henry Clifford was its father.

AUDI ALTERAM PARTEM.

BARON ALDERSON was a great favourite with juries, and, though deep, solid, and acute in his reasoning, delighted in witticisms. At an assize town a juryman said to the clerk who was administering the oath to him, "Speak up, I cannot hear what you say." The baron asked him if he was deaf, and on the juryman answering, " Yes, with one ear," " Well, then," said the baron, " you may leave the box, for it is necessary that a juryman should hear both sides."

SAVING FAITH.

USTICE POWELL, junior, was a profound lawyer, and much respected in private life. Dean Swift represents him as " the merriest old gentleman he ever saw, speaking pleasant things, and chuckling till he cried again." When one Jane Wenham was tried for witchcraft before him, and charged with being able to fly, he asked her whether she could fly ; and on her answering in the affirmative, he said " Well, then, you may ; there is no law against flying." The poor woman was saved from the effects of her own faith, and received the queen's pardon.

TO HAVE NOT TO HOLD.

E have heard lately more than enough and to spare about land bills, land commissions, and that sort of thing. Nevertheless it may interest some of my readers, and be some kind of consolation to others, to know that a worse state of affairs in this particular respect has existed for centuries in a neighbouring country. I allude to the " vested right " (*Beklem-recht*) prevalent in the province of Groningen in the Netherlands, considered by those who profit by it as the chief cause of the extraordinary prosperity of that province. The *Beklem-recht* is the right to occupy a farm on the payment of an annual rent, which the landlord can never augment. This right passes to the heirs of the holder, collateral as well as direct, and he may transmit it by will, may sell it, rent it, raise a mortgage upon it, all without the consent of the landlord. Every time, however, that this right passes from one hand to another, whether by inheritance or sale, the proprietor landlord receives one or two years' rent. The farm buildings belong, in general, to the possessor of the "vested right," who, when his right is transferred, may exact the price of the same. The possessor of the "vested right" pays all taxes, cannot change the form of the property, nor in any way diminish its value. The "vested right" is indivisible. One person only can possess it, and consequently one only of the heirs can inherit it. However, by paying the sum stipulated in case of the passage of the "vested right" from one hand to another, the husband may inscribe his wife, or the wife her husband, and then the consort inherits a part of the right. When the possessor is ruined, or does not pay his rent, the "vested right" is at once annulled. The creditors can cause it to be sold, but the purchaser must first of all pay all outstanding debt.

The origin of this custom is obscure. It appears to have arisen in the middle ages, on the convent farms. The land at that time being of small value, the monks readily granted the possession of certain portions of their estates on the easiest terms, which assured them their rent and exempted them from the charge of the farms. Their income was sufficiently large to enable them to grant the easiest terms without inconvenience. They reserved, however, to themselves the right to dismiss the tenant at the end of every ten years ; but they did not use their right, because, if they did so, they would have had to pay the value of the buildings erected on their lands. During the troubles consequent on the protracted wars with Spain, from 1568 to 1648, the "vested right" became *de facto* hereditary, or, at least, many authorities declared it to be such. Jurisprudence and custom decided the various points subject to question, a more definite formula was adopted, and from that time the "vested right" maintained its place by the side of the civil code.

Sub-letting was formerly rare ; but since the increase in prices of all kinds of food, consequent to the increased trade with England, the profits are so considerable that the possessor of the "vested right" easily can sub-let the farm to a tenant who pays him a much higher rent than he himself pays to the landlord. Thus the original tenant becomes *de facto* landlord : he can let the lands for the term and the sum he likes. The real landlord must rest content with the rent fixed in the middle ages ; and though he sees his land deteriorating, he has no redress. On the other hand, he knows that the farmers roll in wealth, that their dwellings are filled with the finest furniture, pictures, pianos, china, virtu, even gold instead of silver dinner and tea services ; and that the farmers' wives and daughters possess more valuable jewellery than his own woman-kind. And to a properly balanced mind that is certainly some consolation.

TEMULENT LAW.

FAMOUS counsel in Edinburgh, named Hay, who became a judge under the name of Lord Newton, was equally remarkable as a hard drinker and as a lawyer. He considered himself as only the better fitted for business when he had previously imbibed six bottles of claret. One of his clerks declared that the best paper he ever knew his lord-ship to dictate, was done after a drinking bout when that amount of liquor had fallen to Mr. Hay's share. It was of him that the story is told of a client calling for him one day at four o'clock, and being surprised to find him at dinner, when, on the client saying to the servant that he had understood five to be Mr. Hay's dinner hour, " Oh, but, sir," said the man, " it is his yesterday's dinner."

PARLIAMENTARY BILLINGSGATE.

HEN O'Connell said that he was " the best abused man in the world," he might have added that he was also the best abusing. However, he had ample precedent. Sir Archibald Macdonald, who was chief baron of the English

Court of Exchequer from 1793 to 1813, once told Sir Fletcher Norton, afterwards Speaker of the House of Commons, that he was a "lazy, indolent, evasive, shuffling, plausible, artful, mean, confident, cowardly, poor, pitiful and abject creature." This was in parliament, where the decencies of speech are supposed to be observed.

GREAT LAWYERS FROM SMALL BEGINNINGS.

LORD SOMERS'S father was an attorney at Worcester ; Lord Hardwicke's, an attorney at Dover ; Lord King's and Lord Gifford's, both grocers at Exeter ; Lord Thurlow's, a poor country clergyman ; Lord Kenyon's, a gentleman of small estate in Wales ; Dunning's, an attorney at Ashburton ; Sir Vicary Gibbs's, a surgeon and apothecary at Exeter ; Sir Samuel Romilly's, a jeweller ; Sir Samuel Shepherd's, a goldsmith ; Lord Tenterden's, a barber at Canterbury. Lord Mansfield and Lord Erskine were men of family : but all Lord Mansfield got by his noble connection were a few briefs in Scotch appeal cases ; and Erskine, just about the time he was called to the bar, was heard emphatically thanking God that out of his own family he did not know a lord. It would have been more to the purpose to thank God that he *did* know an attorney ; but he judged rightly that his noble blood would have been of no avail.

BIRDS IN THE TEMPLE.

"THERE were formerly rooks in the Temple trees," says Leigh Hunt, writing in 1848, "a colony brought by Sir Edward Northey, a well-known lawyer in Queen Anne's time, from his grounds at Epsom. It was a pleasant thought, supposing that the colonists had no objection. The rook is a grave legal bird, both in his coat and habits ; living in communities, yet to himself ; and strongly addicted to discussions of *meum* and *tuum*. The neighbourhood, however, appears to have been too much for him ; for, upon inquiring on the spot, we were told that there had been no rooks for many years."

Sparrows in abundance still hop and flutter about in the courts and gardens of the Temple. Notwithstanding their irregular existences, they are allowed to find snug roosts and resting-places in the crevices and crannies of the law's local habitation, just as some human nuisances find subsistence in the cracks and flaws of the legal structure. The said sparrows live under the sacred ægis of the law, safe and unmolested, though at one time they appear to have been threatened with wholesale destruction. "When Daines Barrington's treasurership came to be audited," says Charles Lamb, " the following singular charge was unanimously disallowed by the bench : ' Item, disbursed Mr. Allen, the gardener, 20*s*. for stuff to poison the sparrows by my order.' "

I suppose the conduct of the Temple sparrows was outrageous in those days, otherwise the order would be incomprehensible in the friend and correspondent of Gilbert White, the naturalist of Selborne. It was through Daines Barrington, himself a writer on ornithology, that White's papers on the hirundinidæ were presented to the Royal Society ; and by his encouragement, as the fifth published letter of Gilbert White to him shows, the simple-minded unobtrusive parish priest of Hampshire was induced to commence that *Natural History of Selborne*, which ranks among the most delightful publications in the English language.

SUPEREROGATORY ZEAL.

" N the year 1718," says Dr. Doran, in *London in the Jacobite Times*, " a new health was drunk with loud cheers, in the Jacobite taverns, ' To Miss Clarke ! ' This was the name of a pretty girl in Sunderland, who had boldly drunk King James's health in a mixed company. She was called to account for it, of course; but she was only lightly fined, and several of the justices *kissed her*, as she passed in front of the bench, on her way out of court."

COMMON LARCENY.

IN consequence of the efforts which the Lord Chancellor Camden made in behalf of Wilkes, he became so popular that the parishioners of Chislehurst, where he resided, in their patriotism made him a present of ten acres of the common, on which the avenue leading to the seat now stands. Lord Camden, who was a very early riser, was the first to discover, in one of his morning walks, that all the geese of a poor widow who resided on the common had been stolen during the preceding night. Meeting accidentally a labourer going to work, he made some inquiries respecting the geese, asking him if he knew anything about them, and what punishment would be inflicted on the offender who stole the geese from the common. The man answered that he did not know. "Why, then, I'll tell you," said his lordship; "he will be transported for seven years." "If that is the case," replied the labourer, offended at the apparent suspicion of the chancellor, "I will thank your lordship to tell me what punishment the law would inflict on the man who stole the common from the geese?"

A DESTROYING ANGEL.

WILLIAM WAGGETT was for many years a leading man on the Munster Circuit. There was a spirit of originality about his style, which was quite refreshing after the hackneyed oratory of some of his contemporaries. He was a man subject to strong antipathies, and had a great hatred of all base vulgar spirits. Amongst others whom he abhorred, was an attorney who practised in Limerick, and who had obtained an unenviable reputation for dragging people into lawsuits. Waggett lost no opportunities of denouncing this attorney in invectives of withering force. On one occasion a very bad case was brought into court, in which this attorney was agent for the plaintiff, and Waggett leading counsel for the defendant. The case was one which was likely to call forth all Waggett's fine powers, and the court was crowded with persons waiting to hear him address the jury. When his turn came to speak for the defendant, he rose, labouring under emotion, and remained silent for a time. But instead of commencing with " My lords and gentlemen of the jury," he began in his deep and solemn voice, " ' Long live the Sultan Haroun,' said the owl in the Arabian tale." At this singular beginning of a lawyer's speech, the audience was much surprised. The judge looked amazed, and the bar were all eager to hear what would come after so strange a preface. Amid dead silence Waggett continned, " ' Long live the Sultan Haroun,' said the owl in the Arabian tale. ' While he lives we shall have ruined palaces and roofless cottages to roost in. Widows shall bewail their husbands, and orphans weep for their murdered parents. While he lives there shall be gloom upon the land, and the light of day shall shine upon desolation. ' Long live the Sultan Haroun,' continued the owl, ' in order that the birds of ill omen may brood over congenial gloom,' and ' Long live Charley Carroll,' " cried Waggett, turning to the plaintiff's attorney, at whom he pointed his finger contemptuously. " ' Long live Charley Carroll,' says the professor of the law ; ' while he lives clients shall be ruined, and litigation shall fill the courts with half-ruined suitors ; while he lives the lawyer's purse shall be increased, and the trader's wealth diminished ; while he lives there shall be endless contention amongst neighbours, and friends shall be made to hate each other. The father shall quarrel with the son, and brother shall turn against sister.' " He then went on pursuing the metaphor, and denouncing the attorney, who cowered with downcast head under the vehement and wild invective.

BARONIAL JUSTICE.

THE true mark of a true baron in the ancient time was the *curia vitæ et membrorum*, jurisdiction in life and limb. All feudal lords through feudal Europe were equally fond and proud of the right of executing those whom they had first convicted and sentenced to death. The French had the phrase *avec haute et basse justice*, which was equivalent to the *furca* and *'fossa* of this country. The gallow-hill is still an object of interest and of pride near old baronial mansions, and there are some where the surrounding ground is full of the remains of the poor wretches who died by the baron's law. Perhaps the *'fossa*, the pit, was for the female criminal ; for women sentenced to death were, for the most part, drowned. Mr. Cosmo Innis, the Scotch legal antiquary, mentions an old court book, of a regality quite low down in date (*circa* 1640), where the simple form of record in criminal process was to write in the middle of the page the name and offence of the accused, with the name of the assize, and upon the margin to inscribe shortly the words " convickit," " hangit," " drownit." In the rare cases where it was necessary to record an acquittal, the word on the margin is " clengit."

So carefully were matters anciently regulated in some countries, that you knew exactly how low a bow to make to a nobleman by noticing the number of posts to his gallows. A four-legged gibbet was distinctive of a very great baron indeed, and he who had a two-posted one occupied a superior position even among lords. But the smaller fry of nobles were not therefore without the means of getting rid of those that troubled them, without in any way encroaching upon the privileges of their betters. Thus the lords of Aragon hit on the ingenious device of starving to death those whom they might not hang. And this scrupulous observance of the law was by law rewarded, for in 1247 it was, as Ducange records, thus

enacted for the benefit of those who had kept the command-
ments, in word, " Si vassallus domini non habentis merum nec
mixtum imperium, in loco occideret vassallum, dominus loci
potest eum occidere fame, frigore et siti. Et quilibet dominus
loci habet hanc jurisdictionem necandi fame, frigori, et siti in
suo loco, licet nullam aliam jurisdictionem criminalem habeat."

These noblemen of Aragon, it will be observed, amended
the defects of their feudal customs in precisely the same way
as our courts of equity were wont to improve upon the common and statute law of England. "*Fame, frigore et siti.*"
These were also the methods by which suitors in chancery
were put into possession of their inheritance.

DIFFERENCE OF ONE LETTER.

ON one occasion Baron Alderson of the Exchequer was
dining at one of the city feasts, at which, as is not
unfrequently the case, there was so great a noise after
dinner, as to render the toast-master's voice almost inaudible.
This worthy, instead of giving the Army and Navy together,
separated the two services ; when therefore the second toast
was drank, the attorney-general, supposing that "the bar," was
proposed, rose. Mr. Baron Alderson being placed where he
could understand the words spoken, perceived and enjoyed the
learned gentleman's mistake. "Mr. Attorney, Mr. Attorney,"
said he, smiling, "give me leave to tell you Navy is not spelt
with a *K.*"

SENTENCES *PRO FORMA.*

NUMEROUS as the executions used to be in former times,
they did not represent a tithe or hundredth part of
what was pronounced capital crime, nor of the number
of persons who were sentenced to death without the smallest
intention of hanging them. Thus it appears from the records,

that, between 1802 and 1809 inclusive, out of 508 persons capitally convicted in London and Middlesex, only sixty-seven suffered the extreme penalty of the law, in all other instances sentence was commuted. A remarkable incident in connection with these capital sentences *pro 'forma*, is said to have occurred in the judicial life of Edward Willes, son of Lord Chief Justice Willes. " He had many good qualities, but he was much too volatile and inattentive to reasonably grave behaviour upon the bench. He was, however, very anxious to do right. He condemned a boy, I think, at Lancaster," says Lord Eldon, "and with the hope of reforming him by frightening him, he ordered him for execution next morning, though he did not mean that he should suffer. The judge awoke in the middle of the night, and was so affected by the notion that he might himself die in the course of the night, and the boy be hanged, that he got out of his bed, and went to the lodgings of the high sheriff, and left a reprieve for the boy, and then, returning to his bed, spent the rest of the night comfortably."

" This is a very improbable story," observes Serjeant Woolrych, in his *Lives of Eminent Serjeants-at-Law.* " If true, the judge ought not to have remained on the bench. When a judge left the assize town, he was wont to write in the Calendar : *Sus per Coll.*, *i.e.*, let him be hanged by the neck. Mr. Justice Willes must have been *volatile indeed* to make such an escapade. The truth was, no doubt, that he had frightened the boy by telling him that he should be hanged, and hence he tale."

A short time before the abolition of capital punishment for stealing to the amount of forty shillings in a dwelling-house, Lord Kenyon passed sentence of death upon a young woman for that offence. She fell down as dead. The chief justice was much moved. "I don't mean to hang her !" he exclaimed : a pause. "Will nobody interfere and tell her I don't mean to hang her ?"

A SHORT CHARGE.

JUDGE FORSTER, a short time before his death, went the Oxford Circuit in one of the hottest summers that has ever been remembered. He was so far advanced in life as to be scarcely capable of doing the duties which belonged to his office, and when the grand jury of Worcester attended for the charge, he addressed them as follows: "Gentlemen, the weather is very hot ; I am very old, and as you are all very well acquainted with what is your duty, I have no doubt but you will practise it."

HOW NOT TO DO IT.

IN speaking of a learned serjeant who gave a confused and elaborate explanation of some point of law, Curran observed that " whenever that grave counsellor endeavoured to unfold a principle of law, he put him in mind of a fool whom he once saw try to open an oyster with a rolling pin."

PROFESSIONAL EMOLUMENTS.

THE emoluments of the profession of the law have pretty rapidly advanced during the last four centuries. What would a modern lawyer say to the following entry in the churchwarden's accounts of St. Margaret's, Westminster, for the year 1476 : "Also payd to Roger Fylpot, learned in the Lawe, for his counsell giveing, 3*s.* 8*d.*, with four pence for his dinner." Though fifteen times the fee might not seem inadequate at present, yet five shillings would hardly furnish the table of a barrister, even if the fastidiousness of modern manners would admit of his accepting such a dole.

Roper, in his *Life of Sir Thomas More,* informs us that the future chancellor was an advocate of the greatest eminence, and of the most extensive practice ; yet, when he lived in Bucklersbury, " he gained, without grief, not so little as £400 by the year." " Considering the relative profits of the bar, and the value of money," says Lord Campbell, " this income probably indicated as high a station as £10,000 a year in the present day," *i.e.* in 1844 or 1845. Half a century later Sir Thomas Brownlow, one of the prothonotaries in the reign of Queen Elizabeth, made £6000 per annum. He used to close the profits of the year with " Laus Deo," and when they appeared unusually large, his gratitude was vented in a " Maxima laus Deo."

In the reign of James I., the nominal salaries paid to the judges and crown lawyers were extremely low ; their real incomes were derived from certain fees, which had to be paid into court before any suitor could obtain a hearing. " Francis Bacon," says Mr. Hepworth Dixon, " valued his place as attorney-general at £6000 a year, of which the king paid him only £81 6s. 8d." Mr. Dixon goes on to mention several similar instances, adding : " Yet each of these great lawyers had given up a lucrative practice at the bar. After their promotion to the bench, they lived in good houses, kept a princely state, gave dinners and masks, made presents to the king, accumulated goods and lands." Sir Edward Coke had made a still larger income as attorney-general, the fees from his private and official practice amounting to £7000 in a single year." It is difficult to reconcile such figures as these with Lord Campbell's statement about Sir Thomas More. Either within a hundred years the value of money had enormously declined, or Coke was making an income far exceeding anything attainable in the present day.

Bulstrode Whitelock possessed a private practice that brought him in £2000 a year. He stated, as a very uncommon circumstance to have happened to a pleader, that Serjeant Maynard, one of the most eminent lawyers of his day, realized in one circumstance £700. Sir Matthew Hale said that £1000 a year was a great deal for a common lawyer to make ; and when he heard that one made £2000 a year, he said he knew the individual alluded to made a good deal by his city practice, but he doubted if he made so much. Of the lawyers of the time of the Commonwealth an old writer says : " Nor are their fees of mean value, £3, £5, £6 being usual, even for making a motion of five or six lines. Many of them," continues the indignant author, " rise from nothing to great estates, £5000, £8000, nay £12,000 by the year, and purchase baronies and earldoms."

In his survey of the state of England in 1685, Lord Macaulay says, " A thousand a year was thought a large income for a barrister ; £2000 a year was hardly to be made in the Court of King's Bench, except by Crown lawyers." Mr. Jeaffreson, in his *Book about Lawyers*, impugns the accuracy of this statement, holding that the former part of it is based on a passage in *Pepys' Diary*. As long ago as 1668 the Admiralty was a favourite target for parliamentary orators to shoot at, and Pepys, after priming himself with good liquor, made such a spirited speech in behalf of his department, that his friends complimented him hugely, assuring him that if he would put on a gown and plead at the Chancery bar he could not get less than £1000 a year. There is nothing to complain of in this portion of Lord Macaulay's statement, especially as Mr. Jeaffreson adds in a note, " Among advocates in Charles II.'s reign, a professional income of a thousand a year signified a practice and popularity that placed a barrister in the second rank of the unquestionably successful followers of the law. Somers was thought a fortunate and rising counsellor when he enjoyed Lord Chancellor Nottingham's favour, and made £700 a year." But the credit of the second part of Lord Macaulay's statement is certainly shaken by an examination of the fee-book of Sir Francis Winnington, who was solicitor-general to Charles II. In 1673, he received £3371 ; in 1674, £3560 ; and in 1675—the first year of his tenure of the solicitor's office—

£4066, of which only £429 were office fees. Lord Keeper North made £7000 a year as attorney-general, and his brother Roger gives an amusing description of his mode of bestowing the fees in three skull caps—one for the gold, the second for crowns and half-crowns, and the third for the small money. In those golden days the barrister did not open his mouth till his fingers had closed on his client's money, and credit was unknown in transactions between counsel and attorney. A good deal of base money used, however, to be taken on these occasions; and Bishop Burnet gravely praises Sir Matthew Hale for his justice and goodness in not putting this flash coin again into circulation. The worthy judge's virtue was emphatically its own reward. He had gathered together a vast heap of this spurious coin, when some thieves broke into his house, and contentedly carried it off, believing that they were helping themselves to his hoarded treasure.

The practice at the bar does not appear to have become more lucrative in the reign of George II. than it was many years earlier. During the last year of his tenure of solicitor-generalship, Charles Yorke earned £7322. Lord Eldon's fee-book shows a great advance. In 1794, he received £11,592; in 1795, £11,149; in 1796, £12,140. Previous to Erskine's elevation to the bench, he received on an average twelve special retainers in the year, from which he gained at least £3600. Elsewhere we read of Erskine : " It is four years and a half since he was called, and in that time he has cleared £8000 or £9000, besides paying his debts, got a silk gown, and a business of at least £3000 a year." Sir Samuel Romilly is said to have realized an income of upwards of £15,000 a year at the latter end of his life ; and in our own days enormous retaining fees have 'on several occasions been given to counsel. Sir Charles Wetherell is known to have received 7000 guineas for opposing the Municipal Corporations Bill at the bar of the House of Lords ; and it is generally understood that the late Lord Truro's retaining fee in the case of the British Iron

Company against Mr. Attwood, was not less than 9000 guineas. The fee indorsed on the brief was 1000 guineas.

Writing in 1818, H. Crabb Robinson says in his *Memoirs*, " In the winter of this year I heard from Gurney (afterwards Baron Gurney) some interesting facts about fees, which within eleven or twelve years had risen much above what was formerly known. Kaye, the solicitor to the Bank of England, told Gurney once that he had that day carried the Attorney-General Gibbs one hundred general retainers, that is 500 guineas. These were on the Baltic captures and insurance cases. Gibbs did not think that Erskine ever made more than 7000 guineas, and Mingay confessed that he only once made 5000 guineas. He observed that the great fortunes made in ancient times by lawyers must have been indirectly, as the stewards of great men. Otherwise they were unaccountable. I must here add that all this is little compared with the enormous gains of my old fellow-circuiteer, Charles Austin, who is said to have made 40,000 guineas by pleading before parliament in one session." In America David Dudley Field, some years ago, was also reported to make annually over £40,000.

AN UNSPARING HAND.

BACON relates the following anecdote of Lord Ellesmere, who was lord chancellor under James I. : " My Lord Chief Chancellor Ellesmere, when he had read a petition which he disliked, would say, 'What! you would have my hand to this now?' And the party answering 'Yes,' he would say further, 'Well, so you shall; nay, you shall have both my hands to it.' And so would, with both his hands, tear it in pieces." Of this eminent man, Fuller says, " Surely all Christendom afforded not a person which carried more gravity in his countenance and behaviour than Sir Thomas Egerton, insomuch that many have gone to the Chancery on purpose only to see his venerable garb (*happy they who had no other business!*), and were highly pleased at so acceptable a spectacle."

COCKELL-SAUCE.

MR. SERJEANT COCKELL was a very humorous man, and, in his day, leader of the Northern Circuit. He lived when late evening consultations were common, and sobriety by no means a sure attendant upon them. Upon one occasion on the circuit, a worthy farmer contrived to get an introduction—like Pickwick to Serjeant Snubbin—to the great man. Serjeant Cockell had been indulging in joviality, and the farmer began a lengthy tale in the vernacular. There was a pause, and the serjeant rolling in his chair, exclaimed, " Ill —win—your cause." This ought to have contented the farmer ; but he went on with a second tedious tale of his wrongs. The serjeant became impatient, and interrupted him this time with another " I'll win your cause." The stupid man would not stop, upon which the serjeant, highly ebrious, broke out, and said, " Didn't I tell ye I'd win—your—cause ? If you don't get out instantly, I'll kick you out of the room."

SAVE US FROM OUR FRIENDS.

DURING the Gordon Riots in 1780, the benchers of the Temple determined that they should not remain inactive during such times. So they embodied themselves into a company to assist the military. They armed themselves as well as they could, and the next morning drew up in the court ready to follow out a company of soldiers who were there on guard. When, however, the soldiers had passed through the gate, it was suddenly shut in the faces of the benchers and instantly locked, whilst the officer commanding the detachment shouted from the other side, " Gentlemen, I am much obliged to you for your intended assistance ; but I do not choose to allow my men to be shot, so I have ordered *you* to be locked in." And away he galloped. How foolish the benchers looked is quite beyond conjecture.

SCOTT ON ELOPEMENTS.

LORD ELDON'S runaway match, when he was plain Mr. Scott, with pretty Bessy Surtees, is well known. In after life whilst he was on the Lancaster Assizes, it happened that a farmer of some substance desired to retain his services in a suit for damages against another wealthy farmer, who had run off with the daughter of the plaintiff. "Mind, Lawyer Scott," said he, " you are to say that the man who runs away with another man's daughter is a rascal and a villain, and deserves to be hanged." " No, no, I cannot say that," objected Scott. " And why not? why can't you say that?" " Because I did it myself," was the young lawyer's reply ; " but I will tell you what I will say—and I will say it from my heart : I will say that the man who begins domestic life by a breach of domestic duty, is doubly bound to do everything in his power to render both the lady and her family happy in future life—*that* I will say, for I feel it." The farmer had to give up that point, and Scott pleaded so well that the jury, after a deliberation of nine hours, gave a verdict for £800 damages. The most curious part of the affair, however, as Lord Eldon himself related, is that this verdict was actually obtained through the mere obstinacy of a half-drunken juryman.

A BOOK CASE.

THERE is a celebrated reply of the witty Curran to a remark of Lord Clare, who curtly exclaimed at one of his legal positions, " Oh, if that be law, Mr. Curran, I may burn my law books !" " Better read them, my lord," was the sarcastic and appropriate rejoinder.

RELATIONSHIP.

MR. JOHN LEE, afterwards solicitor-general, was a powerful cross-examiner of a witness. Once such a person remonstrated against the torture thus inflicted. The man, who was clothed in rags, said, " Sir, you treat me very harshly, and I feel it the more because we are relations." " We relations, fellow ! " said Lee ; " how do you make out that ? " " Why," said the man, " my mother was such a person, and she was the daughter of such a man, and he was the son of a woman who was the daughter of a person (naming him) who was your great-grandfather, or great-great-grandfather." "Well," said Lee, " you are right ; he was so. And then, my good cousin, my good fourth or fifth cousin, speak a little truth, I beseech thee, for the honour of the family—for not one word of truth, cousin, hast thou spoken yet."

HUMOUR OF LAW BOOKS.

IN *Smith on Contracts*, 5th ed., p. 445, there is the following unique reference : " But the cases most frequently referred to on the subject are *Montague v. Benedict*, and *Seaton v. Benedict*. The name of the defendant probably strikes you as fictitious, and, in truth, it is so, being taken from a play by Shakespeare, called *Much Ado About Nothing*, in which one of the characters is a young officer, named Benedict, who protests vehemently against marriage. The real defendant was a highly respectable professional gentleman." Mr. John William Smith, of the Inner Temple, author of the above text-book, was one of the most learned of modern English lawyers, but he thought it necessary to inform the students to whom he addressed himself that *Much Ado About Nothing* was written by Shakespeare, and that one of the characters in the play was Benedict, " a young officer."

WHOLESALE CHARITY.

AN attorney in Dublin having died in great poverty, a shilling subscription was set on foot, to pay the expenses of his funeral. Most of the attorneys and barristers having subscribed, one of them applied to Mr. Toler, afterwards Lord Chief Justice Norbury, expressing a hope that he would also subscribe his shilling. " Only a shilling !" said Toler, "only a shilling to bury an attorney ! Here is a guinea ; go and bury one and twenty of them."

"THE GLORIOUS UNCERTAINTY OF THE LAW."

CONCERNING the origin of this oft-quoted phrase I find the following in *Notes and Queries:* " Soon after Lord Mansfield in 1756 had overruled several long-established legal decisions, and introduced innovations in the practice of his court, Mr. Wilbraham, at a dinner of the judges and counsel in Serjeant's Inn hall, gave the toast 'The Glorious Uncertainty of the Law.' In 1802, when the prince regent relinquished his claim to the revenues of the Duchy of Cornwall, Sheridan explained in parliament that his royal highness had been induced to do so by 'the glorious uncertainty of the law.'"

UNRE-*LENT*-ING ZEAL.

LORD MANSFIELD was not attached to religious holidays. He even ordered the doors of his court to be thrown open on Ash Wednesday. This disregard of Lent was by no means pleasing to many. But emboldened by success, it is said that the chief justice proceeded to suggest business on Good Friday. He announced this very eccentric intention in court, probably on the Thursday. Serjeant Davy

upon this addressed the peer on the instant, and told him that
"if it were so, his lordship would be the first judge that had
done it since Pontius Pilate."

TERM TIME *TEMP.* CHARLES I.

WYE SALTONSTALL, who published his *Picturæ
Loquentes, or Pictures drawn forth in Character,* in
1631, gives a delightful picture of the general bustle
incident to term time, a curious painting of old-world life, when
term time was what the season is now : "The term is a time
when Justice keeps open court for all comers, while her sister
Equity strives to mitigate the rigour of her positive sentence.
It is called the term because it does end and terminate
business, or else because it is the *Terminus ad quem,* that is,
the end of the countryman's journey, who comes up to the term,
and with his hob-nailed shoes grinds the faces of the poor
stones, and so returns again. It is the soul of the year, and
makes it quick, which before was dead. Innkeepers gape for it
as earnestly as shell-fish do for salt water after a low ebb. It
sends forth new books into the world, and replenishes Paul's
Walk * with fresh company, where *quid novi?* is their first
salutation, and the weekly news their chief discourse. The
taverns are painted against the term, and many a cause is
argued there, and tried at that bar, where you are adjudged to
pay the cost and charges, and so dismissed with 'Welcome,
gentlemen.' Now the city puts her best side outwards, and a
new play at the Blackfriars is attended on with coaches. It

* The middle of old St. Paul's was the fashionable lounge of that
period. The young gallants from the Inns of Court, the western and
northern parts of the Metropolis, and those who had spirit enough "to
detach themselves from the counting houses in the East," used to meet at
the central point, St. Paul's, and from this circumstance obtained the
appellation of "Paul's Walkers." Tradition says that the great Lord
Bacon was a frequent lounger in this spot in his youth.

keeps watermen from sinking, and helps them with many a fare to Westminster. Your choice beauties come up to it only to see and be seen, and to learn the newest fashions, and for some other recreations. Now money that has long been sick and crazy begins to stir and walk abroad, especially if some young prodigals come to town, who bring more money than wit. Lastly, the term is the joy of the city, a dear friend to country-men, and is never more welcome than after a long vacation."

MANUMITTING VILLAINS.

ABOUT the year 1545 Henry VIII. manumitted two villains in these words, which might have been spoken by Wilberforce himself : " Whereas God created all men free, but afterwards the laws and customs of nations sub-jected some under the yoke of servitude, we think it pious and meritorious with God to manumit Henry Knight, a tailor, and Herle, a husbandman, our natives, as being born within the manor of Stoke Clymmysland, in our county of Cornwall, together with all their goods, lands, and chattels acquired or to be acquired, so as the said persons and their issue shall from henceforth by us be free and of free condition."

FORENSIC PROPRIETY.

MR. JUSTICE JAMES ALLAN PARKER was a great stickler for what he called "forensic propriety," which included the supervision of the personal attire of the members of his court. At Chelmsford Assizes the under sheriff thought fit to indulge in a buff-coloured waistcoat. His lordship eyed him for some time with an angry scowl ; at length he could support it no longer : " Really, sir," he said, " I must beg of you to take off that canary-coloured waistcoat ; I cannot sit here, sir, and behold that waistcoat any longer." Upon another occasion a prosecutor who had moustaches appeared before him to give evidence. " What are you, sir ? " inquired the judge. " A schoolmaster, my lord," was the reply. " A schoolmaster, sir ! Then how dare you come before me with those hairy appendages? Stand down, sir, I shall not allow you your expenses."

At the Winchester Assizes Mr. Commissioner Williams, being leader to the plaintiff in an important case of trespass, rose to open a very well digested speech, but was stopped in his exordium by the worthy judge, who exclaimed : " I really cannot permit it, brother Williams ; I must maintain the forensic dignity of the bar." The advocate looked unutterable things at his lordship, and said, " I do not understand you, my lord." " Oh yes, you do ; you have a very extraordinary wig on, a most extraordinary wig indeed ; really I can't permit it. You must change your wig. Such a wig as that is no part of the costume of this bar, as recognized by the jurisprudence of this highly favoured country."

A LEGAL FICTION.

THE words of the oath administered to the bailiff into whose custody the jurymen are delivered, enjoins them to be locked up for the night without eating or drinking, and " without fire, candlelight excepted." " On such an occasion, I had lately to determine," says Baron Campbell, " whether gas lamps could be considered ' candle-light.' *In favorem vitæ* I ventured to rule in the affirmative, and the night being very cold, to order that the lamps should be liberally supplied with gas ; so that, directly administering *light* according to law, they might, contrary to law, incidentally administer *heat.*" It happened lately, says Mr. Forsyth (*Trial by Jury*), a facetious judge being asked by a juror on retiring whether he might have a glass of water, decided that he might, saying that, in his opinion, water was not drink.

THE HALL OF LINCOLN'S INN.

HE first stone of the present noble hall of Lincoln's Inn was laid on the 20th of April, 1843. It bears the following inscription :—

" Stet lapis, arboribus nudo defixus in horto,
Fundamen pulchræ tempus in omne domus,
Aula vetus lites et legum ænigmata servet,
Ipsa novo exorior nobilitanda Coquo : "

which was humorously translated as follows, by the late Sir George Rose :—

" The trees of yore
Are seen no more :
Unshaded now the garden lies.
May the red bricks,
Which here we fix,
Be lasting as our equities.
The olden dome
With musty tome
Of law and litigation suits :
In this we look
For a better ' cook '
Than he who wrote the ' Institutes.' "

MIXED JOY.

R. MADAN, who about the year 1756, changed his bar gown for a clerical one, was the author of a pamphlet wherein he blamed the mistaken lenity of judges, in too frequently reprieving capital offenders. This gentleman was present some years subsequently, either as a magistrate or as one of the grand jury, at the assizes held at East Grinstead, in Sussex, which proved to be a maiden assizes. On the sheriff expressing his happiness in presenting the white gloves to Lord Mansfield, the chief justice observed : " Mr. Madan too, will, no doubt, have a singular pleasure on this occasion, because there is no condemned prisoner to be reprieved."

THOROUGHNESS.

A RELIGIOUS doubt, entangled with mystical metaphysics, and countenanced by his party, had great attractions for the excitable head and Presbyterian taste of Judge Hermand. What a figure! as he stood on the floor declaiming and screaming amidst the divines—the tall man with his thin powdered locks and long pigtail, the long Court of Sessions cravat, flaccid and streaming with the heat of obtrusive linen! The published report makes him declare that " The belief in the being and perfections of the Deity is the solace and delight of my life. It is a feeling which I sucked in with my mother's milk." But this would not have been half utterly utter enough for Hermand; his words were : " Sir, I sucked in the being and attributes of God with my mother's milk !" His constant and affectionate reverence for his mother exceeded the devotion of an Indian for his idol, and under this feeling he amazed the House by maintaining (which was his real opinion) that there was no apology for infidelity, or even for religious doubt, because no good or sensible man had anything to do except to be of the religion of his mother ; which, be it what it might, was always the best. " A sceptic, sir, I hate ; with my whole heart I detest him ! But, moderator, *I love a Turk.*"

DINNERS AT THE OLD BAILEY.

I T was Lord Stowell who said : " The dining system puts people in a good humour, and makes them agree when they otherwise might not : a dinner lubricates business." Some such thought may have been uppermost in the heads of the worthies who introduced the well-known Old Bailey dinners.

Over the court-room in the Old Bailey is a dining-room, where the judges till recently were in the habit of dining when the court was over, a practice commemorated in the oft-quoted line : "And wretches hang that jurymen may dine." " If we are not misinformed," says an amusing writer in the *Quarterly· Review* for 1836, " the fiat has gone forth already against one class of city dinners, which was altogether peculiar of its kind. We allude to the dinner given by the sheriffs, during the Old Bailey sittings, to the judges and aldermen in attendance, the recorder, common serjeant, city pleaders, and occasionally a few members of the bar. The first course was rather miscellaneous, and varied with the season, though marrow-puddings always formed a part of it ; the second never varied, and consisted exclusively of beefsteaks. The custom was to serve two dinners (exact duplicates) a day, the first at three o'clock, the second at five. As the judges relieved each other it was impracticable for them to partake of both ; but the aldermen often did so, and the chaplain, whose duty it was to preside at the lower end of the table, was never absent from his post. This invaluable public servant persevered, from a sheer sense of duty, till he had acquired the habit of eating two dinners a day, and practised it for nearly ten years without any perceptible injury to his health. We had the pleasure of witnessing his performances at one of the five o'clock dinners, and can assert with con- fidence that the vigour of his attack on the beefsteaks was wholly unimpaired by the effective execution, a friend assured us, he had done on them two hours before. The occasion to which we allude was so remarkable for other reasons, that we have the most distinct recollection of the circumstances. It was the first trial of the late St. John Long for rubbing a young lady into her grave.* The presiding judges were Mr. Justice

---

* St. John Long was a quack doctor, who was on his trial for man- slaughtering a Miss Cashir by giving her a mixture for rubbing on her back, which killed her. For this he was fined £250 on October 23, 1830. On the 10th of November he was again before the court for killing a Mrs. Colin Campbell Lloyd, wife of Captain Lloyd, R.N. The verdict returned was manslaughter through ignorance.

Park and Mr. Baron Garrow, who retired to dinner about five, having first desired the jury, amongst whom there was a difference of opinion, to be locked up. The dinner proceeded merrily, the beefsteaks were renewed again and again, and received the solemn sanction of judicial approbation repeatedly. Mr. Adolphus told some of his best stories, and the chaplain was on the point of being challenged for a song, when the court-keeper appeared with a face of consternation, to announce that the jury, after being very noisy for an hour or so, had sunk into a dull, dead lull, which to the experienced in such matters, augurs the longest period of deliberation which the heads, or rather stomachs, of the jury can endure. The trial had unfortunately taken place upon a Saturday, and it became a serious question in what manner the refractory jurymen were to be dealt with. Mr. Baron Garrow proposed waiting till within a few minutes of twelve and then discharging them. Mr. Justice Park, the senior judge, and a warm admirer of the times when refractory juries were carried round the country in a cart, would hear of no expedient of the kind. He said a judge was not bound to wait beyond a reasonable hour at night, nor to attend before a reasonable hour in the morning; that Sunday was a *dies non* in law, and that a verdict must be delivered in the presence of the judge. He consequently declared his intention of waiting till what he deemed a reasonable hour—namely about ten—and then informing the jury that, if they were not agreed, they must be locked up, without food, drink, or fire, until a reasonable hour—about nine—on the Monday, by which time he trusted they would be unanimous. The effect of such an intimation was not put to the test, for St. John Long was found guilty about nine. We are sorry to be obliged to add that the worthy chaplain's digestion has at length proved unequal to the double burden imposed upon it; but the court of aldermen, considering him a martyr to their cause, have very properly agreed to grant him an adequate pension for his services."

In 1807–8 the dinners for three sessions, nineteen days, cost Sheriff Phillips and his colleague £35 per day—£665 ; 145 dozen of wine were consumed at these dinners, costing an additional £450. These dinners were discontinued about 1877.

LAWS, THEIR MEAN.

" IN making laws," said Lord Keeper Finch, "it will import us to consider, that too many laws are a snare, too few are a weakness in the government ; too gentle are seldom obeyed, too severe are seldom executed ; and sanguinary laws are, for the most part, either the cause or the effect of a distemper in the State."

REMEDY AGAINST CHOLERA.

WHEN Lord Thurlow was lord chancellor, Mr. Pepper Arden was master of the rolls. The chancellor greatly disliked Mr. Arden, and frequently showed his distaste with little mitigation. When a messenger once went with his honour's request and regrets that he was too ill to sit at the Rolls, the superior judge demanded in a voice of thunder : " What ails him ? " " Please, your lordship, he is laid up with the English cholera." " Let him take an Act of Parliament "— retorted the ungracious chancellor, with one of those amiable wishes for his organs of vision in which he was in the habit of indulging. " Let him try to swallow that, there is nothing so binding."

THE LAWYER'S BEST FRIEND.

AT a provincial law society's dinner, not long ago, the president called upon the senior attorney to give as a toast the person whom he considered the best friend of the profession. " Certainly," was the response, " The man who makes his own will."

CURIOUS EQUIVOCATION.

IN Siderfin's "Collection of Special Cases" in the reign of Charles II., it is related that a question arose in a marriage agreement (Hookes *v.* Swaine). Plaintiff having undertaken to pay to his son-in-law and daughter the sum of £20 per annum, demurred that the words "per annum" should signify for one year only. The court justly opined that the words meant that maintenance in question should be paid as long as the marriage lasted. Justice Twisden on that occasion related a "nice case" he remembered. A certain Sir William Fish was bound by obligation to pay on a certain day, in Gray's Inn Hall, £50. As the bond did not specify fifty pounds *sterling*, Sir William came into the hall on the day appointed whilst the gentlemen were at supper, tendered fifty pounds weight of stone, and adjudged no tender.

CAPITAL PUNISHMENT.

WHENEVER an execution of some remarkable criminal takes place, the question of capital punishment is sure to crop up. Opinion is greatly divided as to the justice of the death penalty—at present never enforced but in extreme cases. Between fifty and sixty years ago the annual average of executions in England amounted to nearly one hundred, but with the passing of milder laws the number has happily decreased. A glance at the statistics of murder in England and Wales, compiled from the returns of coroners' juries, will show how comparatively seldom the hangman is now called in. For twenty years past the number of culpable homicides, from year's end to year's end, has maintained a remarkably equal average of rather more than two hundred, the highest and lowest figures being two hundred and fifty-seven in 1872, and two hundred in 1875. Attribute the fact to what cause we may, draw every possible deduction from the figures, and the result remains that every succeeding twelve months produces ¸almost the same number of homicides, with but very little variation. During the past fifteen years education has been gradually spreading over the land, material prosperity and refinement have vastly increased. The spirit of gentleness and of culture has permeated downwards, until an ordinary mob of to-day is far less brutal than a similar crowd in the third quarter of the century ; but still, the annual interval between the beginning of spring and the end of winter time produces its comparatively equal tale of murders. How is this sum to be lessened? That is the problem with which statesmen and philanthropists have to deal.

COOL, RATHER.

CHIEF JUSTICE WILLES, of the Common Pleas, though a good lawyer, was scarcely fitted by his habits and character for the high post to which he was appointed. Nor would he readily tolerate the impertinence of any one who ventured to remind him of the inconsistency of his conduct with the dignity he ought to observe on account of his judicial character. It is told by Horace Walpole, who was inclined to be one of his admirers, that a grave person once called on this chief justice to apprize him that certain scandals were reported, impeaching his moral character, particularly the fact of one of his maid-servants being in an interesting position. "Well, sir," replied Willes, coolly, "and what is that to me?" "Oh! my lord, but they blame you for it." "Well, sir, and what's that to you?" was the reply of the chief justice ; the volunteer monitor thought the case hopeless, and left the room.

DIFFERENCES BETWEEN OATHS.

HE oaths used formerly among the Scotch Highlanders in judicial proceedings, contained a most solemn denunciation of vengeance in case of perjury, involving the wife and children, with the arable land and meadow land of the party who took it, altogether in one abyss of destruction. When it was administered, there was no book to be kissed, but the right hand was held up while the oath was repeated. The superior idea of sanctity which this imprecation conveyed to those accustomed to it, may be judged from the expression of a Highlander who at a trial at Carlisle had sworn positively in the English mode to a fact of consequence. His indifference during that solemnity having been observed by the opposite counsel, he was required to confirm his testimony by taking the oath to the same according to the custom of his native hills : " Na, na," said the mountaineer, " ken ye nae thar is a hantle o' difference 'twixt blawing on a buke and domming ane's ain saul ?"

OUTLIVING THE LAW.

HEN old Sir John Maynard waited upon William III. with an address and congratulation from the gentlemen of the bar, the king complimented the old man on his looking so well at his advanced age, adding that he had outlived most of his brother lawyers : " Yes, sire," replied the serjeant, " that is quite true ; and had it not been for your Majesty's arrival, I should have outlived the law itself."

NO SPIDERS IN WESTMINSTER HALL.

"THUS it has been the complaint of all ages," says Godfrey Goodman, one of the chaplains to Queen Anne of Denmark (wife of James I.), in his work *The Fall of Man*, "' Leges esse telas aranearum, vel quia juridici sunt araneæ, vel quia mureas capiunt, et vespas dimittunt.' But I am not of their mind ; for I think that God in his providence hath so fitly ordained it, as prophesying or prescribing a lesson, that the timber in Westminster Hall should neither admit cobweb nor spider : * and God make us thankful for the free course of our justice."

This pleasing application of a very ancient remark, for the comparison of law to cobwebs, which catch the weak but which the strong break through, is attributed by Plutarch to Anacharsis,† who is supposed to have applied this dictum to the laws of Solon. Diogenes Laertius ascribes the saying to Solon himself,‡ whilst Stobæus § names the Locrian legislator Zaleucus as the author. Plato, the comic poet, versified the idea as follows :—

Εἴξασιν ἡμῖν οἱ νόμοι τούτοισι τοῖσι λεπτοῖς
Ἀραχνίοις, ἃν τοῖσι τοίχοις ἡ φάλαγξ ὑφαίνει.
Meinecke, *Fragm. Com. Gr.*, vol. ii. p. 620.

SAT CITO SI SAT BENE.

SIR THOMAS CLARKE, master of the rolls, observed, "There are two things against which a judge ought to guard : precipitancy and procrastination. Sir Nicholas Bacon was made to say—which I hope never to hear

* Fuller speaks of the " cobwebless beams " of Westminster Hall. It is a vulgar belief that it was built of a particular kind of wood—Irish oak— in which, thanks to St. Patrick, spiders cannot live.
† Plutarch, *Sol.* 5, followed by Valer. Maxim. vii. 2, 14.
‡ Diog. Laert. i. 58.
§ Stobæus, *Serm.* xlv. 25, also Theophilact. *Epist.* p. 37.

again—that a speedy injustice is as good as justice which is slow." Certainly a most scandalous maxim.

Sir Thomas More, when he took his seat for the first time in the Court of Chancery, addressing the bar and audience, said: " I ascend this seat as a place full of labour and danger, void of all solid and true honour, the which, by how much the higher it is, by so much greater fall I am to fear." Laborious indeed ·it was ; but Sir Thomas was so indefatigable, that although he found the office filled with causes, some of which had been pending for thirty years, he despatched the whole within two years. Calling for the rest, he was told that there was not one case left, a circumstance which he ordered, with just pride, to be entered on record, and which has been commemorated in the following prophetic and punning epigram :—

> " When More two years had chancellor been,
>   No *more* suits did remain.
> The same shall never *more* be seen,
>   Till More be there again."

Lord Lyndhurst used to say that a chancellor's work may be divided into three classes : first, the business that is with labour done ; second, that which does itself ; third, the work which is not done at all.

SUBMISSIVENESS OF THE BAR.

SO low in point of independence was the profession of the bar in the time of Henry VI., that in the case respecting precedence between the Earl of Warwick and the Earl Marshall, both the advocates for the parties, viz., Sir Walter Beauchamp (the first lawyer, by the bye, who ever wore the spurs of knighthood in England) and Roger Hunt, made most humble protestations, each entreating the peer against whom he was retained not to take amiss what he might be obliged to advance on the part of his client.

Hume, in his *History of England*, speaking of a later period, says : " That the answers given into court by the famous Prynne and his associates, were so full of invectives against the prelates that no lawyer could be prevailed on to sign them." The truth, however, is, that the lawyers allowed themselves to be intimidated by the menaces of the court from defending them at all. Mr. Holt, one of their number, signed Prynne's answer, and was actually told by Lord Chief Justice Finch that " he deserved to have his gown pulled over his ears, for drawing it," though it contained nothing but mere explanations of points of facts, and a dry recital of Acts of Parliament. Afterwards, when it was expunged by order of the judges, and another prepared, Mr. Holt, in excuse for not signing the second, being appealed to by Prynne in open court, submissively replied, that *" he durst not set his hand to it, for fear of giving their honours distaste."*

CURIOUS CASE OF KLEPTOMANIA.

IN 1819 Elizabeth Dunham was tried at the Old Bailey on a charge of stealing two keys, the property of the governor and company of the Bank of England. The prisoner pleaded guilty to the fact of taking the keys, but denied that it was theft. She was respectably dressed, and while Mr. Bosanquet (afterwards Sir John Bernard Bosanquet), a judge of the Court of Common Pleas, was stating the case, appeared to pay great attention to him. He said the only object of the bank in bringing forward this prosecution was, that the prisoner might be sent to a place where she could be taken care of. It appeared that when her room was searched, there were found not less than four thousand keys, all of which were labelled, except about two hundred. Among them were the keys of the Church Missionary Society, Bell's Buildings, of the counting-house of the Duke of York's School, the padlock of Greenwich watch-house ; the key of the College of Physicians ; of the Royal Exchange ; the Temple Stairs ; the

County Prison, Maidstone; the Council Room, Guildhall, and many others. They were all ticketed, and the day carefully recorded on which they were taken.

Shackwell, the porter of the bank, was called for the purpose of identifying the keys, which having been done, the prisoner requested that they might be put into her hands for the purpose of ascertaining whether they were the same found in her room. This being allowed, the moment the poor woman got them into her possession, she exclaimed with an air of triumph, " Now I have got them, I will hold them for the rights of my king, my country, and myself." She then wrapped them up carefully in a pocket-handkerchief, and said nothing should induce her to give them up but a free pardon from the Prince Regent. Being called upon for her defence, she said she had done all this ; that she had taken all the keys for her own rights, which she could not otherwise obtain. She thought that by doing so she would secure her own rights as well as those of her country, as the persons who owned them would thereby come forward and do her justice. The jury, under the direction of the court, acquitted the prisoner upon the ground of insanity, and she was remanded to safe custody.

THE COST OF AN EXECUTION.

TO the Right Honourable the Lord Commissioners of His Majesty's Treasury.

The humble petition of Ralph Griffin, Esq., High Sheriff of the County of Flint, for the present year 1769, concerning the execution of Edward Edwards for burglary :—

Sheweth

That your petitioner was at great difficulty and expense by himself, his clerks, and other messengers and agents he employed in journeys to Liverpool and Shrewsbury, to hire an executioner ; the convict being a native of Wales it was almost impossible to procure any of that country to undertake the execution.

	£	s.
Travelling and other expenses on that occasion	15	10
A man at Salop engaged to do this business. Gave him in part .	5	5
Two men for conducting him, and for their search of him on his deserting from them on the road, and charges on inquiring for another executioner	4	10
After much trouble and expense, John Babington, a convict in the same prison with Edwards, was by means of his wife prevailed on to execute his fellow-prisoner. Gave to the wife . . .	6	6
And to Babington	6	6
Paid for erecting a gallows, materials and labour : a business very difficult to be done in this country	4	12
For the hire of a cart to convey the body, a coffin, and for the burial	2	10
And for other assistance, trouble, and petty expenses on the occasion, at least	5	0
Total £49		19

Which humbly hope your lordships will please to allow your petitioners, who etc.

LEGAL DISPATCH.

AN instance of summary punishment occurred in Derby in 1814. A man was detected picking a pocket. He was taken into custody, the property found upon him, carried before a judge, a bill found by the grand jury which was then sitting. He was tried, convicted, and sentenced to transportation, all within two hours of the commission of the crime.

TWELVE GOOD MEN AND TRUE.

SERJEANT PRIME, without having the slightest conception of humour, yet frequently convulsed the court with laughter. Ridicule did not detract from his real merits as an able advocate. He would tell his facts before the jury " dryly, but weightily," as he found them in his brief. Speaking upon one occasion, he first extolled his own witnesses, and then hastened to depreciate those of his adversary. Having thus called attention to his " gentlemen of repute," " What," said he " is the enemy's battle array ?

> " Two butchers and a tailor,
> Three hackney-coachmen and a corn-cutter,
> But in the rear of the column,
> An alderman of London *solus*."

COMPARISONS ARE ODIOUS.

URRAN, in describing a speech made by Serjeant Hewitt, said, " The learned serjeant's speech put me exactly in mind of a familiar utensil in domestic use, commonly called an 'extinguisher.' It began at a point, and on it went, widening and widening, until at last it fairly put the question out altogether."

REASONABLE GRIEF.

ERJEANT HILL—" Blackletter Hill," as he was called, from his great knowledge of "blackletter law"—married a wealthy heiress, Miss Medlycott, of Cottingham, Northamptonshire. The pair are said to have lived very happily together. " One day," Lord Eldon says, " when I was attorney-general, I met him upon our staircase, after the long vacation, and he addressed me thus : ' My dear friend, you will be shocked to hear what a loss I have sustained since I saw you.' I expressed great concern that anything should have happened which he had so much cause to lament. ' Oh ! ' he said, ' I never had so much cause of grief, or suffered such a calamity.' Before I could express another word, he continued : ' I have lost poor dear Mrs. Hill.' And then pausing for some time, during which I felt greatly and painfully on his account, he at last broke silence, saying, ' I don't know, though, that the loss *was* so great, for she had all her property, Mr. Attorney, to her separate use.' "

A friend called upon the serjeant, to condole with him upon his loss. He found the serjeant sitting very sorrowful and disconsolate. At last he said, " So, poor woman, you find she is gone ! " " Yes, sir ; I merely called to condole with you upon the melancholy occasion." " Ay, she is gone ! But I'll tell you one thing, Mr. ——, if I should ever be induced to take another wife, I would not marry merely for money." The subject was the same, the lament was toned on the same string.

NAUTICAL TERMS.

LORD MANSFIELD, trying an action which arose from a collision at sea, a sailor, appearing as a witness, said, " I was standing abaft the binnacle,——" " Where is ' abaft the binnacle ' ? " inquired Lord Mansfield ; upon which the witness, who had primed himself with strong liquor before coming to court, soliloquized, loud enough to be heard by all present, " A pretty fellow to be a judge, who does not even know where abaft the binnacle is ! " Lord Mansfield, instead of threatening to commit him for contempt, said, " Well, my friend, fit me for my office by telling me where ' abaft the binnacle ' is ; you have already shown me the meaning of ' half seas over.' "

QUICKNESS.

ONE of the best retorts Jeffreys ever received was from a lady, whom he cross-examined in his usual insolent way. Jeffreys' wife had been confined a very short time after her marriage, which excited much ridicule when it became known. Her husband was, shortly after this unfortunate occurrence, cross-examining a fair witness, who gave her evidence

R

with tolerable sharpness. He said, " Madam, you are very quick in your answers." "Quick as I am, Sir George," she replied, " I am not so quick as your lady ! "

PRACTICAL JOKING IN COURT.

AT present no counsel would venture to act as Mr. Newnham, an eminent advocate of the last age, is related, in Serjeant Cradock's *Memoirs*, to have acted towards him. In former times it was the custom at Leicester to have an assize ball, at which, of course, the high sheriff was present. On one occasion, Mr. Cradock, who filled this office, attended the ball, as usual, and did not leave it until it was very late. As he had to dress and wait on the judge very early in the morning, he had not much sleep that night. Next morning, when the judge had taken his seat, Mr. Newnham stood up and said, " My lord, the high sheriff has only been in bed for about an hour, I understand, and I am sure he would be very happy to return to his lodgings, if your lordship would please to dispense with his attendance." Mr. Cradock both felt and looked excessively embarrassed, having never said a word on the subject. The judge looked very condescending, and the court laughed, while Mr. Newnham stood by, enjoying the high sheriff's embarrassment.

LAW FORM-ALITIES.

LORD NORBURY'S law extended scarcely beyond the names of cases, whence he was induced little to respect, and, indeed, sometimes to ridicule, any display of it in others. An entire day having been consumed in very learned argument, he thus wound up a judgment, which, it may readily be affirmed, scarcely deserved that character : " I must say, in conclusion, that counsel have done their duty. They are

not merely all good, but they are all best. I can make no distinctions. However, as to their cases, and their crotchets, and their
quiddities, and their knotty points, they are, every one of them,
like a hare in Tipperary, to be found in *Fern* (Fearne, *Essay on
Contingent Remainders*).

RETENTIVE MEMORY.

MANY great and eminent lawyers have been distinguished
for a retentive memory. Lord Eldon said of Lord
Chief Justice de Grey (Lord Walsingham), who was a
most accomplished lawyer, and of a most extraordinary power
of memory : " I have seen him come into court with both hands
wrapped up in flannel (from gout). He could take no notes,
and had no one to do so for him. I have known him try a cause
which lasted nine or ten hours, and then, from memory, sum up
all the evidence with the greatest correctness."

William Saurin, a member of the Irish bar, was likewise
gifted with a most retentive memory. On one occasion, a fore-
closure suit in Chancery, in which he was retained, came on
for hearing, Mr. Saurin having to state the client's case. The
property was greatly involved ; there were many titles to be
traced, and various denominations of land, with very jaw-
breaking names, as Garrycaghera, Bouladarrigha, Courawad-
lagh, etc. When the cause was called, Mr. Saurin pulled brief
after brief from his huge bag, until he emptied it on the table
in the Court of Chancery. Then leaning over to his apprentice
he whispered, " Have you got the prayer of the bill ? " The
youth handed a paper to him, and opening one of the large
briefs, Saurin commenced his statement. On he went, clear
and precise, with the enumeration of titles and denominations
of land, and nature of incumbrances, until he completed the
statement. Then the proofs were read, and when the decree
was pronounced, and the case over, the apprentice said, " I'll
take your brief home, Mr. Saurin." He smiled as he replied, " It

is on my study table. I was noting it since daybreak, and
forgot it as I was leaving home ; but you see I did not forget its
contents."

LETTERS IN THE TEMPLE.

"APOLLO and Littleton," says an ancient poet, "meet
seldom in the same brain ;" and Wycherley, himself
a Templar, puts the same idea in the address of Old
Fox to the Widow Blackacre : "O lady, lady, all interruption
and no sense between us, as if we were lawyers at the bar ; but,
I had forgot, Apollo and Littleton never lodge in a head together." This may be true in the main ; perhaps it is the rule ;
but exceptions are manifold and brilliant. Nor can I think of
any other profession which has been able to inscribe so many
glorious names in the annals of the literature of this country.
Lord Coke, that revered Nestor of our law, has, indeed, himself
expressly recommended the study of poetry to the diligent fol-
lower of Themis. "Verses at first," he says, "were invented
for the help of memory, and it standeth well with the gravity of
our lawyers to cite them" (*Inst.* 237*a*). So again : "Authori-
tates philosophorum, medicorum et poetarum sunt in causis
allegandæ et tenendæ " (*Id.* 264*a*). Chaucer is thought to have
been of the Temple. But this assertion rests merely on the
word of an unknown Mr. Buckley, who told Speght, the editor
of Chaucer's works, that he had seen "the great poet's " name
in the Temple records. The Temple, however, can afford to let
such a problematical connection slip ; sufficiently well-authen-
ticated names remain. The first English tragedy of any merit,
Gordobuc, was written in the Temple, by Thomas Norton and
Thomas Sackville, the latter a celebrated statesman, and founder
of the title of Dorset. He was also author of a noble work, the
Induction for the Mirror of Magistrates, in which there is a
foretaste of the allegorical imagination of Spenser. Sir John
Davies, afterwards Lord Chief Justice of the King's Bench, wrote

Orchestra; or, a Poem on the Art of Dancing (so lively was the gravity of those days), and a more celebrated one on the *Immortality of the Soul.* His contemporary, Sir Walter Raleigh, was a Templar ; Selden, Lord Clarendon, Beaumont, two others of our old dramatists, Ford and Marston, the latter of whom was lecturer of the Middle Temple ; Wycherley, whom it is said the Duchess of Cleveland used to visit, disguised as a milliner ; Congreve, Rowe, Fielding, Burke, Cowper, and not a few in more modern times. These form a galaxy of names which certainly shed a radiant lustre round

> " those bricky towers
> The which on Thames' broad aged back do ride,
> Wherein the lawyers have their bowers."

LIFE BEFORE FASHION.

THOUGH Lord Mansfield has never been credited with lively sensibilities, yet on one occasion he ordered a jury to find that a stolen trinket was of less value than forty shillings, in order that the thief might escape the capital sentence. The prosecutor, a jeweller, was so mortified by the Judge's leniency, that he exclaimed : "What, my lord, my gold trinket not worth forty shillings ? Why the fashion alone cost me twice the money !" Removing his glance from the vindictive tradesman, Lord Mansfield turned towards the jury, and said, with solemn gravity : "As we stand in need of God's mercy, gentlemen, let us not hang a man for fashion's sake."

DAILY ARRIVAL OF FRESH LAW.

THERE are no regular reports of the Irish cases. All the new authorities are imported from England ; so that the accident of a fair or foul wind may sometimes affect the decision of a cause. "Are you sure, Mr. Plunkett," said Lord Manners one day, "that what you have stated is the law?" "It unquestionably was the law half an hour ago," replied Plunkett, pulling out his watch, "but by this time the packet has probably arrived, and I shall not be positive."

UNRULY LIMBS OF THE LAW.

P to the last years of the reign of Charles II., the space to the north and west of Holborn consisted in fields and meadows, enjoying an unbroken prospect to the hills of Hampstead and Highgate, intersected by hedgerows and green lanes, through which the lawyers of the adjoining Gray's Inn and Lincoln's Inn used to saunter, conning over their Coke upon Littleton, or may be some lighter literature. But in the last year of the reign of the merry monarch, brick and mortar began to assert itself in these pleasant places, greatly to the dismay of the men of law. Under date June 10, 1684, Narcissus Luttrell wrote in his diary : "Dr. Barebone, the great builder, having some time since bought the Red Lion fields, near Gray's Inn walks, to build on, and having for that purpose employed several workmen to go on with the same, the gentlemen of Gray's Inn took notice of it, and thinking it an injury to them, went with a considerable body of one hundred persons, upon which the workmen assaulted the gentlemen, and flung bricks at them, and the gentlemen at them again. So a sharp engagement ensued, but the gentlemen routed them at last, and brought away one or two of the workmen to Gray's Inn. In this skirmish one or two of the gentlemen of the house were hurt, and several of the workmen."

A NEEDLE CASE.

NE of Jekyll's happy sayings was uttered at Exeter, when he defended several needlemen who were charged with raising a riot for the purpose of forcing master tailors to give higher wages. Whilst Jekyll was examining a witness as to the number of tailors present at the alleged riot, Lord Eldon—the Chief Justice of the Common Pleas—reminded him that three persons can make that which the law regards as a riot ; whereupon the witty advocate answered, "Yes, my lord, Hale and Hawkins lay down the law as your lordship states it, and I rely on their authority ; for if there must be three men to make a riot, the rioters being *tailors*, there must be nine times three present, and unless the prosecutors make out that there were twenty-seven joining in this breach of the peace, my clients are entitled to an acquittal." On Lord Eldon inquiring whether he relied on common law or statute law, the counsel for the defence answered firmly : "My lord, I relie on a well-known maxim, as old as Magna Charta, '*Nine* tailors make a man.'" Finding themselves unable to reward a lawyer for so good a oke with an adverse verdict, the jury acquitted the prisoners.

AN ATTORNEY SCARED.

OSEPH YATES—the puisne judge whom Mansfield's jeers and merciless oppression drove from the King's Bench to the Common Pleas, where he died within four months of his retreat—was the finest of fine gentlemen. Before he had demonstrated his professional capacity, the habitual costliness and delicacy of his attire roused the distrust of attorneys, and on more than one occasion wrought him injury. An awkward, crusty, case-hardened attorney one day entered the foppish barrister's chambers with a bundle of papers, and on seeing the young man in a superb, elaborate evening dress, inquired, "Can you say, sir, when Mr. Yates will return?" "Return, my good sir?" answered the barrister, with an air of surprise, "I am Mr. Yates, and it will give me the greatest pleasure to talk with you about these papers." Having taken a deliberate survey of th young Templar, and made a mental inventory of all the fantastic articles of his apparel, the honest attorney gave an ominous grunt, replaced the papers in one of the deep pockets of his long skirted coat, twice nodded his head with contemptuous significance, and then, without another word, walked out of the room. It was his first visit to those chambers, and his last.

ST. IVO, THE LAWYERS' PATRON SAINT.

THE following anecdote occurs in Carr's *Remarks of the Government of the Several Parts of Germany, Denmark,* etc., printed at Amsterdam in 1688. "Give me leave to tell you a story I met with when I lived in Rome. Going with a Roman to see some antiquities, he showed me a chapel dedicated to St. Evona, a lawyer of Brittany, who he said came to Rome to entreat the Pope to give the lawyers of Brittany a patron, to which the Pope replied that he knew of no saint but what was disposed of to other professions. At which Evona was very sad, and earnestly begged of the Pope to think of one for him. At last the Pope proposed to St. Evona that he should go round the Church of St. John he Lateran blindfold, and after he had said so many Ave Marias, that the first saint he laid hold of should be his patron, which the good old lawyer willingly undertook. And at the end of his Ave Marias, he stopped at St. Michael's altar, where he laid hold of the devil, under St. Michael's feet, and cried out : 'This is our saint ; let him be our patron !' So being unblindfolded and seeing what a patron saint he had chosen, he went to his lodgings so dejected, that in a few months after he died, and coming to heaven's gates he knocked hard. Whereupon St. Peter asked who it was that knocked so boldly. He replied that he was St. Evona, an advocate. 'Away, away,' said St. Peter, 'here is but one Advocate in heaven; here is no room for you lawyers.' 'Oh, but,' said St. Evona, 'I am that honest lawyer who never took fees on both sides, or pleaded in a bad cause, nor did I ever set my neighbours together by the ears, or lived by the sins of the people.' 'Well then,' said St. Peter, 'come in.' This news coming down to Rome, a witty poet wrote upon St. Evona's tomb these words—

'St. Evona, un Breton,
Avocat non larron,
Hallelujah.'"

Such the legend. More particulars concerning St. Ivo, "the advocate of the poor," are to be gathered from Baronius, vol. xxiv. p. 498, and the *Acta Sanctorum*, vol. iv. p. 332. The festival of this saint falls on May 19, on which date the Acta give the following notes concerning this honest lawyer. Ivo Haclory was born at Issoire, in Auvergne. From "very trustworthy reports of his life," we gather that he devoted himself from his infancy entirely to the Lord, and having acquired great learning he was appointed a Justice in the Ecclesiastical Court, by the Bishop of Trecœur in Brittany. He always gave judgment with the highest integrity, and as often as he pronounced a rather heavy sentence, he was observed to shed tears. Subsequently he retired from forensic business, and took up the ministration of a parish, in which capacity he exhibited singular care of the souls entrusted to his keeping. Nor did he forget his former profession, for whenever one of his poor parishioners was involved in a lawsuit, if his cause was just he would defend him without accepting any remuneration. Indeed his love towards the poor was so extensive that he exhausted his own resources in their support, till at last, in a time of famine, he had nothing left but a few loaves to share with his poor. But the Lord did not forsake him, for the loaves were multiplied miraculously. Not content with practising virtue, Ivo mortified his very chaste flesh by assiduous fasting, a very hard bed, and voluntary chastisements; at the same time he constantly refreshed his mind by the contemplation of heavenly things, by which virtues he acquired divine grace, and great miracles were worked by his prayer. At the intercession of John, Duke of Brittany, and the clergy of that dukedom, Ivo was ranked among the number of the *beati* by Clement VI., and subsequently canonized by Johannes XXII. in 1330, at the request of Philip, King of France, and his Queen, Guy, Duke of Brittany, and the clergy of the diocese of Bayeux. Miracles are said to have been worked at his tomb.

"NOT THE CHEESE."

JUSTICE SHELLEY, in the sixteenth century, seems to have been somewhat of a humourist on the Bench. A case which he thought overlaboured beyond its merits, he compared to a Banbury cheese, which is worth little in substance when the parings are cut off; "for so this case," said he, "is brief, if the superfluous trifling which is on the pleadings be taken away."

EXTREMES MEET.

THE law's delays were much more general in former times than at the present day, and little effort was made to fetch up arrears. During the Chancellorship of Lord Eldon, the business of the Court of Chancery progressed but slowly, notwithstanding that the proverbial dilatoriness, hesitation, and dubitation displayed by his lordship in his decisions, were more than counterbalanced by the expeditiousness of his colleague, Vice-Chancellor Sir John Leach, who was notorious for the swiftness with which he disposed of the business which came before him. In comparing his summary judgments with Lord Eldon's proverbial delays, the Chancellor's Court was designated the Court of *Oyer sans Terminer,* and Sir John's that of *Terminer sans Oyer.* The following epigram wittily describes the contrast :—

> "In Equity's high court there are
> Two sad extremes, 'tis clear ;
> Excessive slowness strikes us there,
> Excessive quickness here.

> Their source, twixt good and evil, brings
>   A difficulty nice.
> The first from Eldon's virtue springs,
>   The latter from his *Vice.*"

EARLY DAYS OF LORD CHANCELLOR HARDWICKE.

PHILIP YORKE, the great Lord Chancellor Hardwicke, was articled, without a fee, it is said, to an attorney named Salkeld, in Brooke Street, Holborn. It was rather against the wish of his mother, who was a rigid Presbyterian. She expressed a strong wish "that Philip should be put apprentice to some *honester trade;*" and sometimes she declared her ambition to be "that she might see his head wag in a pulpit." However, an offer having been made by Mr. Salkeld, she withdrew her objections, and Philip was transferred to the metropolis, to exhibit "a rare instance of great natural abilities, joined with an early resolution to rise in the world, and aided by singular good luck." He had received an imperfect education—his family being in narrow circumstances —and whilst applying to business with the most extraordinary assiduity, he employed every leisure moment in endeavouring to supply the defects of his early training. "All lawyers' clerks," says Lord Campbell, in his *Lives of the Lord Chancellors,* "were then obliged, in a certain degree, to understand Latin, in which many law proceedings were carried on ; but he, not content with being able to construe 'the chirographs of a fine,'* or to draw a *Nar,*† took delight in perusing Virgil and Cicero, and made himself well acquainted with the other more popular Roman classics, though he never mastered the minutiæ of Latin prosody, and, for fear of a false quantity, ventured with diffidence

---

* Record of a fictitious suit, resorted to for the purpose of docking estates tail, and quieting the title to lands.

† Familiar contraction of *Narratio,* the declaration or statement of the plaintiff's grievances or cause of action.

and trembling on a Latin quotation. Greek he hardly affected to be acquainted with."

By his assiduity he gained the entire goodwill and esteem of his master, who, observing in him abilities and application that prognosticated his future eminence, entered him as a student in the Temple, and suffered him to dine in the Hall during the Terms. But his master's wife, a notable woman, thinking she might take some liberties with a *gratis clerk*, used frequently to send him from his business on domestic errands, and to fetch in little necessaries from Covent Garden, and other markets. This, when he became a favourite with his master, and entrusted with his business and cash, he thought an indignity, and put an end to by a stratagem which prevented complaints or expostulation In his accounts with his master there frequently occurred "*Coach hire for roots of celery and turnips from Covent Garden, and a barrel of oisters from the fishmonger's*," etc.* This Mr. Salkeld observed, and urging on his wife the impropriety and ill-housewifery of such practice, put an end to it.

In Brooke Street Philip Yorke—

> " Three years he sat his smoky room in,
> Pens, paper, ink, and pounce consumin' ; "

when Mr. Salkeld, having been asked by Lord Chief Justice Parker if he knew a decent and intelligent person who might assist as a sort of law tutor for his sons, the attorney eagerly recommended his favourite clerk, Philip. He was immediately retained to assist and direct the youths in their professional studies, and giving the highest satisfaction by his assiduity and obliging manners, gained the warm friendship of the sons, and the weighty, persevering, and unscrupulous patronage of the father. He rose by gradual steps to the Lord Chancellor-ship, an office which he held for twenty years. His reputation

---

* A similar story is told of Lord Kenyon, but in his instance it was a cauliflower carried triumphantly home in a sedan chair, at a legal charge of 1s. 6d.

as a judge was very high. During his Chancellorship not one of his decisions was set aside, and only three were tried on appeal.

TWO SOVEREIGNS.

THE following smart reply to a brow-beating lawyer is historical, and was given in a court of justice in Liverpool, some time in July, 1865. A poor illiterate Irishwoman came forward to prosecute another female, who had robbed her of some twenty-eight shillings. A lawyer who prided himself on his oratorical powers, and his knowledge of common and statute law, rose up to cross-examine the poor unsophisticated daughter of the green island, he being engaged to defend the prisoner, when the following dialogue took place :—Lawyer : " Tell me, good woman, what sort of money had you?" Witness : "Eight shillings in silver, and a sovereign in gold." Lawyer (drawing himself up in the full dignity of forensic elevation) : " Now, tell me, good woman, did you ever see a sovereign in anything else but gold?" The poor woman looked the very personification of humility, but replied without the least hesitation, " Oh yes, your honour ; I saw Queen Victoria, God bless her !" Laughter in court, culminating in an absolute cheer, followed the answer. The lawyer sat down, and was silent afterwards for more than half an hour.

SUBTILITAS LEGUM.

THE present Lord Chief Justice of the Court of Queen's Bench thus discourses on the subtilty of the law :—
" An amusing instance of this *subtilitas* is given by Gaius, in the case of a man who brought an action against another, on a Law of the Twelve Tables, for cutting down his vines. The plaintiff proved the fact, but he was defeated, or, as we should say, non-suited, because the law, in giving the action, had spoken

only of cutting down *trees,* and it was held that the plaintiff ought to have followed the words of the law. I take it there is nothing to beat this to be found in Meeson and Welsby. No wonder that Gaius, speaking of the old legal actions, is led to say : ' Sed istæ omnes legis actiones paulatim in odium venerunt. Namque ex nimia subtilitate veterum eo res perducta est, ut qui nimium errasset litem perderet.' Of this, indeed, the volumes of Meeson and Welsby might furnish us with instances in abundance."

JEFFREYS' LAW.

THE coarseness and tyranny of Justice Jeffreys is well known. One day he is reported to have broken loose upon Serjeant Maynard, one of the most learned lawyers of his time, who had been his instructor, and who was then mellow with age. " You have grown so old as to forget the law, Brother Maynard," was his amiable apostrophe. " 'Tis true, Sir George," was the reply; " I have forgotten more law than ever you knew."

THE HANGING JUDGE.

JOHN PHILPOT CURRAN, the witty and eloquent Irish barrister, was dining one day with Baron Toler (Lord Norbury), who, from the severity of his sentences, was called " the Hanging Judge," and of whom it was said that he had never been seen to shed a tear but once, and that was when, at a performance of " The Beggar's Opera," he saw Macheath get a reprieve. " Pray, Mr. Curran," said the judge, " is that hung beef beside you ? If so, I will try it." Curran's ready reply was : " If you try it, my lord, it's sure to be hung."

GODLY BUTCHERY.

HE horrible punishment formerly inflicted on commoners for high treason was : " That the traitor is to be taken from the prison, and laid upon a sledge or hurdle,* and drawn to the gallows, or place of execution, and then hanged by the neck, until he be half dead, and then cut down ; his entrails to be cut out of his body, and burnt by the executioners ; then his head is to be cut off, his body to be divided into quarters, and afterwards his head and quarters are to be set up in some open places directed," which usually were on the city gates, on London Bridge, or upon Westminster Hall. And to render the crime more heinous to the spectators, the hangman when he took out the heart, showed it to the people, saying, " Here is the heart of a traitor." This sentence was only humanized in the time of George III., by the exertions of Sir Samuel Romilly, which were for a long time baffled by the protest of the Crown officers, " that he was breaking down the bulwarks of the Constitution."

Lord Coke (3 *Inst.* 211), in detailing this butchery, finds conelusive authorities for each act in the Bible. The drawing is justified by 1 Kings ii. 28 ; the hanging, by Esther ii. 23. The embowelling is sanctioned by the circumstances attending the fate of Judas, Acts i. 18. For the extraction of the criminal's heart, he finds authority in 2 Sam. xviii. 14, 15. The beheading he holds justified by 2 Sam. xx. 22 ; and he cites 2 Sam. iv. 11, 12, as authorizing the practice of hanging up the traitor's disjointed body after execution. Psalm cix. in his opinion sanctions the law of corruption of blood in such cases.

* Even this was a mitigation suggested by the monks : originally the culprit was dragged semi-nude over the ground, tied to the tail of a horse.

WILD ANIMALS.

AT the Exeter Assizes in 1872, there was a case in the calendar which usefully illustrates the uncertainty attending the legal definition of a wild animal. The prisoner, a fisherman, was charged with stealing a lobster by abstracting it from the " pot " of a fellow-fisherman, the said "pot" being sunk in the English Channel off the coast of Devon. The counsel for the defence raised the objection that a lobster was a wild animal, and therefore a criminal information could not be maintained. The Judge ruled that a lobster was not a wild animal, and considerable time was wasted in argument before the legal status of the crustacean was fixed. A still more curious instance of the difficulty arose in the same county. A swarm of bees alighted in a lane near the residence of a farmer named Pidsley, who straightway hived them. A neighbour named Llanville declared that the bees were his, and shaking them out of Mr. Pidsley's hive into his own, carried them away. Pidsley sued in the County Court for the recovery of the value of the bees, and the Judge, Mr. Sergeant Petersdorff, after hearing all the evidence, said it would be necessary to withhold his judgment till next Court, "there being a variety of points that suggested themselves to his mind with reference to the ownership of wild animals." The fact of bees being wild animals was a new light for the Devonshire bee-masters.

A CAUTION TO HORSE OWNERS.

SIR JOHN BAYLEY, after the conclusion of a very obstinately contested horse case, is said to have made the following observation : " Take my advice, gentlemen, and accommodate matters of this kind, if possible. For men lose more than 25*l.* in bringing an action on the warranty of a horse, even if they win. And such is the danger, from the evidence common in causes like this, that justice is no security of success to a man. I perceive that the gentlemen below me do not approve of this doctrine ; but the truth must be told sometimes."

NOT RECEIVING HIS DUE.

THE *Gentleman's Magazine*, for 1827, relates that during Alderman Wood's first mayoralty he committed to the House of Correction a journeyman sugar-baker, for having left his employment in consequence of a dispute respecting wages. The prisoner during his confinement *not* having been flogged (as the statute enacted that he should have been), in consequence of 'no order to that effect being specified in the warrant of committal, he actually brought an action against the Lord Mayor, in the Court of Common Pleas, for non-conformity to the law. It was proved that he had not been whipped, and therefore the jury were obliged to allow one farthing damages, but the point of law was reserved.

SHEEP-SHEARING.

AN opulent farmer applied about a lawsuit to an attorney, who told him he could not undertake it, being already engaged on the other side. At the same time, he said that he would give him a letter of recommendation to a professional friend, which he did. The farmer, out of curiosity, opened the note and read as follows :—

> " There are two fat wethers fallen out together,
> If you'll fleece one, I'll fleece the other,
> And make 'em agree like brother and brother."

The farmer carried this epistle to the person with whom he was at variance. Needless to say that the dispute was settled without legal assistance.

33 HEN. VIII., C. 21.

N the reign of Henry VIII., A.D. 1541, a statute was passed, whereby it was enacted, " That every woman to whom the King, or any of his successours, shulde take a faneye in waye of marriage, of what estate, degree, or condition she be, thinking and esteeming her a pure and cleane mayde, when indeade the proofe maye or after shall appere contrarye, either by due testimonye or confession of the partye or partyes, and she yet nevertheless willingly do couple herself with her soveraigne Lorde and King in marriage, withoute plaine declaration before of her unchaste lief to his Majestie, that then every such offence shalbe demed and adjudged high treason, and the offendour therin convicte by thordre of the lawe, shall have and suffre such paines of deth, losse, and forfaytures of landes, tenements, goods, chattels, and debts, as in cases of high treason" (*Stat. of the Realm*, iii., p. 859). This law, which was afterwards repealed, as " trespassing too strongly, as well on natural justice as on female modesty," according to Blackstone, continued in force during the remainder of this reign. Lord Campbell (*Lives of the Chancellors*, vol. ii., p. 108), says it " so much frightened all the spinsters at Henry's court, that instead of trying to attract his notice, like Anne Boleyn, Jane Seymour, and Catherine Howard, in the hope of wearing a crown, they shunned his approach as if he had been himself the executioner, and they left the field open for widows, who could not by any subtlety of crown lawyers be brought within its operation."

PRIME-ARY ELOQUENCE.

ERJEANT PRIME was a good-natured but rather dull man, and an advocate weary beyond comparison. A counsel once getting up to reply to one of his lengthy orations, which had made the jury very drowsy, began, "Gen-

tlemen, after the long speech of the learned serjeant——," " Sir,
I beg your pardon," interrupted Justice Nares, "you ought to say
after the long soliloquy, for my brother Prime has been talking
an hour to himself."

BAR POETRY.

" N my earliest years at the bar," says Sir George Rose,
"sitting idle and listless, rather than listening, on the
back benches of the court, Vesey, junior,* the reporter,
put his notebook into my hand, saying, ' Rose, I am obliged to
go away. If anything occurs, take a note for me.' When he
returned, I gave him back his notebook, and in it the fair report
in effect of what had taken place in his absence in this form :—

> ' Mr. Leach
>   Made a speech,
> Angry, neat, and wrong ;
>   Mr. Hart,
>   On the other part,
> Was right, and dull, and long.
>   Mr. Parker
>   Made the case darker,
> Which was dark enough without;
>   Mr. Cooke
>   Cited a book,
> And the Chancellor said, ' I doubt.'

My short report was so far *en règle* that it came out *in numbers*,
though certainly *lege solutis*. It was about four or five years
afterwards—when I was beginning to get into business—that I
had a motion to make before the chancellor, Lord Eldon.
Taking up the *Morning Chronicle*, at breakfast, I there, to my
surprise and alarm, saw my unfortunate report. ' Here's a
pretty business ! ' said I ; ' pretty chance have I, having thus

---

* This gentleman was so called to distinguish him from his father.
When near eighty he was still called junior.

made myself known to the court as satirizing both bench and bar.' Well, I made my motion. The Chancellor told me to 'take nothing' by it, and added, 'and Mr. Rose, in this case the Chancellor does not "doubt."' Thinking that I might be—as in truth I was—rather disconcerted at so unexpected a *contretemps*, he sent me down a note to the effect that, so far from being offended, he had been much pleased with a playfulness attributed to me, and hoped, now that business was approaching me, I should still find leisure for some relaxation, and he was afterwards invariably courteous and kind ; nay, not only promised me a silk gown, but actually—*credite posteri*—invited me to dinner."

A SINGULAR DECREE.

N the *Thuana, or Miscellaneous Remains of President de Thou*, we read of a whimsical, passionate old judge, who was sent into Gascony, with power to examine into the abuses which had crept into the administration of justice in that part of France. Arriving late at Port Sainte Marie, he inquired " how far it was to the city of Agen ? " He was answered, "Two leagues." He thereupon decided to proceed that evening, although he was informed that the leagues were long, and the roads very bad. In consequence of his obstinacy, the judge was bemired, benighted, and almost shaken to pieces. He reached Agen, however, after midnight, with tired horses, and went to bed in a very bad temper. The next morning he summoned the court of justice to meet, and after having exhibited his commission in due form, his first decree was : " That for the future the distance from Port Sainte Marie to Agen should be reckoned six leagues." This decree he ordered to be registered in the records of the province, before he would proceed to any other business.

CURIOUS COMMUTATIONS.

N the reign of Charles II., one Walcot was executed for participation in the Rye House plot, and twelve years after his execution a writ of error was brought, and his attainder reversed, because in the record of his sentence it had not been stated that his entrails should be burned *while he was alive.* In a similar manner, a prisoner was convicted of a capital felony, and was sentenced to be punished with transportation. On error the judgment was reversed, because he was not sentenced to be hanged, and he was discharged.

A CONTRAST.

AWYERS have always been remarkable, perhaps more than the members of other professions, for displaying the extremes of foppishness and slovenliness in their costume. Erskine was a notable example of the legal fop, Kenyon of the legal sloven. In Erskine's younger days, male attire afforded more opportunity for elegant display than is now possible. Cocked hats and ruffles, with satin small-clothes, constituted the usual evening dress. When Dr. Dibdin called on Erskine at breakfast time, he received him in the smart dress of the times, a dark-green coat, scarlet waistcoat, and silk breeches. Erskine was very particular about the cut and curl of his wigs, their texture and their colour, while the hands he extended in entreaty towards British juries were always cased in lemon-coloured kid gloves. Lord Kenyon's ordinary dress, on the contrary, would have disgraced a copying clerk, and during his later years it was a moot point among barristers, whether his breeches were made of velvet or of leather. He is reported to have gone to court in a second-hand suit, bought of Lord Stormont's valet; and when the war income-tax threatened to abridge people's luxuries and compel economy, Lord Ellenborough observed that Kenyon intended to meet the crisis, by the only retrenchment he could still make, by forswearing the use of handkerchiefs. He had two wigs and two hats, all grievously shabby, but not all equally shabby ; and he always wore the better wig with the worse hat, and *vice versâ.*

SUTOR ULTRA CREPIDAM.

LORD CHELMSFORD relates that a friend of his at the bar was once engaged in a nautical case, in which it appeared that a vessel, in a severe gale of wind, had been thrown upon her beam ends. The barrister, who appears to have had a smattering of nautical matters, asked a sailor who was in the witness-box how it was they did not lower the topmast, upon which the witness replied with a sneer : " If you knew as much of the sea as I do, you would know that that is not a very easy matter in a gale of wind." This incident led the counsel to turn his attention to the subject ; in consequence of which he invented an apparatus for lowering topmasts, for which he obtained a patent, and realized upwards of 20,000*l.* by this invention.

A LEGAL STICKLER.

SAMUEL WARREN relates a case where a client of his had his declaration on a bill of exchange demurred to, because instead of the words " in the year of our Lord 1834," he had written " A.D. 1834." The learned counsel relates that he attended Mr. Justice Littledale at chambers, to endeavour to get the demurrer set aside as frivolous, or leave to amend on payment of a shilling ; but that punctilious, though very able and learned judge, refused to do either. " Your client, sir," said he, " has committed a blunder, sir, which can be set right only on the usual terms, sir ; A.D., sir, is neither English nor Latin, sir, it may mean anything—or nothing, sir. It is plain, sir, that there is a material and traversable fact, and no date to it, sir," and so forth ; whereupon he dismissed the poor summons with costs ! The demurrer had been spun out by a pleader to an inconceivable length in ringing the changes on the above one objection, and Mr. Warren's client had positively to pay out of his own pocket between seven and eight pounds.

MARITAL INDEBTEDNESS.

THE working of the above law has of late been brought before the public in several cases, wherein large drapers sued husbands for debts incurred by their better halves The point in question was a stumbling-block as early as the reign of Charles II. Justice Wyndham, in the Exchequer Chamber (Manby v. Scott, 1 Siderfin 109, 1662–63), specifies the "many inconveniences which must ensue" if the husband shall be bound by the contract of the wife :—

"The husband will be accounted the common enemy ; and the mercer and the gallant will unite with the wife, and they will combine their strength against the husband.

"Wives will be their own carvers, and, like hawks, will fly abroad and find their own prey.

"It shall be left to the pleasure of a London jury to dress my wife in such apparel as they think proper.

"Wives who think that they have insufficient, will have it tried by a mercer whether their dress is not too mean, and this will make the mercer judge whether he will dispose of his own goods or not."

In the same case, Justice Hide, in the Exchequer Chamber, gives his opinion in the following quaint language : " If the wife will have a velvet gown, and a satin petticoat, and her husband thinks mohair or farendon for a gown, and watered tabby for a petticoat, is as fashionable and fitter for his quality, who is to decide the controversy ? Not the wife ; nor a jury—it may be consisting of drapers and milliners—but the husband."

The case was rather strong against the plaintiff, for Dame Scott, who had incurred the bill, had run away from her husband, who thereupon had given due notice to tradespeople not to give her any credit.   After a while Mrs. Scott returned to the conjugal roof, "avec ses batards," claiming cohabitation, which the defendant, Mr. Edward Scott, declined to admit.   The bill—for forty pounds' worth of silk and velvet—had been run up whilst the lady was absent from her lord.   Notwithstanding this, the jury found that, the apparel being "necessaries suitable to the degree" of Mrs. Scott, the husband was liable.   The judges in King's Bench could not agree, and the case was then deferred to the Exchequer Chamber, when judgment was given for the defendant.

LORD THURLOW'S FIRST CASE.

THURLOW had travelled the circuit for some years with little notice, and without having met with any opportunity to exhibit his abilities.   Just then the housekeeper of the Duke of N—— was prosecuted for stealing a quantity of linen, with which she had been entrusted.   An attorney of little note and practice conducted the woman's case.   He knew that he could expect no hearty co-operation if he employed any of the leading counsel ; it was a poor case, and a low case, and it could not be expected that "the foremost men of all the bar" would set themselves tooth and nail against the Duke, whose influence was paramount.   The attorney looked round, therefore, for some young barrister who had nothing to lose, and might have something to win, and he fixed upon Thurlow, who read over the brief with the highest glee, and had an interview with the prisoner.   As he entered the court he jogged a briefless brother, and said in his favourite slang : " Neck or nothing, my boy ; to-day, I'll soar or tumble."   The opening speech of the eminent counsel for the Duke and the evidence completely convicted the woman.   But Thurlow, by his withering cross-examination of

the witnesses, his sneers at the Duke and Duchess, and his powerful address to the jury upon the "grovelling persecution,"
triumphed. The woman was acquitted. And from that day
Thurlow's powers of voice, sarcasm, gesture, and browbeating
became known, and soon raised him to the pinnacle of legal
greatness.

A POT-SHOT.

MR. LAW (subsequently Lord Ellenborough), when on the
Northern circuit, had been very severe one day upon a
rich man who had amassed a great fortune by pottery.
This happened at Lancaster, and the advocate returned to
London. Being at chambers, he received intelligence that the
person he had lectured was coming to challenge him ; upon
which he instructed his clerk, that when the gentleman came,
the clerk should stay in the room. He did come, and requested
a private audience. " What you have come to say, sir," said the
counsel, "may be told before this gentleman." The man of
pottery then stammered out his warlike message; but what was
his surprise when Mr. Law, looking him fully in the face, coolly
answered him : " If it were not for the immense contempt I
should incur, I certainly would have a shot at your crockery."

"BRIEF-ETY IS THE SOUL OF WIT."

BARON MARTIN when at the bar was addressing the
Court of Exchequer in an insurance case, when he was
interrupted by the Momus of Westminster Hall, Baron
Alderson, who said, " Mr. Martin, do you think any office would
insure your life ? " " Certainly, my lord," replied Martin ;
" mine is a very good life, I hope." " Ah ! but Mr. Martin, you
should remember that yours is a *brief* existence," replied the
judge.

"THE MAN WITH THE DYING SPEECH."

WHEN that vacancy happened on the Exchequer Bench which was afterwards filled by Mr. Adams, the ministry could not agree among themselves whom to appoint. It was debated in council, the King, George II. being present, till the dispute growing very warm, his Majesty put an end to the contest, by calling out in his broken English : " I vill have none of dese ; give me de man mit de *Dying Speech,*" meaning Mr. Adams, who was then Recorder of London, and whose business it therefore was to make the report to his Majesty of the convicts under sentence of death.

"ARMS FOUND."

PERSONS in Scotland who glorify in coats of arms pro- cured at the so-called " Heraldic Office " for the mode- rate sum of three half-crowns, are perhaps not aware of the following law, which still stands on the statute-book of Scotland, and has never been repealed. " Act 1672, c. 21, regu- lating the law of armorial bearings in Scotland, is a renewal of the Act 1592, c. 125. By this Act power was given to the Lyon King of Arms, or his deputies, to visit the whole arms of noblemen, barons, and gentlemen, and to matriculate the same in their registers, and to fine in one hundred pounds" (Scots, fortunately, not sterling) ; " as also to escheit all such goods and geir as shall have unwarrantable arms engraved on them." This is strong enough, it might be thought ; but the present Lyon is said to claim a further power, not recited or conferred in the Act of 1672, viz., the power of imprisonments which did form part of the Act of 1592. Thereby the Lyon is " to put inhibition to all the common sort of people not worthy by the laws of arms to bear any signs armorial, that none of them presume to take upon hand to bear or use any arms in time coming, upon any of their household gear, under the peine of the escheating the goods and gear, so oft as they shall be found contravenant this present Act, or whereon the same arms shall be found graven or painted, to our sovereign lord's use. And likewise under the pain of one hundred pounds to the use of the said Lyon and his brother heralds. And failing of payment thereof that they be incarcerate in the nearest prison, therein to remain, upon their own charges, during the pleasure of the said Lyon."

A SECOND DANIEL.

IN 1377, there was a case (*Yearb.* 50 Edw. III. fol. 6, pl. 12) in which a question arose upon a lady's age ; her counsel pressed the court to have her before them, and judge *by inspection* whether she was within age or not. But "Candish, Justice," showing great knowledge of female character, said : " Ill n'ad nul home en Engleterre que puy adjuge a droit deins dage ou de plein age ; car ascun femes que sont de age de XXX ans voilent apperer dage de XVIII ans," which for the benefit of those not conversant with law French may be translated : There is no man in England who can judge rightly in cases of under or over age ; for some women who are thirty years old wish to appear eighteen years.

AN ATTORNEY IN THE SEVENTEENTH CENTURY.

JOHN EARLE, Bishop of Salisbury, who published his *Microcosmography*, or essays and characters, in 1628, draws the following sarcastic and not very flattering character of the attorney of that period :—

"His ancient beginning was a blue coat, since a livery, and his hatching under a lawyer ; whence, though but pen-feathered, he hath now nested for himself, and with his hoarded pence purchased an office. Two desks and a quire of paper set him up, where he now sits in state for all comers. We can call him no great author, yet he writes very much, and with the infamy of the court is maintained in his libels. He has some smatch of a scholar, and yet uses Latin very hardly ; and lest it should accuse him, cuts it off in the midst, and will not let it speak out. He is, contrary to great men, maintained by his followers, that is, his poor country clients that worship him more than their landlord, and be they never such churls, he looks for their courtesy. He first racks them soundly himself, and then delivers them to the lawyer for execution. His looks are very solicitous, importing much haste and dispatch ; he is never without his hands full of business, that is—of papers. His skin becomes at last as dry as his parchment, and his face as intricate as the most winding cause. He talks statutes as fiercely as if he had mooted seven years in the Inns of Court, when all his skill is stuck in his girdle, or in his office window.* Strife and wrangling have made him rich, and he is thankful to his benefactor and nourishes it. If he live in a country village, he makes all his neighbours good subjects ; for there shall be nothing done, but what there is law for. His business gives him not leave to think of his conscience, and when the time or term of his life is going out, for doomsday he is secure ; for he hopes he has a trick to reverse judgment."

HABEAS CORPUS ACT.

ACCORDING to Bishop Burnet, in his *Memoirs of My Own Time*, we are indebted to a jest for that highly prized palladium of English liberty, the Habeas Corpus Act. "The former parliament," he says, writing about the session of 1680, "had passed a very strict Act for the due execution of the Habeas Corpus, which was indeed all they did. It was carried by an odd artifice in the House of Lords. Lord

* Where he keeps the few books he possesses.

Grey and Lord Norris were named to be tellers. Lord Norris, being a man subject to vapours, was not at all times attentive to what he was doing ; so, a very fat lord coming in, Lord Grey counted him for ten, as a jest at first. But seeing Lord Norris had not observed it, he went on with this misreckoning of ten ; so it was reported to the House, and declared that they who were for the bill were the majority, though it indeed went to the other side ; and by this means the bill passed."

A HANDY OBJECTION.

ORD ELLENBOROUGH in a certain lawsuit (*Jones v. Mars*, 2 Campb. 305) was puzzled to decide whether the letter "s" was a fatal variance in this case. A declaration alleged that the defendants, a firm in partnership, made a bill of exchange, "their own *hands* being thereto subscribed." The difficulty was that the word *hand* was in the plural. But he refused to nonsuit.

ADAM IN PARADISE.

ORD COMMISSIONER ADAM was for many years a personal friend of King George IV., and filled some high appointment in the Duchy of Cornwall under his majesty when Prince of Wales. He was appointed to the Jury Court in Scotland upon its first establishment ; upon which a wag asked, "Why is the Jury Court like Paradise ?" and answered his own question by saying, "Because it is a *place* made for *Adam*." This joke Lord Eldon was fond of repeating ; and he always added to it the counter question and answer : "Why is the Jury Court *not* like Paradise ?" "Because there is no getting Adam out of it."

UNCIVIL LAW.

THE causticity of Lord Tenterden sometimes led dramatic scenes between the chief justice and t ⌐ offending counsel. One day in banc a learned ge ʹ tleman who had lectured on the law and was too much addicte to oratory, came to argue a special demurrer. "My client's opponent," said the figurative advocate, "worked like a mole under ground *clam et secrete.*" His figures and law Latin only elicited an indignant grunt from the chief justice. " It is as-serted in Aristotle's *Rhetoric*—— " " I don't want to hear wha is asserted in Aristotle's *Rhetoric*," interposed Lord Tenterde The advocate shifted his ground, and took up as he thougl. a supposition : "It is laid down in the Pandects of Justinian"—— "Where are you got now?" "It is a principle in the civi. law——" "Oh, sir l" exclaimed the judge, with a tone and voice which to a punster's ear would have abundantly justified his assertion, " we have nothing to do with civil law in this court."

LONG LEASE.

ON July 25, 1811, Sir Oswald Mosley, Bart., lord of the manor of Manchester, demised a plot of land at Ancoats in that township, for 9999 years, which term will expire in the year of our Lord 11,810, when his heirs or assigns can eject the tenants, and take possession of all build-ings standing thereon. That leases are made for the term of 999 years because a lease of a thousand years would create a freehold, is a vulgar error.

PRECEDENTS.

IN the last century, when Swiss mercenaries formed part of the armies of various countries, Justice Carr made the following felicitous allusion to these troops in con-cluding his judgment in a case, "It will be observed that I have

ed no cases in support of this opinion ; not that I have not
ıd, and considered, and puzzled myself with the multitude
ıt were commented on in the argument ; but because, finding
ım like the Swiss troops, fighting on both sides, I have laid
ėm aside, and gone upon what seems to be the true spirit of
ʌe law."

In another case, one of the counsel said that he had searched
all the books, " and there is not one case," etc. To which Chief
Justice Anderson responded, " What of that ? Shall not we
ɡive judgment because it is not adjudged in the books before ?
ᶠVe will give judgment according to reason ; and if there be no
ɹason in the books, I will not regard them."

THRICE BLESSED.

HEN in 1802 Sir James Mackintosh was at the bar on
the Norfolk circuit, he had left his wife near her
accouchement. But that " happy event" produced a
most portentous augmentation to his domestic bliss, or rather
his domestic inquietudes. It was an important omen to his
fortunes, which at that time were not prosperous. He was
anxiously looking for letters at Bedford, but received none till
Huntingdon, where he was congratulated upon the birth of a
fine boy. Cambridge was the next circuit town ; there he found
another epistle at the post-office, announcing the birth of a
second pledge. It was with a grave smile that he received the
congratulations of the circuit mess upon the coming of "another
Richard." But he had scarcely reached Bury, when a third
son was announced to him by letter. The letters had indeed
been written after the birth of each of this extraordinary
progeny, but the first only was in time for the post, the second
and third were written after the respective births they related
to, but could not be forwarded by the same mail. This mon-
strous increase to his family was enough to sadden any man's

visage, but Macintosh bore it with great fortitude and philosophy. Nor did George Wilson, the amiable leader of the Norfolk circuit, in the least discompose him, when, in allusion to the Lectures on the Law of Nature and Nations, he proposed with great gravity at the mess, "The health of Mrs. Mackintosh and her three sons—Grotius, Puffendorf, and Vattell."

CHECKMATED.

LORD KAMES, an indefatigable and speculative but coarse man, tried Matthew Hay for murder, at Ayr, in September, 1780. His lordship was an enthusiastic chess-player, and had had many a game with Hay, who invariably beat him when they tried their powers at the beloved game. Kames was not a little mortified by his friend's success, and was not altogether sorry when it became his painful duty to pass the sentence of the law upon his old companion. Having in due form and with suitable solemnity commended the culprit's soul to the divine mercy, he, after a brief pause, assumed his ordinary tone of voice, and nodding humorously to his former friend, observed, "And noo, Matthew, that's checkmate to you for ance." This story is told incorrectly in Lockhart's first edition of Sir Walter Scott's Life. Lord Cockburn in his Memorials relates it with the above names. "Besides general and uncontradicted notoriety," he says, "I had the fact from Lord Hermand, who was one of the counsel at the trial, and never forgot a piece of judicial cruelty which excited his horror and anger. Scott is said to have told this story to the Prince Regent. If he did so he would certainly tell it accurately, because he knew the facts quite well. But in reporting what Sir Walter had said at the royal table, the Lord Commissioner Adam confused the matter and called the Judge Branfield, the crime forgery, and the circuit town Dumfries, and this inaccurate account was given by Lockhart.

THE LAWYER'S FAREWELL TO HIS MUSE.

IR WILLIAM BLACKSTONE, the famous author of the *Commentaries on the Laws of England*, in 1738 entered Pembroke College, Oxford, where he reaped distinction as a classical scholar. An unpublished treatise on the Elements of Architecture, which he wrote at the age of twenty, is said to possess considerable merit. Having determined on the profession of the law, he was in due time entered of the Middle Temple ; and, in 1744, on leaving Oxford, he said farewell to those classical studies which were so congenial to his taste, an era in his life which he feelingly commemorated in an elegant little poem with the above title, published in vol. iv. of *Dodsley's Miscellany*. This graceful performance is distinguished by an early maturity of taste and judgment, and displays powers of expression and versification which have perhaps not been surpassed by the juvenile productions of our most distinguished poets. With accomplished ease and grace it expresses his deep feeling in relinquishing the pleasures of poetry and art, and parting for ever from scenes wherein he had happily spent the days of his youth. In conclusion he describes his anticipations :—

> " Lost to the field and torn from you,
> Farewell ! a long, a last adieu !
> Me wrangling courts and stubborn law,
> To smoke, and crowds, and cities draw.
> There selfish faction rules the day,
> And pride and avarice throng the way ;
> Diseases taint the murky air,
> And midnight conflagrations glare.
> Loose revelry and riot bold
> In frighted streets their orgies hold ;
> Or when in silence all is drowned,
> Fell murder walks her lonely round.
> No room for peace, no room for you,
> Adieu, celestial nymph, adieu ! "

But Blackstone need not have written his *Farewell* to the Muses. If he had been destined to be a poet he could not have taken his leave ; and as an accomplished lawyer, he was always within the pale of the *literæ humaniores.* A strong union ever has existed between the law and the *belles-lettres* highly creditable to the former, or rather naturally to be expected from the mode in which lawyers begin their education, and the diversity of knowledge which no men are more in the way of acquiring afterwards. The greatest practical lawyers, such as Coke and Plowden, may not have been the most literary, but those who have understood the law in the greatest and best spirit have. And the former, great as they may be, are yet but as servants and secretaries to the rest. They know where to find, but the others know best how to apply. Bacon, Clarendon, Selden, Somers, Cowper, Mansfield, were all men of letters. So were the Broughams and Campbells of a later day. Pope says that Mansfield would have been another Ovid· This may be doubted ; but nobody should doubt, that the better he understood a poet, the fitter he was for universality of judgment. The greatest lawyer is the greatest legislator.

THE RIGHT OF THE ROAD.

HE following, from a letter of Lord Erskine to Lord Stowell, in 1821, relating to a judgment of the latter in the Court of Admiralty in a case of collision at sea, is very good :—

" I remember my excellent friend, the late Lord Kenyon, one of the best and ablest judges, and the soundest lawyer, in trying a cause at Guildhall, seemed disposed to leave it to the jury whether the party who suffered, might not have saved himself by going on the wrong side of the road, where the witnesses swore that ample room was left. The answer to which is, the dangerous uncertainty of such an attempt, destructive of all the presumptions of conduct founded upon law. Observing that Lord Kenyon was entangled with this distinction, from his observations in the course of the evidence, I said to the jury, in stating (*sic*) the defendant's case : 'Gentlemen, if the noble and learned judge, in giving you hereafter his advice, shall depart from the only principle of safety (unless where collisions are selfish and malicious), and you shall act upon it, I can only say that I shall feel the same confidence in his lordship's general learning and justice, and shall continue to delight, as I always do, in attending his administration of justice ; but *I pray God that I may never meet him on the road!*' Lord Kenyon laughed, and the jury along with him, and when he came to sum up he abandoned the distinction, saying to the jury that he believed it to be the best course *stare super antiquas vias.*"

INDIAN CURIOS.

NOTHING probably will strike an English lawyer in India more forcibly than the varied and peculiar forms of litigation, of which every court in the country is capable of producing specimens. Immemorial customs create rights which are there brought before our tribunals, such as no courts elsewhere in this world are called upon to consider. It has been said by an ancient Indian lawyer, that when the judges of the Sudder Courts were first set to administer native law, they appear to have felt as if they had got in fairyland, so strange and grotesque were the legal principles on which they were called to act. But after a while they became accustomed to the new region, and began to behave themselves as if all were real and substantial. As a matter of fact they acted as if they believed in it more than did its native inhabitants. Among the older records of their proceedings may be found injunctions, couched in the technical language of English chancery pleadings, which forbid the priests of a particular temple to injure a rival fane by painting the face of their rival red instead of yellow ; and decrees allowing the complaint of other priests that they were injured in property and repute, because their neigbours rang a bell at a particular moment of their (the neighbours') services. Much Brahminical ritual and not a little doctrine became the subject of decision. The Privy Council in London was once called upon to decide in ultimate appeal, on the claims of rival hierophants to have their palanquin carried crosswise instead of lengthwise ; and it is said that on another occasion the right to drive elephants through the narrow streets of one of the most sacred Indian cities, which was alleged to vest in a certain religious order as being in possession of a particular idol, was seriously disputed, because the idol was cracked.

DELIGHTFUL ALTERNATIVE.

IT was Bentham's opinion that the increase of litigation which might follow on the cheapening of justice is not so great an evil as the debarring suitors from their rights by the exaction of a fee at each step of the progress. This opinion may be illustrated by a quotation from Professor Porson's mock examination questions for students : " What happens if you win your cause ? " " You are nearly ruined." " What happens if you lose your cause ? " " You are quite ruined."

A HANDSOME OFFER.

" ONCE," says Sir Lloyd Kenyon, " I had a very hand- some offer made to me. I was pleading for the rights of the inhabitants of the Isle of Man. Now I had been reading in Coke, and I found there that the people of the Isle of Man were no beggars ; * so in my speech I said, 'The people of the Isle of Man are no beggars ; I, therefore, do not *beg* their rights, I *demand* them.' This so pleased an old smuggler who was present, that, when the trial was over, he called me aside and said, "Young gentleman, I will tell you what ; you shall have my daughter if you will marry her, and one hundred thousand pound for her fortune !" That was a very handsome offer ; but I told him that I happened to have a wife, who had nothing for her fortune ; therefore I must stick to her."

TRESPASSERS WILL BE PROSECUTED.

ATTERBURY, the Jacobite Dean of Westminster and Bishop of Rochester, was somewhat of a litigious character. Years before the bishop died, Prior composed the following epitaph for him :—

"Meek Francis lies here, friend. Without stop or stay,
As you value your peace, make the best of your way.
Though at present arrested by Death's caitiff paw,
If he stirs he may still have recourse to the law ;
And in the King's Bench should a verdict be found,
That, by livery and seizin, his grave is his ground,
He will claim to himself what is strictly his due,
And an action of trespass will straightway ensue,
That you without right on his premises tread,
On a simple surmise that the owner is dead."

THE MISSING LINK.

HORNE TOOKE, on his trial, having objected to a particular piece of evidence, he was reminded by Chief Justice Eyre, that if there were two or three links in the chain, they must go to one first, and then to another, and see

* Coke's words are : "The inhabitants of this isle are religious, industrious, and true people, without begging or stealing" (4 *Inst.* ch. 69, concluding paragraph).

whether they amounted to evidence. The defendant demurred to this: " I beg your pardon, my lord," he said, " but is not a chain composed of links, and may I not disjoin each link, and do I not thereby destroy the chain?" " I rather think not," argued the chief justice, "till the links are put together, and form the chain." " I rather think I may," objected Tooke, " because it is my business to prevent the forming of that chain."

A LAY OF ANCIENT LAW.

JOHN WILLIAM SMITH, of the Inner Temple, an eminent barrister, was delighted with Macaulay's *Lays of Ancient Rome.* One evening he sat down and wrote a humorous parody on them, entitled " Lay of Gascoigne Justice," prefaced by an " Extract from a Manuscript of a late Reporter," who says : " I have observed numerous traces in the old reports and entries of the use of rhythm in the enunciation of legal doctrines ; and pursuing the investigation, I àt length persuaded myself that, in the infancy of English law, the business of the court was transacted in verse, or, at least, rhythm, sometimes without, but on grand and solemn occasions with, the aid of music ; a practice which seems to have been introduced by the ecclesiastical advocates." After a humorous argument in support of this notion, he concludes : " The following attempt to restore certain of these *Lays of Ancient Law* is conceived, as the original laws themselves probably were, partly in bad English, partly in dog Latin." Then follows the " Lay of Gascoigne Justice, chanted by Cooke and Coke, serjeants, and Plowden, apprentice, in the hall of Serjeant's Inn, A.D. 15—." The subject of the Lay was the highway exploit at Gadshill of Prince Harry, Poins, and Peto. Poins gets into trouble, being brought incontinently before Gascoigne Justice, "presiding at the Bailey." The concluding verses contain a just satire on certain gross defects in the administration of criminal justice, which have been only remedied not forty years ago :—

"When Poins he spied, ho, ho ! he cried,
　The caitiff hither bring !
We'll have a quick deliverance
　Betwixt him and the king.

And sooth, he said, for justice sped
　In those days at a rate
Which now 'twere vain to seek to gain,
　In matters small or great.

* 　 * 　 *

For sundry wise precautions
　The sages of the law
Discreetly framed, whereby they aimed
　To keep the rogues in awe.

For lest some sturdy criminal
　False witnesses should bring—
His witnesses were not allowed
　To swear to anything.

And lest his only advocate
　The court should overreach,
His advocate was not allowed
　The privilege of speech.*

Yet such was the humanity
　And wisdom of the law,
That if in his indictment there
　Appeared to be a flaw—

The court assigned him counsellors
　To argue on the doubt,
Provided he himself had first
　Contrived to point it out.

Yet lest their mildness should perchance
　Be craftily abused,
To show him the indictment they
　Most sturdily refused.

　* In those days the defendant in accusations of felony, which in most instances touched his life, could not have counsel to speak for him upon the facts of the case, although he might in charges of misdemeanour and in civil actions, which affected only his liberty and his property.

But still that he might understand
The nature of the charge,
The same was in the Latin tongue
Read out to him at large.

'Twas thus the law kept rogues at awe,
Gave honest men protection,
And justly famed, by all was named
Of wisdom the perfection.

But *now* the case is different,
The rogues are getting bold—
It was not so, some time ago
In those good days of old."

The "Lay of Gascoigne" has been published in the *Law Magazine*, vol. xxxv.

AN ATTORNEY TURNED COBBLER.

CURRAN had a younger brother who was an attorney. This man had a good deal of his brother's humour, but his conduct was very dissolute. He was in fact what may be termed the best blackguard of his profession, and that was saying a great deal for him. Curran had justly excluded him from his house, but occasionally relieved his finances, until his calls became so importunate that at length further compliance was refused. There was a small space of dead wall at that time directly facing Curran's house in Ely Place, against which the attorney procured a written permission to build a small wooden shed. He accordingly got a carpenter to erect a cobbler's stall for him, and having assumed the dress of the " gentle craft," he wrote over his stall, "CURRAN, COBBLER. *Shoes soled or heeled. When the stall is shut, inquire over the way.*" Curran immediately despatched a servant to the spendthrift, and gave "something handsome" in order to have the workshop and showboard removed.

WARLIKE BRIEFS.

HE following anecdote, which is almost too good to be true, occurs in the Attorney Cyrus Jay's *What I have seen, What I have heard, and What I have known :* "One morning I met an attorney at the Master's office, taxing the costs of an action for breach of promise of marriage, and I was astonished at the size of his briefs. A month afterwards I met him going to tax costs in another action, with briefs equally long. I asked him how he could make his briefs so bulky. 'Easily enough,' he said; 'I have no library, keep only one clerk, who is a boy, and possess only one book, which is *Napier's History of the Peninsular War.* I draw a fair brief of eight sheets, comprising the whole of the facts of the case. I then give *Napier* to the boy to copy, telling him not to leave off till I give him instructions to do so. When I find there are sheets enough, I tack them to the eight sheets ; but I never got beyond Saragossa.'"

PROFESSIONAL PERJURERS.

ERJURY, though always considered an offence, was in former centuries by no means so severely prosecuted as now, and in fact was by many disreputable characters openly taken up as a profession. From passages in various poets and prose writers, it appears that the inns of court and the purlieus where tribunals sat, were the common haunt of these scoundrels ; there they hung about, waiting for customers, lazily leaning against the posts which in the streets of old London divided the carriage road from the side walks. Hence they were popularly known as " Knights of the Post. " Knights of the Post," says Dr. Nash in his notes to *Hudibras,* " were infamous persons who attended the court of justice to swear for hire to things they knew nothing about. In the fourteenth and fifteenth century [he might have added three centuries after that] the common people were so profligate, that not a few of them lived by swearing for hire in courts of justice."—"A Knight of the Post, quoth he, for so I am termed, a fellow that will swear you anything for twelve pence" (Nash, *Pierce Pennyless,* 1592). When Hudibras consults the lawyer upon the means of obtaining; the widow, he is advised among other modes of entrapping her, to—

> " Retain all sorts of witnesse
> That ply i' th' Temple under trees,
> Or walk the rounds with knights o' th' posts
> Among the cross-legged knights, their hosts,*
> Or wait for customers between
> The pillarrows in Lincoln's Inn,
> Where vouchers, forgers, common bail,
> And affidavit men ne'er fail
> T' expose for sale all sorts of oaths,
> According to their ears and clothes,
> Their only necessary tools
> Beside the gospel and their souls."

Not a century ago professional perjurers used to walk openly in Westminster Hall, and hang about Chancery Lane, with a straw sticking out from one of their shoes—those being the days of knee-breeches—to signify they wanted employment as witnesses. A writer in the *Quarterly Review* (vol. xxxiii. p. 344), treating of Greek Law Courts, says : " We have all heard of a race of men who used in former days to ply about our own courts of law, and who, from their manner of making known their occupation, were recognized by the name of Strawshoes. An advocate or lawyer, who wanted a 'convenient' witness, knew by these signs where to find one, and the colloquy between the parties was brief. ' Don't you remember?' said the advocate. The party

---

* The walks in the Temple and the "round" of Temple Church were among their favourite haunts : "My companions, the worthy knights of the most noble order of the post, your peripatetic philosophers of Temple walks" (Otway, *Soldiers of Fortune,* 1682).

looked at his face and gave no sign ; then the fee increased, and with it the powers of memory : 'To be sure I do.' ' Then come into court and swear it.' And Strawshoes came into court and swore it."

JUDGES' ROBES.

OCCASIONAL visitors to the courts will be puzzled by the somewhat ritualistic change of robes observable in the judges. One day they are attired in black, another in violet, again in scarlet. Puzzling as these changes may appear to outsiders, there is method in this whimsicality, and, as with the garments of the priests officiating in the Roman Catholic Church, so in the courts certain fixed rules are followed. Judges wear black or violet robes in term time, which are to be faced with taffeta from Ascension Day to St. Simon and Jude, and from that day to Ascension Day with miniver. On all holidays scarlet-faced ; scarlet at church, or when they go to a feast; and he that gives the charge, and delivers gaol, is to wear scarlet for the most part. Readers who would desire to know more about this court millinery will find full particulars in the *Penny Post*, 1874, p. 167.

THE COMMON LAW.

THE appellation of " Common Law " originated with Edward the Confessor. The Saxons, though divided into many kingdoms, yet, in their manners, laws, and language, were similar. The slight differences which existed between the Mercian law, the West Saxon, and the Danish law were removed by Edward with facility, and without causing any dissatisfaction. He made this alteration rather famous by a new name than by new matter ; for, abolishing the three distinctions above named, he called it the Common Law of England, and ordained that no part of the kingdom should be governed by any particular law, but all by one. The Common Law, as contra-distinguished from the Statute Law, consists of those rules and maxims concerning the persons and property of men which have obtained by the tacit assent and usage of the inhabitants of this country; the consent and approbation of the people being signified by their immemorial use and practice.

A LONG DAY.

WHEN Sir Thomas More was lord chancellor, he one day ordered a gentleman to pay rather heavy damages to a woman whom he had wronged. The gentleman said, "Then I hope your lordship will grant me a long day to pay it." "I will grant your motion," said the chancellor; "Monday next is St. Barnabas' Day, which is the longest day in the year; pay it to the lady on that day, or I will commit you to the Fleet Prison."

RAISING THE WIND.

IN the *Life and Times of Reynolds* occurs the following amusing anecdote :—"To refuse or grant a patent for a new invention is peculiarly within the province of the attorney-general, who does not, in general, exercise a very strict surveillance. A French count having discovered the means of creating an impelling power by the aid of an artificial wind counteracting the effects of the natural wind, Baron Polnitz thought that this balloon would be seen sailing like a ship, and applied for a patent. At that time Mr. Pepper Arden (subsequently Lord Alvanley—Poivre Ardent, the baron called him) was attorney-general, and being naturally surprised at this extraordinary application, he desired an interview. My father being out of town, I was compelled to conduct the count to Mr.

Arden's chambers, in Portugal Street, when the following curious conversation ensued :—

"'Pray what does this absurd application mean?'

"'Mean, sir,' I 'repeated in surprise; ' it means, sir, that by artificial wind counteracting the effects of the natural wind we can direct balloons.'

"'And what then?'

"'What then, sir?'

"'Ay ; what then?'

"'Why, sir,' I replied, with great consequence and volubility, 'we shall not only raise botany to the highest pitch of perfection, by transplanting fresh roots and plants from one country to another ; we shall not only raise the sieges of towns by introducing armed men and provisions at our pleasure, but we shall discover the North-West Passage.'

"'Ay,' interrupted the attorney-general, scarcely able to suppress his laughter ; 'and in your mighty wisdoms, I suppose, not only defraud the customs and excise, but annihilate the revenue resulting from the Post Office. Pooh! nonsense! artificial wind!'—laughing heartily—'Stuff! Who is to supply the wind? Your client here?'

"The baron, seeing the attorney-general, as he conceived, delighted, smiling, said, 'Que dit l'avocat-général, Monsieur Frederick?'

"I replied, in my usual bad French, made worse by confusion, 'Il demande, baron, si vous êtes le personne qui fait le vent flatulent.'

"'Comment!' exclaimed the baron.

"The attorney-general then rose, bowed, and coolly desired me to tell my father 'that the baron's was less a case for a lawyer than for a physician.'"

COMPLIMENTARY.

HEN a duchess celebrated for her beauty bantered Lord Stowell, then Consistory Judge, and inquired, " How his court would manage if he himself should be guilty of a *faux pas?* ' he answered, with a gallantry becoming the question, " that the idea of such an embarrassing situation had only occurred to him since he had become acquainted with her grace."

TRUTH STRANGER THAN FICTION.

N the danger of admitting presumptive evidence of death, Lord Langdale was in the habit of referring to a very singular case, which happened within his own knowledge while he was on the bench. A sum of money in court was subject to a trust for a particular individual for life, and after his death was to be divided between certain parties. These parties petitioned for payment of the fund to them, on the ground that the individual in question, the tenant for life, was dead. No positive evidence could be adduced of his death; but it was said that his death must be presumed, since there was evidence that he had gone abroad some twenty or thirty years ago, under circumstances of difficulty, and that no human being had heard any tidings of him from that day to this.

This did not satisfy Lord Langdale, and he desired the case to stand over, intimating that, if further evidence could be produced to corroborate the already strong presumption, he would attend to it. Additional affidavits were accordingly filed, after the lapse of some time, and the case then appeared so strong, that he made order for the division of the fund as prayed. The order, when drawn up according to his lordship's directions, was carried to the proper office to be entered, when, lo and behold ! the clerk whose duty it was to enter it, turned out to be

the very individual on whose presumed death the order for payment was made. It seems that in early life he had been
involved in scrapes and difficulties, which led him to fly his
country, and to keep his residence and career a secret from all
his relations ; that he had returned in time, under a fictitious
name, to England, where he at length obtained a situation in
the office in question, but without making himself known to
any one ; that he was ignorant of his right in the fund in question ;
and that, but for the remarkable accident just related, he would
have been deprived of these rights, and the fund would have
been prematurely given over to persons not then entitled to it.

FORENSIC CASUISTRY.

VERY interesting chapter concerning the duty of an
advocate, when he finds that the case of his client is
based on falsehood and fraud, may be seen in a
valuable historical essay, by William Forsyth, Q.C. The question was amicably raised by Quintilian, who declared that
the advocate will not undertake the defence of every one ; nor
will he throw open the harbour of his eloquence as a port of
refuge to pirates ; nor let false shame prevent him from abandoning a cause in which he has engaged under an impression
that it was just, when he discovers, in the course of the trial,
that it is dishonest ; but he ought previously to give notice to his
client of his intention." Of this we have seen many examples,
one of the last that of the counsel of Miss Wilberforce, the
American impostor, on his becoming acquainted with the true
character of that person.

By one of the Edicts of Justinian it was enacted that advocates should take a solemn oath " that they were not to uphold
a cause that was villainous, or supported by falsehood ; and if,
in the progress of the trial, they discovered that a case of that
kind had been entrusted to their care, they were at once to
abandon it."

It was a noble saying of Queen Elizabeth, that she wished her counsel to remember, that they were counsel " not so much pro Domina Regina, as pro Domina Veritate." By the ancient law of Scotland, advocates were required to be yearly sworn " to execute their office of advocation diligently and truly, and that as soon as they understood their client's cause to be unjust and wrongful, they should incontinent leave the same." The advocate's oath, prescribed by a modern ordinance of the representative counsel of Geneva, requires him to swear that " he will not attempt to deceive the judges by any artifice, or by any false exposition of facts or law ; that he will abstain from all offensive personality, and not advance any fact against the honour and reputation of parties."

Sir Edward Coke has declared that " fraud and falsehood are against the Common Law ; " and the illustrious chancellor D'Agnesseau thus addressed the bar of France : " Let the zeal which you bring to the defence of your clients be incapable of making you the minister of their passions and the organs of their malignity." A modern English judge of the purest principles has declared that " the zeal and the arguments of every counsel, knowing what is due to himself and to his honourable profession, are qualified, not only by considerations affecting his own character as a man of honour, experience, and learning, but also by considerations affecting the general interests of justice."

" What shall I say of those," says Bishop Sanderson in one of his sermons, " be they many or few, that abuse the gracefulness of their elocution (good speakers but to ill purposes) to enchant the ears of an easy magistrate with the charms of a fluent tongue, or to cast a mist before the eyes of a weak jury, as jugglers make sport with country people ; to make white seem black, or black seem white ; or setting a fair varnish upon a rotten post, and a smooth gloss upon a coarse cloth ; as Protagoras some times boasted that he could make a bad cause good when he listed? By which means judgment is perverted, the hands of violence and robbery strengthened, the edge of the sword of justice abated, great offenders acquitted, gracious and virtuous men molested and injured. I know not what fitter reward to wish them for their pernicious eloquence, as their best deserved fee, than to remit them over to what David hath assigned them (Ps. cxx.) : ' What reward shall be given or done unto thee, O thou false tongue? Even mighty and sharp arrows, with hot burning coals.' "

Some modern jurists seem to think differently. When Courvoisier, the murderer of Lord William Russell, confessed his guilt to Mr. Phillips, his counsel, at the bar of the court, who, with his colleague, Mr. Clarkson, up to that moment had believed in his client's innocence, the barrister stood aghast, as he well might. On recovering from the shock, he said, " Of course then you are going to plead guilty ? " " No, sir ; I expect you to defend me to the utmost." " I at once came to the resolution of abandoning the case," says Mr. Phillips, " and so I told my colleague." " Had Mr. Phillips yielded to this impulse," reasons Serjeant Samuel Warren, " he would have abandoned his duty ; and we have his own authority for saying that such is now his opinion." " I am satisfied that my original impression was erroneous," says Phillips ; " I had no right to throw up my brief, and turn traitor to the wretch—wretch though he was—who had confided to me." It was the influence of his colleague, Mr. Clarkson, which saved him from committing this grievous error, and overcame his determination by suggesting that they should take the opinion of the eminent judge, Mr. Baron Parke, who sat during the trial beside the chief justice, but did not share in trying the case. Mr. Baron Parke acted with that kindness and discretion in the terrible dilemma so unexpectedly brought under his notice, which the judges almost always exhibit when dealing with the bar. He " requested to know distinctly whether the prisoner insisted on my defending him ; and on hearing that he did, said I was bound to do so, and *to use all fair arguments arising on the evidence.*" The *Jurist* (Nov. 24,

U

1849), in an article in which it admitted the sufficiency of Mr. Phillips' explanations, thus speaks of the duty of the advocate, and Mr. Phillips' due discharge of those duties :—" If the law has laid down for the general protection, some certain rules of evidence, or otherwise, according to which only the legal conclusion of a man's guilt is to be arrived at, it is the duty of counsel to do as Mr. Phillips did—to retain his brief, and to use every endeavour that his intelligence can suggest, to take care that his client shall not be condemned except by a conclusion strictly deducible, by applying the fixed rules of the law to the evidence produced." As it happened, Courvoisier was found guilty and duly executed; but the question arises naturally, what would counsel have done had Courvoisier, thanks to his able pleading, been found " Not guilty," and acquitted? To the uninitiated this case only confirms the truth of the maxim, *Summum jus, summa injustitia.* Why a murderer should be saved from the gallows for a point of legal etiquette passeth understanding.

AN ASTRONOMICAL PHENOMENON.

WHEN Mr. Blackburne (at one time attorney-general, afterwards lord justice, and twice lord chancellor) attended as special counsel during the Cork assizes, Jonathan Henn, Q.C. was counsel on the other side. Alluding to this eminent " special," Henn thus commenced his speech to the jury : " Little, gentlemen, can my poor client compete with the galaxy of talent arrayed against him on the other side, including, if a theatrical phrase might be indulged in, a star of the first magnitude, or rather, I might say [alluding to the ministry which had just resigned], a *comet which has lost its tail.*"

HOC (NON) ERAT IN VOTIS.

WHEN Judge Crampton, a very steadfast total abstainer, was on a vacation ramble in Germany, some one inquired of Chief Justice Bushe, "Where Justice Crampton was?" "In Germany," replied the witty chief justice, "making a *traverse absque hoc(k)*." *

COURT OF SESSIONS AND THE BUTCHERS.

FOR a considerable period after the union of England and Scotland, the Court of Sessions, the supreme civil court of the latter country, appears to have assumed powers of very questionable authority. Among these was the singular and hardly credible one of regulating the sale of beef and mutton by weight in the Edinburgh market. On this subject the following dignified provision occurs in an act of the court dated December 7th, 1734:

"That there be no sale made of mutton or of beef, but by Trois weight, heads, knaps, tongues, and marrow-bones cut out by themselves excepted."

This act seems to have been found grinding or inoperative, for their lordships, by a subsequent act, January 24, 1736, kindly exempted from its operation "the following pieces of flesh, viz. knaplayers, midlayers, shoulderlayers, and craigs or necks." The above will be found printed in the Acts of Sederunt of the Court, published in 1790.

LOGICAL.

THE Statute 1 Edw. II. enacts that a prisoner who breaks prison is guilty of felony; but if the prison be on fire, this is not so, "for he is not to be hanged because he would not stay to be burnt."

* The form of a denial or traverse : *absque hoc quod*, etc.

AN INDICTMENT QUASHED.

RADOCK relates in his *Miscellaneous Memoirs:* "Lord Chief Justice Wilmot gave to a party of us, one evening, a curious account of an innkeeper at Warwick, whom he had tried for having poisoned some of his customers with his port wine ; and that the indictment was quashed by the impudence of the fellow, who absolutely proved that there had never been a drop of real port wine in the hogshead. The indictment, having described it as a 'hogshead of port wine,' had actually to be quashed."

RULES OF EVIDENCE.

ERTAIN rules of evidence which are now considered fundamental, appear to have been altogether unknown in the seventeenth century. In the trial of Hawkins, a clergyman, for stealing money and a ring from Henry Larimore, in September, 1668, Lord Hale admitted evidence to show that the accused had once stolen a pair of boots from a man named Chilton, and that more than a year before he had picked the pocket of one Noble. In summing up, Lord Hale said, after referring to the cases of Chilton and Noble : "This, if true, would render the prisoner now at the bar obnoxious to any jury" (Howell, *State Trials,* 935).

ANTISEMITIC JUSTICE.

RITING about Rome, in 1858, Edmond About, in *Rome Contemporaine,* relates the following curious instance of Papal justice :—"The story of a Jew was lately told me, who derived a singular benefit from his religion. He had committed a crime almost unknown among the Hebrews of our day. He had committed murder—had assassinated his brother-in-law. The crime was proven. Now this was the line of defence adopted by his counsel :—'Gentlemen, why does the law severely punish the crime of murder, as a rule even punish it capitally? Because, when a Christian is murdered, a soul and a body are killed together. A human being is sent before his Sovereign Lord and Judge unprepared, without having confessed his errors and his sins, without having received absolution, and therefore is sent straight to hell, or, at least, to purgatory. That is why murder, I mean the murder of a Christian, cannot be punished too severely. But we, what have we killed? Only a miserable, unbelieving Jew, gentlemen, who is damned beforehand. Even if a hundred years had been granted him for conversion—you know the obstinacy of his race—he would still have died (*crêvé*) impenitent, without confession, like a brute. We have, I admit, hastened his doom, perhaps accelerated the execution of divine justice by a few years ; we have advanced for him an eternity of pain which, however, sooner or later, had to be his fate. But, gentlemen, be indulgent for a venial error, and reserve your severity for those who attempt the life and eternal welfare of a Christian.'"

This plea would have been absurd, to say the least of it, in any other part of the world. At Rome, in those days, it was only logical, and the homicidal Jew was let off with a few months' imprisonment.

PITY THE POOR JURYMEN.

AS the law concerning Juries stands at present, it cannot be said that the position of jurymen is an enviable one. But it was worse in former times. If they could not agree, they were to be *afforced* by the addition of other jurors, as in an assize in the first instance. If the verdict of these men was opposed to the former one, the first twelve jurors were immediately arrested and imprisoned, their lands and chattels were forfeited to the king, and they became for the future infamous, and no longer, as Braeton expresses it, *oathesworth*

At a later period the law added to their sentence with cruel everity : that their wives and children should be turned out of their homes, their houses thrown down, their trees rooted up, and their meadows ploughed (*Co. Littl.* 294 b.). Subsequently this punishment was commuted into a pecuniary penalty.

Mr. Jardine (*Criminal Trials*, p. 118) says that in some extreme cases, when juries obstinately persist in giving a verdict contrary to the direction of the court in matters of law, they are even at the present day liable to be fined ; and he supports this assertion by a quotation from Hawkins's *Pleas of the Crown.* But this is very questionable in point of law, and certainly would never now be attempted in practice.

CALL A SPADE A SPADE.

"WHEN, in 1850, I returned to Westminster Hall," says Lord Campbell, "after an absence of nine years, I found that the *attorneys* had almost all grown into *solicitors.*" This metamorphosis was deeply resented by Lord Tenterden, then chief justice, who could not patiently endure conceit or affectation in the language of others. He was particularly irate if a shop was called a warehouse by its owner, or the shopman dubbed himself an assistant. On a gentleman pressing into a crowded court, complaining that he could not get to his counsel, Lord Tenterden asked, "What are you, sir ?" "My lord, I am the plaintiff's solicitor." "We know nothing of solicitors here, sir," retorted his lordship. "Had you been in the respectable rank of an attorney, I should have ordered room to be made for you."

JOCOPHOBIA.

LORD Tenterden before the public was always afraid of approaching a jest, lest his dignity might suffer. In his book on Shipping he would not, without an apology, even introduce a translation of a passage from a foreign writer which might cause a smile : "If mice eat the cargo, and thereby occasion no small damage to the merchant, the master must make good the loss, because he is guilty of a fault ; yet if he had cats on board he shall be excused (*Roccus*, 58). The rule and exception, *although bearing somewhat of a ludicrous air*, furnish a good illustration of the general principle."

PEINE FORTE ET DURE.

HE Press-yard at the Old Bailey still by its name commemorates one of the cruelties of our old statute-book.

In all cases where a criminal refused to plead on his trial, the horrible punishment of pressing to death was inflicted. This punishment was established in 1406,* as a substitution for the old punishment of imprisonment with scarcely enough food to sustain life. At a time when human life was held very cheap, it was, as Blackstone † remarks, intended as a species of mercy to the delinquent, by delivering him the sooner from his torment. The original form of the judgment was as follows : " That the prisoner shall be remanded to the place from whence he came, and put in some low dark room, and there laid on his back, without any manner of covering, except for his privy parts ; and that as many weights shall be laid upon him as he can bear, *and more ;* and that he shall have no sustenance but of the worst bread and water, and that he shall not eat the same day on which he drinks, nor drink the same day on which he eats; and that he shall so continue till he die.‡ The following were added in 1476 to the word *room* : " That he shall lie without any litter or other thing under him, and that one arm shall be drawn to one quarter of the room, with a cord, and the other to another, and that his feet shall be used in the same manner."§ The same authorities substitute for that part

* Yearbook, 8 Hen. IV. 1. † *Comment.*, iv. p. 328.
‡ Hawkins, *Pleas of the Crown*, ii. p. 469.
§ 14 Edw. IV. 8 pl. 17, and 2 *Inst.* 178.

of the sentence which follows the word *more* and ends with *water*, the following : "That he shall have three morsels of barley-bread a day, and that he shall have the water next the prison, so that it be not current."

Instances are on record of lunatics, and even of persons reputed deaf and dumb, having been submitted to this terrible death. Frequently also criminals possessed of rank and fortune refused to plead in order to preserve their property from being forfeited to the Crown, as would have been the case had they been found guilty. Such was in the sixteenth century the case of a Mr. Calverly, of a very ancient family in the north of England. Having murdered his wife and seven children in a fit of jealousy, he surrendered himself to justice ; but distressed at the thought that his only surviving child, if he confessed the crimes, should be deprived of the estate and the dignity of his ancestors, resolved not to plead. He therefore stood mute upon being arraigned, and, in accordance with the law, was crushed to death. The estate was thus preserved for the child, which was a male, from whom, if I am rightly informed, the present family of Blackett, in Yorkshire, are lineally descended. This tragical event seems to have furnished the subject of the play, " The Yorkshire Tragedy," attributed to Shakespeare.

Another remarkable application of this torture took place in 1659, when a Major Strangways endured it for a similar motive. He and his elder sister had shared a farm peacefully enough, till the sister married a lawyer named Fussell, whom Strangways disliked. He had been even heard to say that if ever his sister married Fussell, he would be the death of him in his office or elsewhere. One day Fussell was shot at his lodgings in London, and suspicion fell on Strangways, who consented to the ordeal of touch. At his trial, however, wishing to avoid the ignominy of the gallows, and to be able to bestow his estate on some friends, he refused to plead. Lord Chief Justice Glynn then passed the sentence in the words given above, qualifying the word *weights* with " as much iron and stone as he can bear ; "

allowing him three morsels of barley bread every alternate day, and three drinks " of the water in the next channel to the prison door, but of no spring or fountain water." Adding, " and this shall be his punishment till he die." Provision is here made for an agony of several days' duration, but this was mitigated in the execution.

On the Monday following Strangways was clothed in white from head to foot, and wearing a mourning cloak, for, indeed, it was his own funeral to which he was going. His friends placed themselves at the corner of the press, and when he gave the word commenced putting on the weights. This was done till he uttered the words, " Lord Jesus, receive my soul ; " but the weight being too light to produce instant death, those present stood on the top of it, as a ghastly and last act of friendship. The poor fellow bore this some eight or ten minutes, when he expired without uttering another word.

In the *Nottingham Mercury*, of January 19th, 1721, the following paragraph is given as part of the London news, from which it appears that as late as that year the law was practically put in force : " Yesterday the sessions began at the Old Bailey, where several persons were brought to the bar for the highway, etc., among them the highwaymen lately taken in Westminster, two of which, viz. Thomas Cross, alias Philips, and Thomas Spigot, refusing to plead, the Court proceeded to pass the following sentence upon them " [here follows the sentence in the usual form]. " The former, on sight of the terrible machine, desired to be carried back to the Sessions House, where he pleaded not guilty. But the other, who behaved himself very insolently to the ordinary who was ordered to attend him, seemingly resolved to undergo the torture. Accordingly when they brought cords as usual to tye him, he broke them three several times like twine thread, and told them if they brought cables he would serve them after the same manner. But, how-ever, they found means to tye him to the ground, having his limbs extended ; but after enduring the punishment an hour, and having three or four hundredweights put on him, he at last submitted to plead, and was carried back again, when he pleaded not guilty."

The following, extracted from the *Annals of Newgate*, published by the Rev. Mr. Villette, ordinary of that prison in 1776, describes the torture suffered by Spigot : " The chaplain found him lying in the vault upon the bare ground, with 350 pounds weight upon his breast, and then prayed by him, and at several times asked him why he would hazard his soul by such obstinate kind of self-murder. But all the answer that he made was : ' Pray for me ! pray for me !' He sometimes lay silent under the pressure as if insensible to pain, and then again would fetch his breath very quick and short. Several times he complained that they had laid a cruel weight upon his face, though it was covered with nothing but a thin cloth, which was afterwards removed, and laid more light and hollow ; yet he still complained of the prodigious weight upon his face, which might be caused by the blood being forced up thither, and pressing the veins as violently as if the force had been externally on his face. When he had remained for half an hour under this load, and 50 pounds weight more laid on, being in all 400, he told those who attended him he would plead. The weights were at once taken off, the cords cut asunder ; he was raised up by two men, some brandy was put into his mouth to revive him, and he was carried to take his trial."

After the almost total abolition of this cruel punishment, it was the custom to force prisoners to plead if possible by screwing their thumbs with whip-cord. As early as 1721 Mary Andrews was tortured thus. The first three whipcords broke, but she gave way with the fourth. The same year the cord was tried first on a criminal named Nathaniel Hawes, and when this proved insufficient, a weight of 250 pounds was imposed upon him, under which pressure he consented to plead. Barrington, in his *Ancient Statutes*, says that he had been furnished with two instances of the application of the press in the reign of

George II.   One of these happened at the Sussex Assizes before Baron Thompson, and the other at Cambridge in 1741, when Baron Carter was the judge: In both these instances the press was not inflicted until, by direction of the judge, the experiment of the minor torture with the cords had been tried, "though this course was wholly unauthorized by law."

The *Peine Forte et Dure* was abolished by the statute of 1772,* which enacts that if a prisoner upon his arraignment stands wilfully mute, or does not answer directly to the offence imputed to him, he shall be convicted of the offence as if he had been convicted by verdict or by confession of the crime.   But now, by the statute of 1827–28,† in such cases a plea of not guilty can be entered for the prisoner, which is to have the same effect as if he pleaded it.

* 12 Geo. III., c. 20.   † 7 and 8 Geo. IV. c. 28, s, 2.

INDEX.

PRINTED BY WILLIAM CLOWES AND SONS, LIMITED, LONDON AND BECCLES.

SD - #0034 - 230125 - C0 - 229/152/18 - PB - 9781333656782 - Gloss Lamination